British Gothic Cinema

The Palgrave Gothic Series

Series Editor: **Clive Bloom**

Editorial Advisory Board: **Dr Ian Conrich**, University of Nottingham, UK, **Barry Forshaw**, author/journalist, UK, **Professor Gregg Kucich**, University of Notre Dame, USA, **Professor Gina Wisker**, University of Brighton, UK.

This series of gothic books is the first to treat the genre in its many inter-related, global and 'extended' cultural aspects to show how the taste for the medieval and the sublime gave rise to a perverse taste for terror and horror and how that taste became not only international (with a huge fan base in places such as South Korea and Japan) but also the sensibility of the modern age, changing our attitudes to such diverse areas as the nature of the artist, the meaning of drug abuse and the concept of the self. The series is accessible but scholarly, with referencing kept to a minimum and theory contextualised where possible. All the books are readable by an intelligent student or a knowledgeable general reader interested in the subject.

Barry Forshaw
BRITISH GOTHIC CINEMA

Margarita Georgieva
THE GOTHIC CHILD

Catherine Wynne
BRAM STOKER, DRACULA AND THE VICTORIAN GOTHIC STAGE

The Palgrave Gothic Series
Series Standing Order ISBN 978–1–137–29898–0 (hardback)
(*outside North America only*)

You can receive future titles in this series as they are published by placing a standing order. Please contact your bookseller or, in case of difficulty, write to us at the address below with your name and address, the title of the series and the ISBN quoted above.

Customer Services Department, Macmillan Distribution Ltd, Houndmills, Basingstoke, Hampshire RG21 6XS, England

---

British Gothic Cinema

Barry Forshaw

palgrave
macmillan

Softcover reprint of the hardcover 1st edition 2013 978-1-137-30030-0

First published 2013 by
PALGRAVE MACMILLAN

Palgrave Macmillan in the UK is an imprint of Macmillan Publishers Limited, registered in England, company number 785998, of Houndmills, Basingstoke, Hampshire RG21 6XS.

Palgrave Macmillan in the US is a division of St Martin's Press LLC, 175 Fifth Avenue, New York, NY 10010.

Palgrave Macmillan is the global academic imprint of the above companies and has companies and representatives throughout the world.

Palgrave® and Macmillan® are registered trademarks in the United States, the United Kingdom, Europe and other countries.

ISBN 978-1-137-30031-7   ISBN 978-1-137-30032-4 (eBook)
DOI 10.1057/9781137300324

A catalogue record for this book is available from the British Library.

A catalog record for this book is available from the Library of Congress.

Typeset by MPS Limited, Chennai, India.

Contents

Introduction

A gruesome bout of bloodletting had cinema audiences of the day gasping at its graphic nature. An Englishman on holiday in the Carpathian Mountains has been stabbed to death in the secluded castle to which he and his party have been lured. His murderer utilises a rope and pulley to hoist the dead man's body above an empty sarcophagus. What follows is an act of horror that is all the more disturbing for its resemblance to the butchery of an animal in an abattoir. The dead man's throat is cut, and gouts of blood rain down upon ashes which have been spread beneath them. Sometime later, the murdered man's wife – a repressed and (it is hinted) frigid Victorian bluestocking – is transformed into a ravening, sexually voracious monster, her buttoned-up, body-concealing clothes replaced by a diaphanous gown that reveals ample cleavage. What follows are acts of implied vampiric lesbianism reminiscent of Coleridge's 'Christabel' and (as an appalling finale) an act of ecclesiastical murder with hammer and stake that comes across like a gang rape.

These scenes riveted (and shocked) audiences in Terence Fisher's 1966 film *Dracula, Prince of Darkness* – one of the sequels to Hammer Films' original revivification of Bram Stoker's murderous nobleman. And while modern audiences have become accustomed to much more operatic bloodletting, the film still carries a considerable charge in the twenty-first century. But – a contentious question – does Fisher's visceral melodrama (which somehow combines an almost delirious surrealist quality with a precisely arranged, geometric and non-kinetic use of cinematic language) represent the final popular debasement of the Gothic form inaugurated by such writers as Stoker and Coleridge, or is it a transmuting of the Gothic impulse into something very different from the original expressions of the form, but equally worthy of consideration? This book, a labour of love, is an attempt to engage

1

with that question: to examine whether the Gothic impulse is now a mongrelised, cheapened form or a thoroughgoing re-invention of still-potent tropes – tropes, in fact, which are still energising filmmakers at the beginning of the twenty-first century quite as much as they did such British directors as Terence Fisher half a century ago. The Gothic form is, it seems, as indestructible as Bram Stoker's vampire count.

The romantic strain in nineteenth-century literature found its most delirious expression in the British horror film. From a tentative flirtation with the macabre in the otherwise mainstream Gainsborough studio films of the 1940s and 1950s (which similarly explored a kind of damped-down eroticism, with female flesh tightly squeezed into bustiers as blue-blooded characters leered and lusted), popular cinema of the day was on a dangerous collision course with moralists. The refulgently coloured horror and carnality of late 1950s and early 1960s exploitation cinema was to come up against the brick wall of the British censors, who responded to the moral panics of local watch committees by Draconian cutting of this unrespectable genre. Ironically, such Pavlovian responses were not a million miles away from similar vapours inspired by the more discreet bloodletting of Mary Shelley, Bram Stoker and other eighteenth- and nineteenth-century progenitors of the horror genre, but the producers of the Sadean movies of the mid-twentieth century could not adduce literary respectability, even in the case of direct adaptations, so free were the spins given to the new widescreen versions of Dracula, Frankenstein and co.

To the horror of the prudish, the most seductive (and most commercially successful) purveyor of this new breed of unabashed gruesomeness and eroticism was, of course, the bijou-sized Hammer Films studios, nestling in genteel Bray just outside London. And while the studio's then-sensational products initially inspired loathing of passionate intensity in mainstream critics and commentators, such disapproval was counterpointed by massive commercial success. While the audiences who flocked to pulse-racing (though often sedately paced) films directed by the likes of Terence Fisher were unlikely to be aware of the antecedents of the Gothic product they were consuming (apart, that is, from the monochrome Universal Studios adaptations of the same literary material 20 years earlier), the vehement establishment disapproval was grist to the commercial mill of the films.

After a time such objections grew less strident, even as Hammer and its rivals began to up the ante in terms of copious nudity and bloodshed; the studio even bagged a much-deserved Queen's Award for Industry. In fact, the impeccably spoken English of such actors as Christopher

Lee and Peter Cushing (intoning the dialogue of Jimmy Sangster, some way after Bram Stoker or Guy Endore) was often the first British accent heard by many Americans, so successful was the company's product in the United States.

Pugnacious Hammer Films was not the only game in town, and a remarkable Gothic strain was to be discerned in such then-outrageous films as Michael Powell's complex *Peeping Tom* and Sidney Hayers' nigh-operatic *Circus of Horrors* (both Anglo-Amalgamated). These censor-baiting films proffered a sometimes highly sophisticated blend of sexual abandon and grotesquely imaginative carnage (Arthur Crabtree's energetic *Horrors of the Black Museum*, from the same company, utilised a pair of deadly binoculars which, when adjusted, produced eye-piercing spikes – this claimed to be an authentic object drawn from a real-life English murder case), and other more sober black-and-white studies in the Gothic were produced by Richard Gordon, starring ageing British expat Boris Karloff, who returned to his native shores for such films as *Corridors of Blood* (a surprisingly intelligent piece which dealt with the discovery of anaesthetics). Interestingly, all three of the Anglo-Amalgamated films also treat sex and female semi-nudity in a provocative fashion barely attempted elsewhere – as ever, the Gothic impulse is a libidinous one.

Such films, while pleasing mass audiences (and upsetting self-styled moral guardians), were quickly lionised by the more unorthodox aesthetic commentators (notably, as so often, the French) and celebrated for their reinvigoration of a long-moribund Gothic tradition. The nation which gave birth to the gushing blood of Grand Guignol in a Pigalle theatre (with discreet boxes for those patrons erotically aroused by the horrors onstage) was quick to acknowledge the surprising fact that the staid British had found the perfect cinematic expression of this subversive branch of literature. What made the genre so intriguing was its surreal concatenation of moral values: Christianity traditionally supplied the necessary accoutrements for the destruction of supernatural evil, while less noble instincts were stimulated by violent death and generous displays of female cleavage. Hammer Films (and the genre in general) proffered the kind of erotic display that was otherwise unavailable in the British cinema. Interestingly, the British Board of Film Censors (BBFC) nourished one particular shibboleth which invariably produced the scissors: the sight of blood on breasts (almost *de rigueur* in many a Hammer product – the company was the first to spot the ineluctable link between vampirism and displaced sexuality).

Inevitably, of course, the Hammer Films revolution ran out of steam, and a new breed of horror film (signalled by the phenomenal success of William Friedkin's *The Exorcist*, with its bloody masturbation-by-crucifix, in 1973) and a period of stasis for the Gothic genre followed. However, in the last decade of the twentieth century, a major revival of interest in the field (in both Britain and the United States) took place, a revival which is proceeding with fresh vigour as the tropes of Gothic literature find new and inventive forms of expression. It is the latter trend which makes a study such as this ever more apropos, drawing together the antecedents of the genre, its mid-century filmic flourishing and its all-conquering success in the early years of the twenty-first century. The aim of *British Gothic Cinema* is to discuss every major film from both the Hammer Films studio and elsewhere (from Tod Slaughter's creaky, unsophisticated shockers in the early 1930s to the big-budget Hammer revival with such films as the highly successful *The Woman in Black* (2012) and beyond), attempting to illuminate a variety of facets (such as all-pervasiveness in the genre of the sexual impulse), along with career studies of the major (and minor) directors, stars and other creative personnel (from directors such as James Whale to actors such as Christopher Lee) – and largely in a spirit of generosity; my overriding agenda is to celebrate.

This study begins with a brief examination of the origins of the Gothic genre in English literature, along with an examination of the early proponents of the form and the eroticism and horror found in such works as Keats' 'La Belle Dame sans Merci' and Coleridge's aforementioned 'Christabel' (which combines two familiar elements of British Gothic cinema: vampirism and lesbian sex). There is, of course, the crucial importance of two key works of English literature: Mary Shelley's *Frankenstein* and Bram Stoker's *Dracula*, which enjoy continual re-invention stretching into the twenty-first century.

I have also attempted an analysis of the English influence on the first important wave of adaptations of Gothic literature in Hollywood in the 1930s (concentrating on the achievements of the massively influential James Whale, director of the seminal *Frankenstein* and several key movies of the genre), while also discussing the fashion in which later British-made adaptations were both reactions to and departures from the earlier films, with certain elements moved from the periphery to centre stage. I look at other treatments of English Gothic in American and world cinema in general, establishing templates for the form which have remained influential to this day; the exodus of British writing, directing and acting talent to the USA creating a specifically English vision in American cinema and the foregrounding of the literary aspects in these adaptations (e.g. English actress Elsa Lanchester playing Mary

Shelley – as well as the bizarrely coiffured bride of the creature). The Appendix includes interviews I have conducted with a variety of writers, actors, directors and other personnel.

The first wave of British horror films in the 1930s and 1940s and their reception is instructive, such as the now-hilariously camp Grand Guignol sequence of Tod Slaughter films (notably *Sweeney Todd: The Demon Barber of Fleet Street*, also a peculiarly British horror myth, and *Crimes at the Dark House*). And there are early examples of respectable English theatrical actors not too proud to appear in horror films (Ralph Richardson in *The Ghoul*, Charles Laughton in Whale's *The Old Dark House*) – with the same phenomenon to be found in Hammer films; the importance of the English actor Boris Karloff and his work in the UK after his Hollywood success must be noted, along with the contemporary discussions of the cinema of cruelty as diversion or depravity. Gothic horror elements incorporated in non-genre or other film products of the day are also fertile ground. The notorious 'H' for 'Horrific' certificate of the 1930s heralds the major censorship furore created by the then-unprecedented popularity of horror films in the UK (with banning campaigns by local watch committees and questions in the Houses of Parliament; there were outright bans on much Gothic material, including serious adaptations from such writers as H.G. Wells, who was not at all pleased by the films of his work).

The sporadic appearance of horror material and the continuing use of elements of the macabre in non-genre films is an intriguing phenomenon (cf. the celebrated opening sequence of David Lean's *Great Expectations* with Pip in the graveyard). Prestigious literary adaptations of the genre in the late 1940s included such fascinating work as the 1949 film of Pushkin's *The Queen of Spades* (with a memorably grotesque Edith Evans) and the crucial importance of early television and radio versions of Gothic subjects are similarly noteworthy. TV was a broadcast medium which would furnish key material for the first horror wave of the mid- to late 1950s (Hammer's first major horror/science fiction genre initiative being a striking, intelligent adaptation by Val Guest of Nigel Kneale's seminal *Quatermass* series, initially just one of its copious rejiggings of other media, but setting the standard for the company from that point onwards).

At the heart of *British Gothic Cinema*, though, is the worldwide impact of Hammer's cottage industry in an examination (and celebration) of the great worldwide success of the tiny British studio, with its imaginative (and, for the time, sensational) re-invention of Gothic material, incorporating both nonpareil production design and the cream of the British acting profession. There were (cannily) conspicuous sexual elements knowingly incorporated into the films at a time when British cinema was notably chaste and largely libido-free; the workings of the studio resulted in a highly efficient, machine-tooled product (which nevertheless allowed striking creativity within commercial parameters, with journeymen directors such as Fisher blossoming into true auteurs) and the studio's forging of a new film language for its Gothic adaptations is significant, as is the typical outraged critical response of the day to the Hammer product (blind to any filmic virtues in light of the horrific/sexually suggestive material). These films, of course, are now perceived as relatively understated (by modern standards), almost fairy-tale fables utilising classic material. Similarly, the crucial influence of the English ghost story tradition (as exemplified by M.R. James) on British Gothic cinema is discussed here, as is the concentration in this particular strain of monochrome film on more subtle atmospheric narrative devices as opposed to the more graphic bloodletting of the colour rivals. Most notable, perhaps, is the influence of M.R. James on British cinema (notably in what is generally considered to be the finest single Gothic film ever made in this country, Jacques Tourneur's *Night of the Demon*, a creative and rich expansion of James' classic story 'Casting the Runes'); there is a detailed celebration of the other great British horror film of the 1940s, Ealing's portmanteau classic *Dead of Night* (with its celebrated Michael Redgrave ventriloquist dummy sequence), and later offshoots of this trend including *The Innocents* (after Henry James' novella 'The Turn of the Screw'), *The Haunting* and *Night of the Eagle* (after Shirley Jackson and Fritz Leiber, respectively).

In the modern age, the revival of Hammer has been much remarked-upon (oft-attempted but only now bearing fruit with such films as the commercially successful *The Woman in Black*, after Susan Hill). Other iconoclastic films have rejuvenated the horror field both in this country and abroad, with quirky new approaches to the genre: we have millennial horror, with an end-of-the-century mindset creating a new fatalistic (and often apocalyptic) strain; the revival of the zombie movie, with the Walking Dead now given to sprinting; and the massive current success of the vampire genre (both in the cinema and television) aimed at a younger demographic, along with the growth of knowing parodies of the genre in such films as *Shaun of the Dead*. The traditional forms have been customised for the new millennium and auguries for the future of the genre are in rude, sanguinary health.

1
Gothic Fiction: English Terror and Carnality

The origins of the Gothic genre in English literature demonstrates, even in its nascent form, a delirious mix of eroticism and horror, as found in such works as Keats' 'La Belle Dame sans Merci' and Coleridge's 'Christabel'. The poet Percy Bysshe Shelley nurtured a fascination with horror and cruelty which was to prove (as we shall see) highly influential, while the haunted novels of Ann Radcliffe provided several key elements. Similarly (in other fields), the German romantic painters left their mark on the visual character of British horror. But, above all, it's essential to note the crucial importance of two key works of English literature: Mary Shelley's *Frankenstein* and Bram Stoker's *Dracula*; their continual re-invention and rejuvenations, as noted earlier, have continued into the twenty-first century.

An influential literary offspring came not from the poet Shelley but from his 19-year-old inamorata Mary. The latter, with *Frankenstein*, created the most enduring Gothic myth alongside that of the vampire, utilising ideas of the God-usurping creation of life (adumbrated in such works as E.T.A. Hoffmann's 'The Sandman' in 1812, in which the dancing doll Olympia is granted a grotesque half-life), as well as the myth of the monstrous, stalking Golem, which the young Mary Shelley had found grimly fascinating. The notion of audacious scientific experimentation was also familiar to her from the experiments of Erasmus Darwin, grandfather of the author of *Origin of Species*.

Mary Shelley's original notion for Frankenstein was that of a short story, but the canny Lord Byron, recognising that something much more ambitious might be created from the young woman's tentative idea, encouraged her to expand it to novel length.

The narrative of Victor Frankenstein's creation of life has (in the twenty-first century) lost its shocking power in a secular age, despite the growing influence of fundamentalist Middle Eastern theocracies and the unstoppable rise of the Religious Right in the USA, so the notion of a man playing God and creating life no longer has the blasphemous charge that it would have had for Mary Shelley's original readers (and the suggestion by Charles Darwin that life on Earth might be the product of natural selection and evolution rather than the seven-day creation of a deity was to cause even more seismic upsets, even among scientists such as Philip Henry Gosse). What made the story that Shelley created particularly disturbing was not just the usurpation of the creator's role by a man, but the basic materials utilised by Frankenstein, the gruesome stitched-together remnants of mortuaries, and the book's first appearance in three volumes in 1818 was not at all well received. Early reviewers included Sir Walter Scott, who (while acknowledging the commendably flesh-creeping qualities of the narrative) expressed a slightly school-marmish revulsion towards the whole enterprise via a curious backhanded compliment, suggesting that the author's undoubted skill made her macabre narrative more disturbing than a poorly written tale might have been – and thus, for him, more deserving of condemnation.

But tut-tutting moral condemnations of works of art often have a corollary (something that is as true today as it was in the nineteenth century): they inspire a keen interest in their target audience, hungry for the transgressive and the forbidden. A dramatisation of the novel some three years later was (unsurprisingly) highly successful, making a considerable mark first at the new Covent Garden Theatre in London with a subsequent transfer to the highly appropriate setting of the Grand Guignol theatre in Paris. The creature was played by the actor T.P. Cooke, a sort of Boris Karloff *avant la lettre*, whose Grand Guignol repertoire included vampires, murderous wizards and assorted monstrous types. His performance is inevitably lost to history, although we do have a fragmentary record of the very first filmic Frankenstein monster (played by Charles Ogle in J. Searle Dawley's 1910 silent film). Theatrical productions continue to hold the stage to this day, with a recent London production in which the actors Benedict Cumberbatch and Jonny Lee Miller alternated as the (sometimes naked) creature and his creator, drawing large audiences.

While Shelley's novel has inspired a host of literary imitators (among them the British writer Brian Aldiss' *Frankenstein Unbound*, its title a play on the original novel's subtitle *The Modern Prometheus*), it is of course the cinematic legacy which has proved the most enduring – far more people have seen actors from Boris Karloff to Christopher Lee and beyond incarnating the creature than have ever read the novel.

In fact, an acquaintance with the grim finale of Shelley's book (set in frigid Arctic wastes) is often surprising to viewers of the many films, given that so few have chosen to represent Shelley's concluding selection, either for budgetary or artistic reasons. The choice of the name of Prometheus as a subtitle for Shelley's novel referred to the Greek myth of the God who presented mankind with the gift of fire, only to pay a heavy price at the hands of his fellow gods; punishment, Shelley was suggesting, for responses to destabilising advances in scientific knowledge which stretch from Galileo being shown the instruments of torture by the Inquisition (for suggesting that the Earth was not the centre of the universe) to the modern day, when science is once again under siege from newly confident religious movements of various kinds. Mary Shelley herself was punished to some degree and was not pleased by the suggestion that she had been inspired to write *Frankenstein* because of the popular perception of her father William Godwin as a dangerous outsider. But her success (now that the dust of history has settled) extends across many areas, not least her status as a feminist heroine. It's interesting that her first cinematic representation was via a sympathetic portrayal by the English actress Elsa Lanchester in a film directed by another English artist, the highly unorthodox James Whale, in the Hollywood film *The Bride of Frankenstein* (1935). This film is considered later in this study, but by the time of Hammer's groundbreaking late 1950s spin on the characters, Mary Shelley had become to some extent just a name in the credits.

Initially, several Gothic novels were infused with a certain Anglican perspective that (among other things) aligned the sinister influence of the Church of Rome with the locations where Catholicism reigned (notably France, Spain and Italy), concomitantly identified as a fertile breeding ground for eldritch evil. A corollary of this was a certain fascination with the French Revolution (among such writers as Mary Wollstonecraft, who was to give birth to the creator of Frankenstein, Mary Shelley), which also provided much of the gruesome imagery, including the copious shedding of blood and severed heads. The 'threat from abroad' scenario was an infinitely serviceable plot engine, using strategies similar to those that were to be used later on in the golden age of crime fiction in England. A settled status quo is presented in order to be disrupted by a malign presence before order is wrested from chaos (the *locus classicus* here is Bram Stoker's *Dracula*). Italy was often located as a source of potential corruption and decay; the notion of *Il Bel Paese* as a place in which the destruction of hapless Englishmen was wrought was still finding expression in the writings of Daphne du

Maurier a century and a half later in such books as *My Cousin Rachel* (1951), with its dark, corrupting Italian influences. The latter even sports the metaphor of a 'vampiric' woman whose sexual involvement with an Englishman in Florence brings about his weakening and subsequent death. Sexuality as a harbinger of destruction is very much the central notion of British vampire films, where the undead monster is often presented as a charismatic, sexually attractive figure, is also to be found in Coleridge's 'Christabel', notably in the beautiful and seductive figure of Geraldine – who also, of course, embodies the lesbian sexuality to be found in Sheridan Le Fanu's 'Carmilla' (1872). The latter has proved to be an almost boundless source of inspiration for many lesbian-themed horror films, both foreign (Harry Kümel's *Daughters of Darkness* (1971)) and British (the 'Carmilla' cycle that begins with *The Vampire Lovers* (1970)).

But as well as producing the negative, destructive aspects that would be so serviceable and re-usable for Gothic cinema, the age of romanticism (concurrent with the Gothic impulse), as well as drawing on the eldritch, might also be said to reflect the rational figure to be set against unspeakable evil – the avatar here would be Stoker's Van Helsing, who would appear in a variety of guises and names throughout (for instance) the Hammer horror cycle.

Coleridge's moody 'Christabel', however, with its encounter between the virginal innocent maiden of the title and the dark destructive succubus Geraldine, is actually something of a cornucopia of Gothic themes (not least the reference to 'heaving breasts'). We are given the classic Gothic setting (in which darkness cloaks the evil impulses of the non-human characters, with an obbligato of animal noises, similar to those that will accompany Dracula and his ilk); there is also the channelling of unconscious impulses which was to prove so suggestive, particularly in the 1950s innovations of the Hammer company, which allowed the studio's writers and directors to deal with themes that would otherwise have been *verboten*, but which slipped by the censor as the settings and locales drew attention away from the often barely disguised libidinous impulses that powered the characters.

Geraldine in Coleridge's poem is initially presented as a figure of light and is contrasted with the dark woods in which she is discovered, apparently in distress after a brutal kidnapping. And as in so many subsequent British Gothic films, a naïve protagonist is drawn into a monstrous web against which their lack of worldliness is no protection; a parallel here might be with Henry James' innocent Americans abroad, unable to cope with the machinations of older – and possibly malign – Europeans (one might think here of the figure of Dracula, against whom his English victims are quite unable to cope without the aid of another older, sager European figure).

However, the vampirism of the poem remains nebulous, particularly when compared with Bram Stoker's influential *Dracula*, in which the dead Prince of Darkness becomes a far more interesting figure than his historical antecedent Vlad the Impaler; the latter's sadistic pleasures (notably dining surrounded by the tortured, stake-impaled bodies of his victims) is less interesting than Stoker's character's immortality and ability to transmogrify into a variety of animal forms. The sexual impulse of the novel is incarnated in the Count's diaphanously clad, ravenous brides who are denied their blood feast, and this can truly be seen as a sexual consummation. Such themes were later to be confronted head-on, notably in the films starring Christopher Lee. Whether or not Stoker was working out feelings about his browbeating employer, the celebrated actor Henry Irving (who is now seen as vampirising his much-abused employee and who was cruelly dismissive of the latter's attempts at writing) is beside the point – the impulses that gave birth to Dracula are perhaps less interesting than the myriad possibilities the character opened up for Gothic cinema, both in the United States and Great Britain. And Dracula's progeny flourish to this day, although the first cinematic incarnations of the vampire count did not involve British talent – it was to be Mary Shelley's Frankenstein creature which would be brought to murderous life by some eccentric and unorthodox British talents working in a foreign country.

2
Through American Eyes: Stoker and Shelley in US Cinema

'It's alive! It's alive!' gasps the English actor Colin Clive, working himself into a paroxysm over the twitching, scarred body of the patchwork corpse he has reanimated in *Frankenstein* (1931). It's a seismic moment in several senses, freezing the derisory laugher it might prompt in an age of more subtle performances. An analysis of the English influence on the first important wave of adaptations of Gothic literature in Hollywood in the 1930s is obliged to concentrate on the achievements of the massively influential James Whale, director of *Frankenstein* and several key movies of the genre (sometimes informed by his irreverent gay sensibility). Later British-made adaptations (e.g. from the Hammer studios) were both reactions to and departures from the earlier films, with certain elements (including copious bloodletting) moved from the periphery to centre stage, but Whale (and his cadre of the British talent) set the gold standard for other treatments of English Gothic in US and world cinema in general, establishing templates for the form which have remained influential to this day. The exodus of British writing, directing and acting talent to the USA created a specifically English vision in American cinema, along with the foregrounding of the literary aspects in these adaptations (e.g. English actress Elsa Lanchester playing Mary Shelley).

For the purposes of this study (which, after all, is called *British Gothic Cinema*), we must note – relatively briefly – the 1931 Hollywood film version of *Dracula* (directed by Tod Browning and starring, of course, the larger-than-life Bela Lugosi), as the British element of the film lies merely in the residue of what is left of the original novel. It is the superior UK-made version produced several decades later (with Christopher Lee as a notably more sophisticated – and sexually attractive – Dracula) that will demand attention. As an aside, it should be noted that a few bars of Tchaikovsky's *Swan Lake* under the title (as inappropriately utilised by Universal in its inaugural version) must have seemed a curious choice, even before the grinding dissonances of James Bernard's brass-based score heralded the appearance of Lee's vampire count, but that is not the only element which requires a certain tolerance in modern audiences. The Gothic elements of the opening scenes set in the Carpathian Mountains suggest that some justice might be done to Stoker's original, not to mention the production design of Dracula's splendidly dilapidated castle (with its wandering armadillos), but the more prosaic orientation of the London scenes deadeningly suggests the proscenium arch of the play from which the film is adapted; ironically, the constraints of the Bray Studios locales for the later *Dracula* are used far more creatively, even though budgetary restrictions meant that Lee's Count never reaches London.

The key problem for modern audiences, inevitably, is Bela Lugosi's eye-rolling, outrageously camp Dracula. The actor, while undoubtedly charismatic, betrays his phonetic learning of the lines (the Hungarian Lugosi's English was never secure, even at the end of his career) by some truly bizarre emphases and articulations which are more likely to prompt mirth today than shudders of dread. What's more, the latent eroticism of the count's nocturnal activities is left largely inert and may really only be read in the interstices of how the count is presented. This first film Dracula (leaving aside the unauthorised version *Nosferatu*) is, these days, more of a fascinating curio than a fully realised piece of Gothic cinema – that phenomenon was to arrive with a far superior film, directed by an expatriate Englishman and starring two fellow Brits as a scientist and the gruesome, barely human result of his experiment.

Even before the completion of *Dracula*, Universal Studios had considered filming Mary Shelley's *Frankenstein*, and the talented director Robert Florey (later to make the deliriously inventive *The Beast with Five Fingers*) was in the frame – long-lost screen tests had even been made with Lugosi as the monster in make-up which apparently owed something to the Paul Wegener version of *The Golem*). But the Florey/Lugosi *Frankenstein* was not to be – an impeccable Englishman of iconoclastic manner named James Whale stepped into the frame and created (*pace* Browning's Dracula) the first great universal Gothic film with this extremely free adaptation of Mary Shelley's novel. Whale had made his mark with two much-acclaimed films, a 1930 adaptation of R.C. Sherriff's anti-war play *Journey's End* (which he had directed in 1929 both in London's West End and New York) and the more workaday

Waterloo Bridge (1931, which, significantly, starred Mae Clarke as a prostitute – the director was subsequently to cast her as Frankenstein's endangered fiancée in his Shelley adaptation). Whale came to America as one of the many European talents that early US cinema was beginning to assiduously collect (and domesticate); his sophisticated manner and homosexuality were regarded as aspects of the 'otherness' which distinguished these 'exotic' foreign talents from US directors. What was not immediately apparent was his pitch-black sense of comedy. To modern audiences, the opening scenes of *Frankenstein* (with its outré components: grave-robbing, a grotesquely scarred hunchback, the driven, shibboleth-defying Frankenstein hiding behind headstones) are now clearly infused with a delicious gallows humour (literally so, when the hunchbacked assistant Fritz, played by Dwight Frye, cuts down a body from a gibbet – and there is the lovely moment when the dishevelled Fritz carefully adjusts his sock before scuttling up a staircase). None of this wry underlay provided by Whale would have been immediately apparent to the film's original audiences, who would have focused on the macabre atmosphere and who would never have seen scenes so redolent with horror before. This judicious balance of irony and dread was new in this nascent genre, demonstrating how Whale was ahead of his time.

The British expats in Hollywood often favoured each other's company, so it was hardly surprising that Whale employed the actor Colin Clive (with whom he had made *Journey's End*) for his Frankenstein (now renamed 'Henry'; Shelley's 'Victor' is assigned to another character). Clive's performance, viewed today, has a curious duality, with some remarkably contemporary underplaying alternating with scenery-chewing excess. But as an organic part of Whale's idiosyncratic conception, Clive cannot be faulted. The film's definitive coup, however, was Whale's hiring of an English actor (of Anglo-Indian antecedents), the prosaically named William Henry Pratt, who was to be granted the memorable stage name Boris Karloff. As with Christopher Lee's later assumption of the role for the Hammer studios, this judicious piece of casting is one of the film's several master strokes, furnishing a mimed, virtually silent performance which is one of the cinema's great assumptions of a monstrous outsider (finessed, of course, by Jack Pierce's brilliantly utilitarian make-up which allowed the actor to retain and use much of his own facial expressivity).

Those looking for a faithful channelling of Mary Shelley's literary original would be disappointed; once again (as with Browning's *Dracula*), a variety of stage adaptations as much as the original novel had been utilised for the film version, jettisoning Shelley's Arctic finale. The device of the theft of a supposedly 'abnormal' criminal brain (clearly – and rather ludicrously – labelled to that effect), as opposed to the carelessly dropped 'normal' brain which was to be placed in the monster's cranium, suggests that a more quotidian rather than a poetic approach was taken in adapting Shelley's narrative.

One might read another significant change from the novel as evidence of early 1930s dumbing-down: the creature's loquaciousness is reduced to a series of inarticulate grunts and cries – but in the context of Whale's schema, this is greatly to the benefit of the presentation of Frankenstein's creation as something of an *enfant sauvage*, a badly served innocent whose violent actions are the result of taunting (the hunchback Fritz's sadistic wielding of a flaming torch) or tragic misunderstanding of games (the monster's inadvertent killing of a little girl by tossing her into the river like the flowers she had been throwing). Of course, this interpretation is muddied by the fact that we now know the monster has a 'criminal' brain, but little in the creature's behaviour suggests these actions to be the results of criminality.

The death of the little girl famously resulted in a particularly egregious piece of censorship – the removal of the latter half of the scene after the monster reaches down towards her (followed by a shot of her father carrying her soaked body with one stocking askew) encouraged audiences to infer more sinister behaviour by the monster than this elision now suggested. The first appearance of the monster (in the series of jump cuts echoed years later by Alfred Hitchcock in a similarly shocking view of a gruesome face in *The Birds*) still carries a remarkable charge today and marks out the fearful territory in which we are to regard the monster, however much sympathy we are invited to extend towards him later. He is, of course, the outsider, as both Whale's Britishness and homosexuality made him in Hollywood – although both of these things were hardly novel in the circles in which he moved. The youthful Frankenstein's portrayal as an outsider with his taste for the forbidden (articulated in one of his more subtle moments by Colin Clive) is also readable as a metaphor for the director's wry perception of his own status; Bill Condon's 1998 film *Gods and Monsters* constructs a plausible picture of Whale's later life in Hollywood, aided by a nuanced performance by Ian McKellen as the director. And any reading of the monster (as played by Karloff) as a classic outsider to whom the director has extended sympathy is consolidated by the readings of virtually every other actor (with the honourable exception of Christopher Lee) who has essayed the monster, with performances in which the physical mutilation and capacity for murderous violence are foregrounded at the expense of the alienated loneliness.

More than Browning's *Dracula*, the prodigious success of Whale's film virtually forged the horror film industry and spawned multiple progeny, mostly at the mercy of the law of diminishing returns – with the splendid exception of this film's immediate sequel. It also popularised a certain (somewhat reduced) quotidian perception of Gothic motifs in the public mind, motifs which were almost parodically treated by Whale even before they had established themselves in any iconographic sense. But viewed in the twenty-first century, the concatenation of elements that make *Frankenstein* work so well are still easy to discern: the aforementioned stressing of the creature's outsider status; the utterly persuasive mime utilised by Karloff to characterise his tragic misfit; and (above all else) Whale's intoxicated, endlessly inventive utilisation of the newish medium of sound cinema. The film functions as both as a blackly comic horror fable and as a serious study of misguided human striving. What's more, the defining, status quo cliché of so many horror and science fiction films – the rosary-clutching suggestion that man should not trespass onto the territory of God – is given little force by the director, a man perfectly prepared to defy the deity.

The success of the film consolidated James Whale's position as one of Universal Studios' most bankable directors and their ace practitioner of the horror film (a position he was further to consolidate with what many considered to be his best work, the sequel to *Frankenstein*, which would place on screen for the first time the novel's diminutive female creator).

After *Frankenstein*, the other James Whale films which creatively utilised Gothic elements are an atmospherically eccentric adaptation of J.B. Priestley's now-unread novel *Benighted* as *The Old Dark House* (1932); a darkly comic, very English take on H.G. Wells' *The Invisible Man* (1933); and what many consider to be Whale's *chef d'ouevre*, the delirious *The Bride of Frankenstein* (1935). All of the Catherine wheels and Roman candles in the director's box of fireworks are gleefully detonated here: his luxuriating in the theatrical, his taste for unorthodox close-ups, staggered camera angles and (for the time) ambitious tracking shots. All of these, along with his very British sense of irony, informed *The Bride*, as did his background as a graphic artist and newspaper cartoonist (a characteristic he shared with another, later filmmaker of similar exuberance, Federico Fellini). The film is further enhanced (unlike the virtually music-free *Dracula* and *Frankenstein*) by a fully realised orchestral score from another talented expat, Franz Waxman, adding a nigh-operatic dimension to Whale's already grandiose conceptions.

As previously mentioned, Whale's reluctance to give the standard Hollywood 'trespassing on God's domain' piety any force in the film may have been a reaction to his mother's almost fanatical devotion to religion. Similarly, the director's channelling of his homosexuality in his work is by no means as straightforward as it might first appear – the failed relationship with a woman with whom he was in love, Doris Zinkeisen (who designed the costumes for his highly successful film of the Jerome Kern/Oscar Hammerstein musical *Show Boat* (1936)), was, Whale would repeatedly tell people, a traumatic event for him, and he remained concerned with the creation of an ideal relationship with an ideal woman (an off-kilter metaphor for themes to be found in his work).

The J.B. Priestley adaptation, *The Old Dark House*, was a film that the director himself was keen to make, persuading a reluctant Universal Studios that they should purchase the rights to Priestley's then-popular novel *Benighted* as a project for both himself and Boris Karloff (with whom he had earlier enjoyed such conspicuous success).

The theme – a diverse group of travellers (including a battle-weary First World War veteran) finding themselves in a secluded house whose inhabitants are a truly bizarre group of misfits – drew from the director some of his quirkiest work, as the endangered visitors struggle to survive a night of horrific happenings. As always with Whale, darker undercurrents are present in the film (darker, that is, than the putative narrative menace). Despite the playful, blackly comic surface of *The Old Dark House*, Whale was able to infuse into even a piece of uncomplicated popular entertainment such as this a noting of Priestley's observations about the grim consequences of the First World War – and even issues of personal responsibility as embodied in the film's soldier, Penderel (played by Melvyn Douglas).

Inevitably, of course, Whale is fascinated by the film's monsters, notably the demented, fire-raising Saul (played by Brember Wills), who is kept in a locked room. Whale's audacious transformation of the lumbering psychopathic beast that the character was in the original novel into a twitchy reined-in little man given to endless sinister quotations from the Bible renders Saul as actually the most sinister figure in a house not short of threatening presences. Particularly significant, of course, is the characterisation (as Horace Femm) of the effete, precious English actor Ernest Thesiger (subsequently to be encouraged by Whale to shamelessly steal scene after scene in *The Bride of Frankenstein*), and the treatment of the character here is provocative, given the director's own sexuality. The deeply effeminate, self-deluding character played by Thesiger invites both derision and fascination on the part of the viewer, inviting speculation on the way in which the director viewed himself. Karloff's hulking butler, however, is a largely just a satisfying bogeyman, but hardly stretches the actor in the fashion in which the Frankenstein monster had for the director.

Prior to *The Bride of Frankenstein*, Whale's enjoyably irreverent version of H.G. Wells' 'scientific romance' *The Invisible Man* (1933) is perhaps the film in which the director finds his sardonic approach perfectly at the service of the blackly comic material. And while the film's provenance undoubtedly lies in the category of science fiction, Whale treats its absurdities as he does his customary Gothic material, pointing up the corollaries with the latter genre. The deranged megalomaniac protagonist (played by Claude Rains with all his customary acumen) is a splendid addition to the gallery of grotesques which the director delighted in creating. The film is significant in that the dire results of a misguided scientific experiment are encapsulated not in some monstrous synthetic creation, but in the scientist himself. And, ironically, the English village setting of the film points up the increasingly murderous psychosis of Griffin, the eponymous Invisible Man, in wry counterpoint – no other English director (with the exception of Alfred Hitchcock) took such an ambiguous attitude to his own country (in terms of attraction/repulsion: a rich contempt for the eccentricities of the English character combined with a deep affection for the same).

The film also allows Whale to confront the English class system in a way that had not been possible in his other works: Griffin's attempt to better his social standing leads to him being an 'invisible man' in several senses (even Thomas Hardy's *Jude the Obscure* might be cited here: a working-class figure destroyed by his attempt to better himself; it might be argued that Hardy, Wells and Whale all regarded the English class system as pernicious, although all were to some extent seduced by it). The fact that the murderous, rule-breaking Griffin is treated to a large measure of sympathy by his director is one of several ways in which the Hammer studios (and later heirs of James Whale such as that studio's signature director Terence Fisher) were to extend a similarly qualified admiration for the single-minded, utterly ruthless and amoral behaviour of figures such as Frankenstein – Claude Rains' Griffin may be more demented than Peter Cushing's implacable Baron Frankenstein, but there is a key resemblance. The attitude of the Invisible Man (in the adaptation by R.C. Sherriff) is extremely modern in his nihilistic, amoral view of murder which the viewer is almost encouraged to accept (and certainly relish the commission of), and although Griffin dies in a hospital (giving us our only glimpse of Claude Rains' face) paying lip service to the fact that there are the customary things which 'man must leave alone', the deepest logic of the film is that Griffin at least attempted to follow a course of action, however destructive, and did not vanish into a faceless bourgeois existence as those around him (with more limited horizons) had done. The similarly taboo-scorning James Whale must have sympathised with this impulse at least.

Inevitably, Universal Studios had responded to the immense success of *Frankenstein* in a fashion which has now become *de rigueur* – in other words, feed the appetite of hungry audiences by producing more material in a similar form: a sequel. But Mary Shelley herself had produced no further suitable source material, so the project that was originally known as *The Return of Frankenstein* was to be based on original material (although using elements from Shelley's book that had not featured in the original film). The new film (as a response to James Whale's lack of interest in a sequel) was to be offered to another director, specifically another expatriate, Kurt Neumann (who was later to make one of the most memorable 1950s science-fiction/horror films, *The Fly*). But Universal executives were no fools and were well aware that the success of the first film owed a great deal to its radical, immensely creative English director. As an added inducement to his helming the new project, he was offered nothing less than complete creative control – and this turned out to be the offer that Whale found himself unable to refuse.

The film he was to make was to be Universal's finest entry in the Gothic cinema genre, even though its divergence from the standard tactics of the field rendered it unlike most other contemporary work, notably in its refusal to deploy the straightforward shock tactics of other films in both Whale's own oeuvre and those of other directors (the moments of menace in the film are relatively rare). Ironically, however, the director's new impatience with the techniques that he himself had forged resulted in a fresh infusion of creative impulses. In *The Bride of Frankenstein* (as the new film was now called), the religious impulse treated so unsympathetically in other works by the director had been transmuted into something different. Henry Frankenstein's creation is specifically aligned with the figure of Christ during the film, carrying further a motif which had appeared in the original *Frankenstein,* and the monster is at one point actually crucified. But this does not suggest an overweening seriousness in the film, as is immediately apparent from the humorous prologue which features Shelley (played by Douglas Walton), his wife Mary (English actress Elsa Lanchester, in a career-making double role – her later appearance in the film as the bride of the monster is to be one of the cinema's most indelibly iconic moments) and Lord Byron (played by Gavin Gordon). The trio (in elaborate period costume) present a prologue to the film which actually consists of a précis of Whale's earlier *Frankenstein* outing. Ken Russell was to make a whole film based around this fecund literary meeting, *Gothic* (1986), written by Stephen Volk (see Appendix: Interviews) and featuring a typically unsettling image in which a woman's naked breasts sport eyes instead of nipples.

The narrative proper picks up at the burning mill of the first film, and we are presented with a now-unsympathetic picture of the revenge-hungry mob which has become a critical motif that will appear throughout the work. When the monster – which did not perish in the mill fire at the end of the first film, as we thought it did – escapes (as it must), we are subsequently presented with another scene touching upon one of Whale's recurrent motifs (the outsider who must perforce live apart from the world – in this case, a sightless hermit played by O.P. Heggie, with whom the monster takes shelter and even develops an embryonic relationship). The dual misfit theme is handled as strikingly as we might expect.

The monster's real nemesis is not so much the unthinking mob as the camp Dr Pretorius (played at full throttle by Ernest Thesiger), who utilises the theatricality of Frankenstein as presented in the earlier film (in which the monster's creator had staged the scene in his laboratory for his audience as if it were a proscenium arch) and whose outrageous concept of a mate for the monster is to bring about the destruction of nearly everyone involved. Once again, the notion of an ideal mate tailored to the specific requirements of an individual (a theme, as we have seen, which possessed a personal resonance for Whale himself) is illusory, although the director, as so often in his career, presents this hopeless dream as something both simultaneously attractive and repellent. Elsa Lanchester's make-up for the bride (courtesy of the maestro Jack Pierce) with a bandage-cocooned body, grotesquely stitched neck and electrified hairstyle has become one of the most celebrated (and caricatured) cases of character make-up in the history of the cinema, beautifully matched with the actress' striking mime performance (as finessed by her director); her jerking, spasmodic head movements and hissing vocal interjections rendering her both hypnotic and otherworldly. The sexual consummation between the monster and his bride to which the narrative has been leading (though she is inevitably as repelled by him as the villagers have been) can only end in catastrophe and conflagration, after Boris Karloff's memorably intoned line 'We belong dead'. This *Liebestod* moment – and the film itself – represents the apogee of Whale's career, and even though that career continued with several other films, he was unable to reach this operatic pitch again. After the loss of his physical health, his mental state became more fragile until he was discovered dead in the pool of his home at Pacific Palisades in 1957. A note discovered after his death suggested suicide, but the official verdict was accidental death. Whether or not the man who brought about the annihilation of a variety of romantic dreams in the cinema was the architect of his own destruction we shall never know.

3
Undermining British Cinema: Gothic Horror in the 1930s and 1940s and Censorship

Macaulay's pithy observation that 'We know of no spectacle so ridiculous as the British public in one of its periodical fits of morality' is a phase that might have been coined for the prissy British reaction to the first wave of horror films in the 1930s and 1940s; even the now-camp, pantomimic Grand Guignol sequence of Tod Slaughter films (notably *Sweeney Todd: The Demon Barber of Fleet Street* (1936)) provoked outrage. No ice was cut in the wave of general disapproval for early examples of respectable English theatrical actors prepared to appear in horror films, such as Ralph Richardson in *The Ghoul* (1933) or Charles Laughton in *The Old Dark House*. Such tongue-clucking reactions are, inevitably, cyclical: the same phenomenon was to be replicated two decades later when Hammer Films began to make its mark with singularly non-respectable fare. The common factor might be seen in horrified contemporary discussions of what was perceived as a new cinema of 'cruelty as diversion', and the films were identified as indexes of depravity; Gothic horror elements incorporated into non-genre or other film products of the day were less vilified, as public disapprobation had already found its target. And who could defend such films?

An essential ingredient for the British horror film has long been its unfaltering ability to upset those seeking the experience of being upset (and thereby gleefully recording falling moral standards). And filmmakers have been more than happy to oblige. 'Épater les bourgeois' has long been the philosophy (even a badge of honour) of many a director and writer in the genre, and those same confrontational filmmakers experience a grim acceptance when the British establishment brings its guns to bear in terms of swingeing censorship. In cyclical fashion over the years, self-styled or government-appointed guardians of decency have become vexed over what was perceived as the unredeemable imagery of the horror film, the flames often fanned by the headline-grabbing exploitation of popular newspapers as well as the usual elective upholders of morality, religion and public decency. The argument that one of the *raisons d'être* of such material has always been its ability to disturb cuts no ice with those who would extirpate horror films, and the suggestion that a film might be 'too exciting' (a criticism levelled at the earliest British essays in the macabre) is salutary, given that an enthusiast for rock music (or, for that matter, the symphonies of Shostakovich) would be unlikely to complain that a particular concert played on the senses in an unpleasantly exhilarating fashion and advocate the removal of the offending passages of music.

In the same fashion, the viewer who enjoys the frisson produced by horror material is unlikely to lament that they found the experience too frightening or disturbing – indeed, these are the very qualities that genre enthusiasts are usually seeking. Most such aficionados clearly relished the Aristotelian catharsis experience afforded by bloody horror films, in which the darker impulses which we all possess are harmlessly slaked by pantomime terror, while we sit safely in our armchair or cinema seat.

Many commentators on the genre have taken the position that any censorship is a dangerous precedent to establish, particularly so in a field that is unlikely to find respectable defenders (as E.M. Forster defended D.H. Lawrence's literary reputation against the would-be prosecutors of the 1960s). And when the frequently recurrent comment is made about the dangerous effects on children of violent entertainment, the response is customarily along the lines that censorship should be a matter of parental responsibility and that the notion that all adults should be obliged to watch only films that qualify as being of a wholesome family nature (because some people take no account of what their children do) clearly strikes many as a ludicrous proposition. However, the most strident advocates of public decency from the 1930s to the present day routinely maintain that all adult material on film should be banned outright, as certain parents cannot be relied upon to be sufficiently vigilant (this tenet was maintained for films from the beginning of the industry, but became more apropos with the advent of home video and, latterly, DVD). Whether such a ban would reduce juvenile crime without any attention to the quantifiable roots of crime (urban deprivation, alienation, joblessness, etc.) is simply not an argument that is taken into consideration.

Frequently rehearsed – but largely ignored by the would-be censors – is the argument that Grand Guignol is often utilised by serious artists specifically to disturb. *Macbeth* and *The Spanish Tragedy* have multiple bloody murders, but invoking the blood-soaked carnage of high art since the Greeks is inefficacious, as supporters of British Gothic have discovered. The fact the Shakespeare packed *Titus Andronicus* with tongue-severing, limb-lopping and enforced cannibalism (atrocities lovingly recreated, ironically, in a British horror film, Douglas Hickox's lively *Theatre of Blood* (1973)), or that Sophocles utilised bloody patricide, incest and blinding in *Oedipus Rex* doesn't cut any ice with the forces of homogenisation. These sanguinary endeavours are, after all, art and *sui generis*, though it has to be said that the censors have never really liked the notion of freedom of expression in the fine arts: Richard Strauss' opera *Salome* (after Oscar Wilde) had the censors' scissors snapping in this country – John the Baptist's severed head could not be presented on a silver platter to the erotically aroused Salome, only the sword which performed the severing, ironically substituting a phallic object for the heroine to salivate over. But the censors are well aware that a strong case for the defence can be made out for high-powered literary or artistic figures.

The much-maligned horror film, however, has few articulate defenders, even though the appetite for the spilling of blood to which this medium caters is precisely that cheerfully exploited by Shakespeare, Dostoevsky, Poe and Homer, all of whom were fully aware of the delicious thrill provided by horror and unblushingly used its frissons to captivate audiences.

Margaret Thatcher's Conservative government commissioned the Williams Committee (chaired by the well-respected moral philosopher Sir Bernard Williams) to examine the effects of graphic material on audiences with a view to altering film censorship. The Committee's exhaustive survey, which appeared in 1979, by far the most comprehensive ever conducted, principally concentrated on obscenity, but sex and horror were being conflated as 'pornography' by now (as in the subsequent Video Recordings Act of, appropriately, 1984). Williams and his colleagues came up with the unacceptable (to the government) conclusion that the 'deprave and corrupt' argument against films was simply unproven and unprovable. And as canny juvenile delinquents quickly realised that magistrates and press pundits eager for a story were all too ready to listen to cries of 'I did it after watching violent films', the Thatcher administration quietly buried the findings of the report, its implications perhaps throwing too much emphasis on the necessity of dealing with the social causes of juvenile crime.

A principal argument of the censorship brigade is the desensitising effect of too much exposure to violence and horror, but a reference to our greatest writer is surely appropriate here. The putting out of Gloucester's eyes onstage in *King Lear* remains deeply shocking and disturbing in any well-staged production, however often audiences have seen this gruesome scene enacted. To some degree, aficionados of the genre must admit that a certain desensitising process is at work, and the films that once terrified audiences now seem distinctly sedate. But the corollary of such a normalising process is not that audiences will rush out to perform the atrocities enacted by Dracula and co. D.H. Lawrence talked about the necessity of maintaining a sense of the reality of pain, something that the better horror films incorporate along with the honest imperative of (as Dickens' fat boy enjoyed) making our flesh creep.

The critic Derek Malcolm, when defending in court a prosecution of the indifferent American horror film, Romano Scavolini's *Nightmares in a Damaged Brain* (1981), made some attempt to defend the film on artistic grounds (even though he admitted that his heart was hardly in it – an echo of E.M. Forster's defence of *Lady Chatterley's Lover*, which the writer considered one of the weaker novels by D.H. Lawrence, but nevertheless maintained his defence as a point of principle). But the judge in the later case regarded a discussion of the technical expertise or creativity involved in a horror film as simply beside the point – whether it was well made or badly made was, quite simply, immaterial; the genre itself was, quite simply, beyond the pale.

The suggestion that horror films routinely put audiences in the position of (and thereby in sympathy with) the monster or killer also does not stand up to much scrutiny. The extensive use of subjective camera point-of-view in films from the 1980s onwards may go some way towards shoring up this canard, but the ultimate imperative of most such horror films is the final survival of the heroine or hero, and this remains the principal source of the generation of suspense (we may be exhilarated by the brilliantly edited depictions of murder and mayhem, but in the best films we feel an acute sense of waste and loss, while audiences unquestionably want the beleaguered heroine or hero to survive).

Defenders of the genre customarily hold that viewers maintain a clear-sighted ability to deal with the excitement of the horror film without becoming immune to the effects of violence in real-life situations; it is possible to enjoy the dramatic recreation of such things while being filled with an abhorrence at an encounter with the real thing. But such debates are hardly new, and one of the most acrimonious exchanges of views led to a seismic change in the way in which British authorities regarded horror films in the 1930s.

The major censorship furore created by the unprecedented popularity of horror films in the UK in that era led to what we can now see as an all-too-predictable response, one that was to be repeated over the years: enthusiastic banning campaigns by local watch committees and furiously voiced questions in the Houses of Parliament by MPs who (it might be argued) were thereby guaranteed of column inches and attention from their Whitehall supremos. However, the most significant result of the hysteria was a now-forgotten initiative: the creation for contentious films of the 'H' for 'Horrific' certificate (predecessor of the 'X' certificate), with parallel outright bans on much Gothic material, including serious adaptations from such writers as H.G. Wells – the impressive film of the writer's *The Island of Doctor Moreau* starring Charles Laughton was only to enjoy wide currency (in uncut form) in the twenty-first century, when the furore was long over. Re-christened *Island of Lost Souls*, Erle C. Kenton's 1932 film was unseen for many years. This once-banned classic showcases a wonderfully sly (and, at times, camp) performance by Laughton, but this asset apart, the film now looks like one of the great horror/science fiction films from Hollywood's Golden Age. Wells hated the film and welcomed its banning, but leaving the creator's displeasure aside, it now appears a truly remarkable, delirious piece of work.

Simmering rather than boiling over: that might be an accurate description of the diversity of the Gothic field in British cinema before the revolution wrought by a small, savvy and industrious British studio with canny commercial instincts. There had been sporadic appearances of horror material in the UK (fallen upon with gratitude by aficionados of the macabre in the days when such fare did not hold the prodigious sway it does today), though crumbs had been thrown to audiences by the continuing use of elements of the genre in non-genre films (cf. the opening sequence of David Lean's 1946 film of *Great Expectations*). Other prestigious literary adaptations sampling the genre included Thorold Dickinson's creepily atmospheric film of Pushkin's *The Queen of Spades* (1949), and the cartography of the (pre-Hammer) terrain should include the crucial importance of early television and radio versions of Gothic subjects, which would furnish the material for the first horror wave of the mid- to late 1950s. These green shoots (or should that be 'red shoots'?) of the coming horror revolution could be tied into the beginning of the mass paperback market and its use of Gothic material, which was soon to be employed in a determinedly synergistic fashion.

The British cinema's interest in the macabre had been present from the very beginning, with significant early titles such as Maurice Elvey's *Maria Marten or the Murder in the Red Barn* (1913; the subject enjoyed multiple film adaptations). The director, who was to have a long and successful film career, took a suitably lip-smacking melodramatic approach to the scenario, a tale of a *crime passionel* (a famous nineteenth-century murder in which the criminal is apprehended when a dream by the victim's mother reveals the location of her corpse). The film inevitably looks quaint today, but was considered strong stuff in its time and set the stage for such later films as *The Wraith of the Tomb* (directed in 1915 by Charles Calvert); Calvert's film is unseeable today, but appears to be the first treatment of an actual horror theme in which the spectre of a Egyptian princess wreaks revenge on the man who made away with her severed, mummified hand. The public's taste for such fare was noticed by enterprising producers from the start, but dissenting voices were also to be heard (as, indeed, they would continue to be throughout the history of the genre). However, the tone of public pronouncements in this area was more along the lines of a sad, fatalistic acceptance that the public should be drawn to such unpleasant fare rather than hectoring demands that such films should be banned.

In the silent era, one of the most impressive films made in the genre of the macabre was directed by a young man who would go on to become Great Britain's greatest filmmaker. Alfred Hitchcock's film version of the Jack the Ripper story, *The Lodger: A Story of the London Fog* (1927), was made at the Islington studios of Gainsborough Pictures (a company which would enjoy a profitable relationship with the Gothic), and it was a calling card film for the youthful Hitchcock, heavily influenced by the German Expressionists he was so impressed by (he had previously worked in the German film industry). But while some of the film's most striking atmospheric effects are the product of this Expressionist influence, others are merely hallmarks of the fizzing, coruscating talent that was to carry the director from this country to an even more successful career in the United States (where his American sojourn was inaugurated with another Gothic subject, a polished adaptation of Daphne du Maurier's *Rebecca* in 1940). The film abounds with Hitchcock touches, such as the suddenly transparent floor which conveys the steady pace of a character in the room above whose presence is obsessing those in the room below. The film was written by Elliott Stannard and was an adaptation of the novel by Mrs Belloc Lowndes written in 1913. In recent years, *The Lodger* has been remastered and has enjoyed modern acclaim to match the enthusiastic reception it initially received, and modern audiences will have no problem accepting the actor Ivor Novello in the role of the mysterious Jack the Ripper figure now that he is perhaps best known for the music awards that bear his name – not to mention the fact that his distinctly effete matinee idol presence has long been forgotten by audiences. The Novello character arrives at the boarding house of an ageing couple who are obsessed with the bloody murders which are plaguing London. The killer is called 'The Avenger' rather than the historical Ripper and his victims are always young blonde women. When viewed in the twenty-first century, the visual style of the film is still astonishing, with everything directed (as is often the case with Hitchcock) towards the implacable manipulation of audience response: we are forced to share the landlord and landlady's apprehensions about their new tenant (is he the ruthless killer?), but also to be involved in the lodger's terror when he is pursued by a vengeful mob (this is an early example of the director's penchant for forcing the audience to identify totally with the villain of the film, although, in the case of *The Lodger*, things are not quite so clear-cut). In fact, the marked expressionist style utilised by Hitchcock in this film was to be abandoned by him fairly speedily, although its concerns would remain paramount throughout his career: the seductively sympathetic killer, the virtuoso treatment of scenes of violent murder and the utterly unerring manipulation of audience responses. Despite the bleakness of its subject, the director posits a certain basic humanity – possibly a kind of personal cockney fellow-feeling – which is set against the implacability of the mob, and the director's celebrated 'transference of guilt' theme makes an early appearance. *The Lodger* was also significant in terms of the Gothic in Great Britain: with this film, Hitchcock had directed the first masterpiece in the genre, and his successors were to find the film a difficult act to follow.

No great impact was made by such films as *The Face at the Window* (filmed by Wilfred Noy in 1920) with its electrically revived, vengeful corpse or, nearly a decade later, *Chamber of Horrors* (1929) directed by Walter Summers, which featured the results of a night spent in Madame Tussauds. Neither film – nor most of those made in the intervening period between the two – made any serious attempt to engage with the darker currents of the English terror film. The subject was sometimes played for laughs and, almost inevitably, derisory laughter is the response (in the modern era at least) to the films of a man whose name for audiences of this era was virtually synonymous with horror and threat: Tod Slaughter.

It would be difficult to underestimate the impact of the cheaply made and audience-pleasing, censor-bothering films which invariably featured a desperately mugging Slaughter as a corrupt and murderous authority figure (invariably brought to his own destruction after a catalogue of killings). But to modern eyes, the killings seem ineptly staged and the biggest problem remains, inevitably, the performances of Slaughter himself, who took the eye-rolling, moustache-twirling villainy (almost literally so in the latter case) of his theatrical performances and transferred them directly to the screen without any attempt to modify his outrageous effects for the more analytical eye of the camera. His performances now seem hilarious to us (in a way that later actors of a not-dissimilar ethos such as Donald Wolfit do not), but this is to view Slaughter's films through the prism of twenty-first-century expectations; there is no gainsaying the fact that audiences of Slaughter's day lapped up these films and even (as is suggested by contemporary critics) realised that they were not to be taken too seriously. Nevertheless, for those early viewers of Slaughter's films, there may have been smiles on their faces, but they were frozen ones; the actor was still considered to be a frightening figure. This apprehension has been totally lost today.

As the 1930s progressed, it was clear that the most innovative work in the Gothic genre was being done in America with such expat film-makers as James Whale (and with talented actors including Charles Laughton and Boris Karloff finding new careers for themselves there). But Slaughter needs a little attention – even if only as a footnote.

The Tod Slaughter films are perhaps a true representation of the kind of touring company productions (or at least the brand of acting they contained) which entrepreneurs like Slaughter would tour around the country. At the centre of all these, often catchpenny, productions – and the subsequent films made of the company's 'greatest hits' – would be the overwhelming (and, at times, overweening) central performance by the bulky, imposing figure of Slaughter himself, with all the actors around him (at least those who might qualify for the noun 'actor') tacitly encouraged not to take attention away from the individual who the public had paid money to see. Slaughter, in defence of his centrality to these films, would no doubt have argued that he was simply giving the public what they wanted, but there are few films where the concentration on one performer at the expense of all those around him does the piece any favours (and the cannier actors know this). No such thinking was part of Slaughter's mindset, but there is no denying that when he is onscreen, viewer attention will be firmly fixed upon him. Like many repertory-trained performers of his generation, the actor came late to films, and at the time of his first appearance in 1935, he was almost 50 – hence the liberal use of hair dye through most of his subsequent performances. Not that the actor ever tried to present any image of attractiveness, which was not his métier: lantern-jawed, gimlet-eyed and heavy-set, Slaughter utilised his intimidating bodily presence with no sense of nuance but with a great deal of gusto. His remake of *Maria Marten or the Murder in the Red Barn* (directed in functional fashion by Milton Rosmer in 1935) is played as one imagines it might have been done on some Victorian provincial stage, and the film marked the beginning of Slaughter's exhaustive plundering of a variety of villainous parts, all rendered in melodramatic colours and employing a certain uniformity of staging and style which makes it difficult retrospectively to judge between them (they all have in common the fact that modern audiences might wonder why the slow-witted characters dealing with Slaughter's clearly malign protagonist did not instantly realise they were being taken to the cleaners – or being set up to be murdered).

Slaughter was born in Newcastle in 1885 and in his teens was already treading the boards at a variety of theatre companies. But when in middle life he began filming the kind of performances that he had become most famous for, such as the evil Squire Corder in *Maria Marten* (with lascivious designs on the heroine) committing a variety of evils from rape to murder, the comeuppance that audiences keenly expected was always delivered. It was inevitable in the Slaughter gallery of villains that he would play one of the most famous, *Sweeney Todd: The Demon Barber of Fleet Street* (for George King in 1936), but this was well before such artists as Stephen Sondheim added a variety of levels to the previously one-dimensional character; Slaughter's version of *Sweeney Todd* removed the bloodletting preparations by the homicidal barber for the ingredients for Mrs Lovett's pies, working on the dual assumption that the censor would ruthlessly remove any such scenes and that, in any case, audiences would be perfectly well aware just what Todd got up to with his specially built barbering chair, the folk legend being common currency.

Slaughter always ensures that his actions suit his name, and such films as this and the subsequent *Crimes of the Dark House* (for the same director four years later) may be enjoyed on a simple primary level, as well as being cogent reminders of the kind of acting that might be seen in theatres of the day. Moreover, such exercises can be instructive – the 1929 film *The Show of Shows* includes a snippet of John Barrymore's Shakespeare, demonstrating that acting styles for the Bard have changed considerably since those days.

But none of this is to suggest that Slaughter's canon is not worth investigating, simply that the correct, indulgent attitude of mind will be necessary. As historical artefacts, they have their use, but the actor's way with his monsters was to seem particularly antediluvian when compared to the infinitely superior playing of villainous roles that was to become the norm from the Hammer studios a decade later.

Since Victorian times, when the attentions of the censorious decisively moved Thomas Hardy away from such forthright novels as *Jude the*

Obscure into less controversial poetry, art (particularly of the popular variety) had always been seen as somewhat subversive, and through the 1930s and 1940s, close attention was paid to the burgeoning phenomenon of popular art and the horror film, with both magazines and censors keen to strip both American and home-grown material of its dangerous, unsettling effects. Rouben Mamoulian's American film of *Dr Jekyll and Mr Hyde* (1931), despite its British setting and origin, was extensively cut in the UK; other casualties were the Universal Pictures/ Lew Landers adaptation of Edgar Allan Poe's *The Raven* (1935), and it was finally decided that a new category should be created to deal with such 'unacceptable' films. In early 1937, the BBFC announced the existence of a new certificate, with the nomenclature 'H' for 'Horrific', ensuring that only audiences of 16 or over were able to see the film (a precursor, in fact, to the 'X' certificate). Interestingly, this particular initiative looked forward to the Video Recordings Act of 1984 (the 'Bright Bill', after the Conservative MP who sponsored it); both claimed that they were not censorship initiatives, but nevertheless (hopefully) stated that they would have the effect of removing such objectionable material completely (classic pieces of 'Orwellian doublethink'). And to some extent, the 'H' certificate did just that – compared to later decades, genre films of a macabre nature became markedly thin on the ground. The certificate was awarded to a film starring an imported star (from Hungary via Hollywood), Bela Lugosi, who came to the UK to film an adaptation of the British writer Edgar Wallace's *The Dark Eyes of London* (1939), essentially a story of the underworld, but with horrific elements – such as disfigurement – that earned it the new certificate. Viewed today, the film seems a naïve melodrama with unsophisticated effects that match the playing of its never-subtle Hungarian leading man, but the response to the film in Britain at the time was as if the very gates of civilisation were being shaken by the Barbarians. The director was Walter Summers, who had previously handled 1929's *Chamber of Horrors*, as mentioned above.

However, despite the best attempts of the censors, the Gothic genre obstinately refused to die, and such films as Brian Desmond Hurst's adaptation of Poe's 'The Tell-Tale Heart' (filmed in 1933) continued to appear. Hurst's film barely clocked in at an hour and is now of historical interest more than anything else; its intrinsic merits are slim. The Gothic impulse was to find its way insidiously into the melodramas produced at Islington's Gainsborough Pictures, where the cruelty of such leading men as the Byronic James Mason could partake of the psychopathology of the horror film without ever trading in its more graphic effects (such as Leslie Arliss' *The Man in Grey* of 1943: sadistic cruelty, but no bloodshed). Hence, such films enjoyed less unwelcome attention from the censor, although moral guardians, sensing the relish with which the material was attacked (and noting the enthusiastic female response to the films), remained unhappy with their success. But there was one consolation – at least (thank God) they were not in the despised, dangerous genre of the horror film.

Edgar Allan Poe (American, but schooled for a period in England – in Stoke Newington, in fact) remained an occasional preoccupation of British filmmakers during the 1930s and 1940s, his name (even at this period) virtually a synonym for Gothic horror; an adaptation of *The Fall of the House of Usher* was directed by Ivan Barnett in 1949. Compared to such handsome-looking versions as Roger Corman's later colour remake for American International Pictures (AIP), this was a threadbare affair, poorly acted with all of Poe's melancholy poetry and febrile ambience leached from the film. Moreover, the embroidery on the writer's brief original was far less creative and in sympathy with the material than that practised by Richard Matheson for the later Corman version. Nevertheless, despite its paucity of effects, the film achieved the distinction of being the second British film (after *The Dark Eyes of London*) to be granted the 'H' certificate. But unlike the later 'X' certificate which the wily Hammer Films studios parleyed to considerable commercial advantage (suggesting to sensation-hungry audiences that the restrictive category meant that they would be party to some kind of forbidden fruit), this lacklustre version apparently did very little business.

After the wonderful, all-too-brief phenomenon that was Ealing Studios' *Dead of Night* (1945), and apart from the later Thorold Dickinson's unsettling adaption of Pushkin's *The Queen of Spades* (both discussed separately), attempting a similarly malign atmosphere, the macabre was an under-visited genre in the UK, and little evidence appeared to suggest that Britain still had the capacity (or the will) to make arresting movies in the Gothic genre. But as the 1940s shaded into the 1950s, a small, ambitious company which had specialised in opportunistic radio adaptations (such as the now-forgotten police show *PC 49*) was to revive the Gothic film (after some science fiction laced with horrific elements) – and, what's more, to rejuvenate the field with such colourful panache and inventiveness that the entire British film industry was to undergo a sea change, with effects that have lasted into the twenty-first century.

4
Bloody Revolution: The Worldwide Impact of Hammer's Cottage Industry

Who could have foreseen that the burgeoning success of a tiny British film studio would effect seismic changes on the industry? Or that it would establish a hegemony that would flourish until big-budget US successes in the field (such as William Friedkin's *The Exorcist* in 1973) would hasten the progress of the death-watch beetle already at work in the studio?

The pocket-sized Hammer Films studios, which established its dominance in premises at Bray, near Maidenhead in Berkshire, quickly established its penchant for the imaginative (and, for the time, sensational and graphic) re-invention of Gothic material, incorporating both nonpareil production design and top creative personnel with (cannily) conspicuous sexual elements at a time when British cinema was notably chaste (such then-shocking films as Jack Clayton's *Room at the Top* (1959), with its frank post-coital discussion of sexual intercourse, would hardly raise an eyebrow today). The studio nourished directors such as Terence Fisher, helping to forge a very personal vision of the Gothic.

Gothic poetry had a marked effect upon romantic verse, most notably in its obsessive concentration on the accoutrements of death, decay and other morbid preoccupations, not to mention its liberating loosening of sexual repression (at least in an indirect fashion). But the sexual impulse in the Gothic – both in this noteworthy first literary appearance and in the films it was to engender from Hammer and other studios – hardly represented a positive, ameliorative attitude to the erotic. In defining fashion, Eros became inextricably linked to Thanatos (ironically, this was to become a particularly useful strategy for British film studios in their dances with the censor – had the films been more straightforwardly about sex, the already over-active application of the censor's scissors would have gone into overdrive).

The product of Hammer Films and co. was clarion evidence that the Gothic impulse (tied so ineluctably to an imperishable erotic impulse) was capable of almost continual re-invention (both creatively and in lacklustre fashion), much as it had been through the eighteenth and nineteenth centuries. And as the poetry of Coleridge and Poe formed a body of work which thoroughly identified the genre, several other lesser writers (who traded in the same doomy tropes) gained the attention of readers, much as the studios which attempted to imitate Hammer product owed some of their commercial success to hanging onto the coat-tails of that studio (a film from the Baker and Berman studios, *Blood of the Vampire*, is still routinely described as a Hammer film, a fact that would not have upset the duo at all). The stress on medievalism in literary Gothic was to bear less fruit in subsequent cinematic incarnations, where the time period was almost invariably Victorian; the latter period inevitably lent itself to the *de rigueur* repression of libidinous impulses, with the concomitant orgiastic sense of release when those impulses are unleashed (particularly significant here is the bodice-bursting sexual transmutation of the repressed Barbara Shelley character in Fisher's *Dracula, Prince of Darkness*).

If the wide diversity of the literary Gothic genre (Radcliffian terror, melodrama and even philosophical tenets) was not to be reproduced in the cinema, the imaginative scope of many of the talents who worked for Hammer and the other studios nevertheless hinted (however unconsciously) at the range of material available to the filmmakers from the genre's past. And it might be said that the thirst for novelty (as individual motifs began to become exhausted through over-use) forced filmmakers to try – sooner or later – most of the strategies that the original practitioners of the Gothic had essayed. No stone – or tombstone – was left unturned. The Hammer studio turned out some of the finest British films (whether considered as part of the horror genre or not), bolstered by the cream of British acting talent, before the law of diminishing returns (and the emergence of modern-day-set horror films) put paid to the studio's period product.

So Long at the Fair (1950), the last film that Hammer's signature director Terence Fisher was to make at Gainsborough Pictures (where he initially began to display the skills that he was later to finesse), is a fascinating curio when looked at in the context of his later career. Co-directed by Antony Darnborough, this period-set piece trades in growing unease (with an ingenious plot that has seen much service subsequently) and is crammed with intriguing pre-echoes of elements that the director would later move centre stage in his filmmaking portfolio.

Jean Simmons plays a naïve young English girl in Paris whose brother goes missing during the 1889 Grand Exposition – and whose very existence is denied by staff at the hotel where they were staying. An English artist working in Paris (played by Dirk Bogarde) is the only person who believes her, having encountered the missing brother the night before he vanished. The film's final revelation, in which it is discovered that the missing brother has contracted the plague and is being held incommunicado so as not to empty the city of alarmed tourists, has a certain disturbing force, and the atmospheric treatment of several earlier scenes now look like vintage Fisher, such as an investigation of the slightly sinister Paris hotel from which the brother's room has inexplicably vanished. There are also foreshadowings of the director's *Dracula, Prince of Darkness* with an English couple abroad destined for a sinister fate (one of whom has no patience with the foreign people and customs they are obliged to deal with), and the final ushering of the Jean Simmons character into a cloistered room to see her desperately ill brother has the kind of understatement that Fisher often demonstrated subsequently (in the teeth of the fact that he is often regarded as a unsubtle, over-specific director); we are not shown the brother ravaged by the plague and we are allowed to fill in our own suggestive mental image of his unseen visage. The smashing of a false wall in a hotel room also suggests similar moments in later Fisher films, and the conjuring of the unspeakable concealed beneath a minatory, subtly off-kilter surface is again characteristic of the director.

But the film which announced Fisher to the world as the definitive horror director was *The Curse of Frankenstein* in 1957. Interestingly, Hammer's move into the horror genre was actually occasioned by the success of its adaptation of Nigel Kneale's BBC *Quatermass* serial as *The Quatermass Xperiment* (1955), which, although being firmly in the science-fiction genre, achieved many of its most memorable effects through the use of horror tropes (such as the hideous, sucked-dry husk of a corpse). And it was the latter genre which was to prove the studio's most enduring legacy in filmic terms.

A recurrent refrain over the years – from both Peter Cushing and Christopher Lee – was their combined, slightly prickly (in Lee's case at least) defence of the horror films they made in the late 1950s and 1960s; their tactic was to repeatedly attack the unrelenting gruesomeness of the current product (from the 1980s onwards). Their position (in essence) was that in their heyday, working for Hammer, Amicus and co., they made what were essentially classically oriented colourful fantasies – harmless and closer to the Brothers Grimm than to the real world – with distancing period settings, unlike the in-your-face modern-day-set evisceration and bloodshed that dominated later films. Lee, in fact, preferred the term 'terror' to that of 'horror', although one might wonder how he came to feel about the hijacking of that word for religiously inspired attacks on Western targets.

But were Cushing and Lee being disingenuous (and indulging in a certain special pleading) when trying to suggest that the films they made were more innocent and less offensive than those that followed? Nietzsche's aphorism about memory might be on the nail here: '"I did this", says my memory; "I could not have done this", says my pride. Eventually memory yields.' It would appear that the actors had forgotten the mountain of outrage and opprobrium that greeted *The Curse of Frankenstein* on its first release in May 1957; one of the less horrified epithets used by critics queuing up to excoriate the film was 'repulsive'. In fact, the tone of most of the reviews went beyond merely hostile, with suggestions that the Hammer Films ethos represented a wholesale attack on the decent values in society (*pace* Cushing and Lee, the films of such modern-day horrormeisters as Eli Roth outraged their critics rather less than this). But if the Hammer actors had remembered such vitriolic attacks of 50 or so years earlier, they would no doubt regard them as quaint and hilariously outmoded when set against the context of modern horror films. It was, after all, an era when such product had virtually no cultural cachet – the British Film Institute magazine *Sight & Sound* famously (and dismissively) reviewed Hitchcock's *Psycho* in 1960 in terms of a sorrowful lament as to just how far the Master had fallen (ironically, this was in a portmanteau review with Billy Wilder's *The Apartment* of the same year – and exactly the same point was made about the director of that now-highly regarded film).

So do vintage Hammer Films in the twenty-first century look harmless and quaint, much removed from the grisly, flesh-stripping torture of such profitable franchises as the *Saw* and *Hostel* films? Has *The Human Centipede* (with mouths stitched to anuses) seen off the lovable old Frankenstein monster with his more acceptable stitching? If Christopher Lee, whose acting career has stretched impressively into his ninth decade, were to put a Blu-ray of *The Curse of Frankenstein* into his home movie system, he might find that his memory has been playing him false. Certainly, the first 45 minutes of the film are relatively sedate, as we are shown a youthful Frankenstein (played at this point in the film by Melvyn Hayes) beginning his studies in primitive spare parts surgery with the occasional macabre moment. These include the long-censored scene in which Peter Cushing gazes at an eyeball in a jar – Fisher can't resist a joke here, enlarging the actor's own eye as he gazes at the repulsive object through a magnifying glass. But from the moment when Frankenstein discovers that his creature, wrapped, mummy-like in bandages, has become ambulatory, the tempo of the film abruptly changes from *andante* to *accelerando*. As the Baron opens a door and sees the creature standing awkwardly (like a puppet that has had its strings cut), we are in a very different kind of horror film than had previously been shown to audiences. The creature reaches haltingly towards its own bandaged face, and with a juddering zoom Fisher propels us in for a close-up of the most ghastly horror film make-up – in full colour – that audiences had hitherto ever seen. And from this point on, the elderly Christopher Lee (watching the film today) would see how wrong he was about how relatively innocent this film that made his name was. The violence and power of *The Curse of Frankenstein* (with the creature clutching his face after a gunshot as blood streams through his fingers) still carries a charge in the twenty-first century, and that first sight of the creature's mutilated face is a harbinger of a new era in macabre cinema.

It is worth considering for a moment Phil Leakey's famous creature make-up, utilising rubber solution and morticians' wax. Had Universal Studios realised early on just what a cash cow they had in these Hammer remakes of their own classic product, they might have been more cooperative. At the time, no sanction was granted for a re-use of the image created by Jack Pierce for Boris Karloff's monster, so Leakey was obliged to come up with something very different – the result, he later claimed, was conceived and created in haste, and he was not happy with it. But looked at today, the make-up provides the perfect metaphor for the kind of cinema in which Hammer was to trade. At the time, Lee's creature was described as having the face of a traffic accident victim, and certainly, with the opaque eye and horrendous, swollen scars, this was a nightmare visage some considerable distance from Karloff's more abstract and perhaps less realistic appearance (there was of course no medical precedent for the square forehead of Karloff's creature, no matter how iconic it became). The hideous green tinge of Lee's make-up suggested the charnel house origins of the creature's head, and for a generation of filmgoers, the striking image was to be a calling card for the studio – rivalled only by the appearance of another very different form of make-up for Christopher Lee: that created for his Dracula. The violence and threat that follows in the third act of *The Curse of Frankenstein* remains deeply visceral even today and gives the lie to the notion that these films are now denatured historical artefacts.

Certainly, the period settings in this film and its stablemates grant a certain distance (the audience is not watching, say, a victim strapped into a torture chair in contemporary Europe, as in the *Hostel* films), but no retrospective allowances need to be made for Fisher and his cohorts in dealing with the volatile, violent activities of his characters. For Fisher, *The Curse of Frankenstein* – at a stroke – established him as the *de facto* director of such product for the studio, although critical respectability was not to come till much later, and there can be few directors whose stylistic fingerprints went from being regarded as evidence of a talentless hack/journeyman director to those of an authentic auteur.

What is perhaps most astonishing about the unified elements of this first Hammer colour film is just how many of the important constituent elements are already in place – and, what's more, functioning from the off at maximum effectiveness. There is Fisher, of course; the writer Jimmy Sangster (whose first major Gothic enterprise for the company this was, and who produces a stripped-down scenario some considerable distance from Mary Shelley, but absolutely utilitarian and at the service of the film Fisher and his associates wanted to make); the composer James Bernard, with an effective score (if scrawnily recorded), albeit lacking anything as distinctive as the plangent leitmotif he was to compose for the subsequent *Dracula* and which would see perhaps too much service in further films in the series; the cinematographer Jack Asher, responsible as much as any other member of the creative crew for forging a strong visual identity for the film and its successors; and the production designer Bernard Robinson, whose particular skill was to manufacture a facsimile of sumptuousness on extremely restricted budgets. While Hammer films rarely have the air of spaciousness of their Universal Studios predecessors, the British studio's more confined spaces are dressed in the most creative and evocative of fashions, affording a pleasure as keen as anything else within the film.

With *The Curse of Frankenstein*, comparisons to James Whale's more excessive, operatic approach to his material are inevitable, but essentially pointless. These are two very different films, and within the parameters that the two English directors set themselves, they signally achieve their precise aims (the differences might be encapsulated in Whale's steady accumulation of dread as opposed to Fisher's abrupt and visceral use of shock cuts, the latter set against a more ordered and precise dramatic schema). Similarly counterpointing the moments of gruesome jolts are the shafts of black humour: the elderly professor (from whom the ruthless Baron is to farm a brain of genius for his creature) being shown Rembrandt's 'The Anatomy Lesson of Dr Tulp' (which Frankenstein claims that his father owned) before pushing the elderly man over a balcony (the stuntman taking the fall, landing, ironically, on his head); the aforementioned shot of Cushing's eye being set against the one he is inspecting for his creature; and the famous joke after the Baron has arranged for the dispatch of an inconvenient serving girl by the creature (he is seen listening to the unseen assault in another room), cutting to breakfast the next day with Frankenstein drily asking his fiancée to pass the marmalade.

Recent restored Blu-ray editions of the film present an interesting question: how would a modern audience, used to regularly timed injections of pulse-raising horror, respond to these rather sedately paced opening scenes? Have contemporary viewers lost the art of patience or waiting for deferred pleasure? A similar question might be posed concerning Alfred Hitchcock's *The Birds*, which takes a considerable time before delivering the principal reason why the audience is in the cinema: the avian attacks. In both cases, while the directors' choices may have to be justified to a modern viewer, they remain specific strategies rather than a misreading of the material. Similarly, audiences might be expected to be impatient with the character of Frankenstein's tutor-turned-assistant, Paul Krempe, whose dramatic function is principally to irritatingly remind the Baron how dangerous his unorthodox activities are, and be, essentially (in Freudian terms), an ever-cautious super-ego to Frankenstein's unrestrained id. It might be said that modern impatience with Krempe's notion that Frankenstein is tampering with God's work is quickly dispensed with by the Baron's sardonic replies (and inevitably audience awareness) to the effect that all medical advances are, to some extent, doing just that. But does Krempe have a point when he talks about the dangerousness of these activities? Even when he is proved right – as in Frankenstein's murder of the elderly professor or the monster's psychopathic nature – we still find the character of the ever-critical Krempe (ably enough played by Robert Urquhart) a tiresome one.

The suggestion was also made that the film was really suitable for sadists only, and given the immense commercial success of the film, this would suggest that the fairly specialist taste was more endemic than might have been thought. But the critical superciliousness (not entirely unanimous, it should be noted) had an intriguing subtext.

In the same way that Eunice Gayson is fondly remembered as the first Bond girl, Hazel Court does similar duty here as the first Hammer heroine, Elizabeth (although Valerie Gaunt as the luckless serving girl Justine murdered by the monster is the first Hammer victim). Given the sombre warnings Elizabeth receives from Paul Krempe – and the fact that she is actually living in a house in which Frankenstein is conducting his arcane experiments – she perhaps seems either a little naïve or a little incurious, but (unlike Barbara Shelley in later Hammer films) her role is largely a decorative one, with her prominently displayed cleavage accentuated in the film's posters.

In keeping with a more cynical modern age, the creature here – while pathetic – is not the vaguely sympathetic victim that Karloff makes it, but quickly begins to show signs of the homicidal behaviour which is to be the hallmark of Hammer's treatment of the creature throughout its long series; it's a measure of Christopher Lee's splendid mime performance that we do not despise Frankenstein's patchwork creation (a key scene here is the one in which the Baron forces the monster to stand up and sit down awkwardly, treating it like a performing dog).

Modern audiences have to use a certain imagination, mentally filling in the rich colours of the film which were so much a part of its original shocking effect on audiences. Even with the careful restoration it has recently received, the Eastmancolor process is still a touch faded but (interestingly) becomes more vivid and forceful from the midway point of the film, prior to the monster's first appearance. And there is no doubt that this is the best that the film will ever look in modern times.

In terms of its place in the history of Gothic cinema, *The Curse of Frankenstein,* as written by Sangster, has little interest in the Promethean themes of the original novel and is more concerned with (for instance) such issues as the niceties of social position, as demonstrated in Elizabeth's mother virtually pimping her daughter to the Baron (on whom she relies for financial support, as she had done with his father); modern audiences might wonder why the adult Elizabeth (although affianced to Frankenstein) comes to live in his house without the benefit of a chaperone (apart, that is, from the unhappy Krempe, who quickly appears to fall in love with her). More modern sexual attitudes are revealed when we learn that Frankenstein and the maid Justine are sleeping together, something that would have been unthinkable in the James Whale version.

With this first important Hammer horror film, Terence Fisher had raised the bar high for himself. His problem now was to produce material as striking is this first entry. *The Revenge of Frankenstein* in 1958 is an early example of the kind of ingenuity in ringing the changes on pre-existing material which became (perforce) Hammer's stock in trade, as the eponymous Baron cheats the guillotine. Substituting for his own execution a priest who has been dispatched to perform the last rites for him, Frankenstein is soon once again primed to resume his experiments. The fact that the audience does not immediately despise him for the ruthless (and homicidal) deception that brought about his freedom is due as much to the casting of Peter Cushing in the part as the writing and direction, which would not have been the case had the part been played by (say) another Hammer alumnus, the far less sympathetic Michael Gough, who was noted at the time for his sneering expression and supercilious voice. Interestingly, when the director Tim Burton, a long-time Hammer aficionado, was (many years later) to cast the latter as Batman's obliging butler in his highly successful revival of the Bob Kane/Bill Finger superhero, he was to uncover surprisingly likable facets of the actor's personality which had been ruthlessly stamped down and repressed in the heyday of Gough's career as a horror actor. But Cushing allows a certain winning charisma to inform his portrayal – one that Terence Fisher knows precisely how to showcase.

As such, it isn't long before the Baron is bloodily plying his old trade (under the name of Dr Stein), using the sanatorium for charity patients he now runs as a sort of body bank for his real vocational work. Once again, the real sleight-of-hand here lies not so much in the grisly bag of tricks with which the audience is pleasurably shocked, but in the easily assumed complicity we adopt towards the Baron's ruthless practices. Unlike Colin Clive's inaugural Frankenstein for James Whale (with whom we were hardly involved and who is regarded as *sub specie aeternitatis*), the real achievement of Fisher and Cushing is to make us (by proxy) as keen as the Baron is to advance science in his own particular, take-no-prisoners fashion (however queasily we may regard his moral code). In some ways, the complicity invited here is along the lines that Shakespeare creates for his equally cold-blooded Richard III, but with the black and sardonic humour incorporated into our observation of the Baron's actions, rather than via a wry address to the audience.

While in the first entry in the Frankenstein series, Jimmy Sangster appeared to be trying out a variety of approaches to the character (approaches finessed into something more nuanced and interesting through the treatment of the text by Cushing and Fisher), *The Revenge of Frankenstein* demonstrates a growing confidence and ambitiousness – and even more ambiguity – in the way in which the Baron is realised. In his confrontation with the Medical Council in the second film, we see a brisk professional man set against his peers (the latter always *comme il faut*), and a syndrome is established which will be repeated several times in the course of the series. Frankenstein, despite the obvious impatience he feels towards his more intellectually limited colleagues, maintains, initially, at least, a certain professional decorum – until, that is, the bourgeois limitations and (as he sees it) desperately limited horizons of his colleagues drive him into a cold anger.

We also see a more pronounced and nuanced picture of the class distinctions which are a small but resonant part of the Frankenstein scenarios. The Baron, of course (for the benefit of audiences), speaks English, but in a carefully enunciated received pronunciation which often suggests a social difference between him and those he encounters (again, although we are nominally in places with names like 'Karlstad', English remains the lingua franca) and those lower down the social scale (such as the numerous landlords suspicious of but deferential towards their betters, who they regard as corrupt) utilise non-specific regional British accents, maintaining the division. The Baron's apparently worthy social gesture in *The Revenge of Frankenstein* of working in a hospital where the patients are not drawn from the aristocratic classes is inevitably a sham, given that his real agenda is (as ever) to harvest human body parts for his creation of a human being. But compared to the Medical Council (as we see on a visit they make to the hospital), the Baron is not constrained by any particular social expectations and has a briskly authoritative (but not alienating) manner towards *all* those he deals with, whatever their class. Here, as written by Sangster and as acted by Cushing, Frankenstein is a modern, genuinely *deraciné* figure uninterested in the finer points of social behaviour that might be expected of someone from his class. But this is not because of any healthy democratising instinct; it is the product of the Baron's egomaniacal sense of superiority to the whole human race. He considers himself not only above class, but above all the stultified mores of the time; the mores, in fact, which repeatedly prevent him from being allowed to continue with his work. Science is his god, and the utter ruthlessness with which he worships at this particular altar is (unsurprisingly) what makes his charisma and energy so attractive, however murderous his actions. Parallels might be drawn with the cinema's customary preoccupation with the high-achieving but ultimately doomed gangster whose rise and fall we watched with fascination. The difference from such figures, though, is that Frankenstein may appear to die at the end of several of his films, but we know that (like his supernatural *confrère* Dracula) he will be back again in another film, doing his bloody work.

The strategy for sequels has frequently become calcified into a fairly tight rendering of the perceived elements that made the first film successful, but Terence Fisher's second Frankenstein film is a particularly surprising piece of work, not conforming to this pattern, showing that both the director and the writer (Sangster again) were clearly prepared to try something more audacious, eschewing certain components of the first film which probably contributed to its success (such as a straightforwardly repulsive monster, which the second film does not (quite) possess, a risky tinkering with the formula before, in fact, it had become a formula). This was something that clearly worried the film company publicity department – the lurid poster for *The Revenge of Frankenstein* is particularly mendacious, converting Michael Gwynn's unpleasant looking 'creature' into something more closely resembling the monstrous make-up utilised by Christopher Lee in the first film, whereas a certain coarsening of the features is the actual extent of Gwynn's transformation.

Frankenstein is once again the single-minded, agenda-setting *force majeure* surrounded by others who (we as viewers are made to feel) prevent him from completing his life's work. After cheating the guillotine with a substitute, a newly energised Baron (showing greater attention to his elegant raiments than before) sets about the task of transplanting the brain of a disabled man into a new body. But, unlike the preceding film, the Baron's creation, Karl, is not initially monstrous, but is possessed of both conscience and feeling. The luckless Karl (sensitively played by the always-reliable Gwynn, one of the best British character actors of the day) is humanised to a greater degree than the creature played by Lee in the preceding film, and we are party to his anguish in a way that puts us more firmly on his side, so that (on this occasion) we are obliged to take a more jaundiced view of the ruthlessness of the Frankenstein character, charismatic though he remains.

The notion of dualism of character which was to become so central to many Hammer films is here located with particular cogency in Karl's character, notably when he learns that his new, transformed condition may produce an urge for cannibalism – and the monstrousness of this condition is brought home with some force (the metaphor regarding his creator's consumption of human bodies for scientific purposes is not over-stressed). A scene in which the now-terrifying Karl bursts into a room full of horrified onlookers – like some grotesque illegitimate child of Frankenstein that has been kept hidden from view – has palpable Freudian resonance, but Fisher saves his most disturbing extrapolation of the central theme until late in the film. The notion of brain transference is re-introduced when, in a savage and horrific attack by the patients in his sanatorium, Frankenstein himself is reduced to a pathetic bloody ruin. His own brain is transferred by an assistant into another body. Once again, the various outrageous (and, for the nineteenth century, blasphemous) notions of asexual reproduction – and a ruthless supplanting of accepted religious notions – is conveyed for a modern cinema audience with some dramatic impetus. And it should be noted that in a secular age (such as Britain was beginning to enter), the fact that such strategies were not distancing in terms of the film's impact is a measure of the achievement of Fisher and his colleagues. Having said that, the displacement of the more horrific, Gothic elements of the scenario into the realms of moral quagmires more than physically realised bloody violence (though that element is present) meant that the film did not quite deliver what its contemporary audience expected, and (the usual morally disapproving voices aside) did not please its audience as much as its predecessor had. The film's reputation over the years has fluctuated, but a variety of persuasively argued advocacies for *The Revenge of Frankenstein* has ensured that its reputation is now relatively secure.

In many ways, Terence Fisher's film of *Dracula* (from an economical screenplay by Jimmy Sangster) is not only one of the most perfectly constructed films made by the studio, it is also an encapsulation of just how filmmakers conflated the various elements that made the product function so well (and for those aware of such things, the way in which budgetary constraints had occasioned a level of inspiration in Fisher and his colleagues, not to merely conceal the paucity of their resources but to make a positive virtue of such realities).

When Merian C. Cooper's *King Kong* (1933) was remade (both in the crass and indifferent John Guillermin 1976 version and in the far more successful Peter Jackson reimagining in 2005), there was a significant change by these filmmakers to one key aspect of the inestimable original. One might speculate that the makers of the 1933 film did not seem to realise quite how sympathetic we would feel towards the giant ape, wrenched from his natural habitat and propelled towards his doom by human greed, so that when the entrepreneur Carl Denham (who is basically responsible for Kong's fate) intones over his corpse 'It was beauty killed the beast', there is little sense that the filmmakers knew how much we would resent this complacent remark from the man responsible for Kong's destruction. There is a much more knowing attitude on the part of the makers in the later versions; we're openly invited to disapprove of Denham by this point in the films, and we are well aware that the real bad guy is not the towering simian, however many people he has killed.

All of this is a preamble to wondering just how well the filmmakers understood the real implications of the Hammer version of *Dracula*, in which the vampiric count is not presented as the straightforwardly monstrous creature of the Browning Bela Lugosi version, but (in Christopher Lee's mesmeric interpretation) as an elegant, dangerously attractive and cultivated figure with immense erotic appeal. However little his character is inclined to (or, for that matter, able to – who knows?) indulge in straightforward sexual activity, there is a metaphor for sexual threat implied, with a libidinous charge more insidious than any more conventional erotic presentation would be. Certainly, the actor who played the part claims to have been unaware in advance of the erotic effect his playing of the character would have, and has repeatedly said that he was greatly surprised at the matinee idol-type following his bloodsucking monster quickly acquired.

Ironically, the censorship problems that British horror films were plagued with during their heyday in the late 1950s and 1960s were customarily directed at the more sanguinary aspects of the films, although various censors were invariably disturbed by what they perceived as the linking of sexual and violent aspects. John Trevelyan of the BBFC (with whom Hammer was to have many battles, both amicable and acrimonious) was exercised by this particular conjunction, but not as much as one of Trevelyan's successors, James Ferman, who decided that 'blood on breasts' (needless to say, a standard image in Hammer films) was a trigger for rapists and routinely attempted to excise such images. But the more deep-seated eroticism of the earlier Hammer films (such as *Dracula*) appeared to go over the heads of – or at least be (tacitly?) ignored by – the censors. The erotic submission to the vampire count by his female victims in their various states of *déshabillé* was self-evident (such as Melissa Stribling's clearly sexual surrender in Fisher's film, an image foregrounded in the posters, à la Bernini's Saint Teresa of Avila's orgasmic response to Christ).

Such notions were actually more subversive in an era when female sexuality (at least in terms of its representation in films) was a subject far less open to discussion than it is in the much freer twenty-first century. Inevitably, of course, looked at in terms of the gender politics of the later era, the clearly expressed sadomasochism and dominance/submission of the relationships between the vampire and his victims could hardly be said to be a positive expression of female sexuality. But discussions of the moral dimensions concerning these illegitimate offspring of Leopold von Sacher-Masoch remain as complex as ever (and are still debated within the lesbian community, both in terms of straight and gay S&M, the latter being considered more acceptable, as the power plays are seen as less problematic). And this territory has assumed a particularly pertinent relevance towards the end of the first decade of the twenty-first century with the phenomenal success of the female writer E.L. James' crudely written but self-evidently reader-friendly erotic trilogy beginning with *Fifty Shades of Grey*. At the time of Fisher's film, the Dracula character might have been said to represent a variety of archetypes: the untrammelled libido wreaking havoc within the repression of the Victorian era; the dangerous masculine image forged by such female writers as Charlotte Brontë and Jane Austen: the devilishly attractive but unyielding and controlling male figure with a barely concealed contempt for the female sex; and, finally, even as a challenge to clear-cut notions of good and evil. Dracula, as played by Christopher Lee, is hardly – in Nietzschean terms – beyond good and evil, but his challenge to the established order, and the verities of Christian belief, is given an energy and power mostly lacking in his opponents, whatever spiritual grace was conferred upon them, with the conspicuous exception of the Count's nemesis, the savant Abraham Van Helsing, who (as played by the forceful Peter Cushing) is a very different figure from the more sedate and philosophical incarnation of the role as played by Edward Van Sloan in Tod Browning's film of the Stoker novel. Of course, those who chose to dismiss such films as immoral and depraved were closing their eyes to a recurrent theme: the ultimate triumph of religious belief over seemingly insurmountable supernatural power. The accoutrements of religion (notably the crucifix and holy water) are routinely utilised to re-establish order out of the chaos brought by Dracula, even if the films are carefully drained (for the contemporary era) of the religiosity of standard Hollywood products.

Attention must be paid to the actor Peter Cushing; his significance is prodigious and his position in the pantheon of the British horror film cannot be over-estimated. Cushing is as important (in a very different way) as his friend and colleague Christopher Lee – the pitting of the two actors against each other in innumerable films might initially seem to represent a bifurcation of intellect and reason against the forces of destruction (most frequently, Cushing for the former and Lee for the latter). However, there are levels of nuance (and even direct contradiction) in the use of both actors' personae: in terms of the physicality versus intellect conflict, one of the conspicuous successes of Hammer Films is to invert this notion whenever possible, though Cushing is the studio's arch personifier of intellect and learning (the template no doubt being the success of Cushing's Van Helsing in the first Dracula film). Cushing had enjoyed considerable television success before his typecasting as a horror actor (apart from a memorable Winston Smith in a controversial television adaptation of Orwell's *Nineteen Eighty-Four*, set against the malign torturer O'Brien of Andre Morrell with whom Cushing was work again in later years, most notably in *The Hound of the Baskervilles*, and an acclaimed Darcy in a TV adaptation of *Pride and Prejudice*). Aside from the mellifluous speaking voice – one of his principal assets as an actor – Cushing was famous for his teasing out of the physicality of the characters he played (in parallel with the intellectual acumen), a skill he was particularly fastidious about cultivating. In order to make (for instance) Frankenstein's ministrations over a bloody operating table plausible, the actor would consult doctor friends in order that his physical movements presented an image of verisimilitude, however unlikely the activities of his character. This physicality was extended to the famous final conflict played out in the most energetic of terms in Fisher's *Dracula*. Unlike Edwin Van Sloan's disappointing off-screen staking of Bela Lugosi, Cushing's destruction of the vampire is splendidly energetic: he makes an athletic leap from a table to tear down the drapes that will expose Dracula to the exterminating sunlight (*inter alia*, it should be noted that the subsequent speedy putrefaction of the vampire was something audiences had not seen before and made all previous vanquishing of vampires seem rather genteel; recently, censored footage of this spectacular decay has been found and restored to prints of the film). But the intellect/physicality codification of the two actors Cushing and Lee was (fortunately) not to become set in stone, as Lee was repeatedly prove quite as capable as his colleague in characterising rationalist men of action (he was to play Sherlock Holmes for Terence Fisher in the inert German film *Sherlock Holmes and the Deadly Necklace* (1962), not made under the Hammer aegis, but it was a film which added no lustre to either man's reputation; however, Lee's Duc de Richelieu for the company in *The Devil Rides Out* is one of his great performances). And it is the fact that both men are able to convey these different levels of striation in their characters that rendered their performances more multifaceted than Jimmy Sangster's sometimes quotidian screenplays might have initially suggested.

In the modern era, when virtually all films are made in colour, it's hard to remember quite what impact its use could have when the output of the cinema was largely divided between black-and-white and colour (later use in film of the medium of black-and-white cinematography, such as Tim Burton's tribute to the exploitation director *Ed Wood* and Michel Hazanavicius's silent film homage *The Artist*, utilise monochrome as a way of self-consciously conjuring up a vanished era). This impact of colour is a factor that cannot be underestimated in the impact of the early Hammer films such as *Dracula* – the startling splash of blood which appears in the subterranean lair of the Count in the credit sequence was doubly shocking both in an era when monochrome was often the norm and also in this sudden unexpected appearance of a body fluid which was seen far less in the more understated era in which the film appeared. Jack Asher, the director of photography, utilised the vintage Eastmancolor process to create a canvas which was redolent of influential art movements of the past – not so much the Impressionists, although Asher's use of chiaroscuro would have pleased the French Masters, but in the coordination of often jarring blocks of colour in the manner of such Cubists as Georges Braque. The director Terence Fisher realised that a more subtle, understated use of cinema technique (including, for instance, an avoidance of fast cutting) would allow this innovative colour palette to make its best effect. This shows a highly professional approach to new methods which may be at risk in the twenty-first-century; Peter Jackson's 2012 film of Tolkien's *The Hobbit* utilised an accelerated 3D technology in the number of frames, which had its first preview audiences feeling something akin to motion sickness. If Fisher destabilised and disturbed his audience, it was precisely in line with the agenda he had intended.

Viewed in the modern age, *Dracula*'s virtues now looks positively classical (not least in its orthodox framing of individual scenes) which perhaps ties in with what many considered to be the narrative's embrace of patriarchal attitudes, although any attentive viewing of the film will show that it cannot be shoehorned into any ideological stance. Perhaps the deepest logic of its makers was to produce the best-made piece of exploitation cinema for the day that they could (and in that mission Fisher and his colleagues succeeded admirably), but *Dracula* remains ineluctably modern in its refusal to be interpreted in any single fashion. And it's that fact – as much as the frisson of pleasure that the film still produces in the viewer – that is *Dracula*'s greatest achievement.

Time has a way of displacing existing (flawed) judgements, particularly when it comes to both the serious and the popular arts. In his day, the composer Louis Spohr commanded almost as much attention as Beethoven, but which of the two do we remember today? Both the Nobel Prize in Literature and a variety of Academy Awards have been granted to artists to whom posterity has not been kind, while less acclaimed work has proved extremely durable (the *locus classicus* here is Alfred Hitchcock, who was belatedly – and guiltily – granted a lifetime achievement award by the Academy, but enjoyed no such recognition for his individual films, which have outlasted many other more fêted products). In similar fashion, certain projects from the Hammer Films had a distinctly underwhelming response on their first appearances (and often collected a crop of mostly negative reviews).

But several of these films have retrospectively been accorded much more affection and respect. A notable example here is Terence Fisher's first *Dracula* sequel – but one which did not, in fact, feature the count himself: 1960's *The Brides of Dracula*. The Dracula figure here is Baron Meinster, played by David Peel. It was the actor's finest hour, famous for a shot of Peel, still handsome (and impressively coiffed) but in gruesome mutilation make-up. The film is undoubtedly Peel's *chef d'oeuvre* (nothing else in his unspectacular career proved so memorable); at the time of the film's release, the company considered that although they had not as before used Christopher Lee as the source of seductive evil in this film, they had another potential in the attractive (if effete-seeming) Peel and anticipated much female fan mail. In the event, they were to be disappointed in these hopes, as they were also to be on the next occasion when they self-consciously groomed a good-looking younger successor to their now-ageing principal stars: the raven-haired and intense Ralph Bates. Although the latter was a striking presence in Hammer films, his career as a horror star was short-lived (not helped by Jimmy Sangster's woeful *The Horror of Frankenstein* (1970) and ended by indifferent TV sitcoms which ruthlessly siphoned off any charisma he may have possessed).

Peel, though not the stellar presence Hammer hoped for, is nevertheless a particularly interesting case. To modern eyes, his performance is notably camp and feline, and offers a distinct contrast to the saturnine, understated elegance of Christopher Lee's vampire. But Peel was undoubtedly charismatic, and the very different dynamic his performance brings to *The Brides of Dracula* is to its advantage. When combined with the other elements that Fisher introduced to the mix, what resulted was something subtly different from most Hammer films (even though the reliable Peter Cushing is on hand to provide an antidote to the insidious evil of Baron Meinster). The film compensates for its absent eponymous monster by being full of scenes charged with a poetic intensity, such as a grimly obsessed, middle-aged woman (Freda Jackson) straddling a grave and imploring its occupant to emerge and accept her new vampire identity. There is also the ageing mother of the monstrous nobleman (played with customary eccentricity by the glorious character actress Martita Hunt), vampirised by her son (an act that has an unsettling incestuous quality) and delicately covering the tell-tale incisions in her neck with a nervous smile as if to reveal such things would be more of a social faux pas than to present herself as the victim of supernatural evil. This intriguing strand of Debrett-style misdemeanour in the presence of vampiric evil was later to be echoed in Kim Newman's novel *Anno Dracula*, in which bad form involving the blood of serving girls is socially infra dig. *The Brides of Dracula* has a more phantasmagoric air than many of its bedfellows. Fisher was seemingly ready to finesse the surrealistic elements of his work; while the more unemphatic presentation of evil in his other films creates an effect by virtue of its almost quotidian quality, the dreamlike, narcoleptic effect of *The Brides of Dracula* often makes it seem like a Hammer-style overlay in primary colours on a different palimpsest – the more horrific engravings of Gustave Doré, perhaps.

Given the unenthusiastic welcome it initially received, it is perhaps somewhat surprising that Fisher's *The Brides of Dracula* is now regarded by many as one of (if not *the*) definitive Hammer film. To some extent, this might be attributed to the familiar syndrome whereby a neglected child is extolled (almost wilfully) as the best of the breed. Sir Arthur Conan Doyle, for instance, always considered his now largely unread *The White Company* as far superior to his much-loved Sherlock Holmes stories, and there are many who regard *On Her Majesty's Secret Service* as one of the very best James Bond movies, even though, for all its considerable virtues, it has an inexperienced non-actor struggling with the central character. So what are the reasons for this seemingly perverse promotion of *The Brides of Dracula* into the upper echelons of critical esteem? It may be able to boast the presence of Peter Cushing, but Dracula (in the person of Christopher Lee) himself is notable for his absence – although, as noted above, David Peel's Baron Meinster provides a piquant, one-off substitute. Jimmy Sangster's original screenplay featured the Count, but Lee's refusal to be shoehorned into public perception as synonymous with the character (as he ruefully observed had happened to Bela Lugosi) led to his absence. The screenplay was perhaps a case of 'too many cooks': Jimmy Sangter's first draft was reworked by Peter Bryan, and Edward Percy, with a final wash-and-rinse from producer Anthony Hinds. The resulting film from this polyglot screenplay – for all its dreamlike atmosphere – is often incoherent and has yawning gaps in its narrative credibility. But it might be argued that for this very reason, the effect that the film has on the viewer is more complex and allusive than many a more linear piece; we are, at times, not a million miles away from the almost narrative-free imagery of Buñuel and Dali's *Un Chien Andalou* (1929), which also featured physical mutilation. Needless to say, the disparate elements here required integuments to allow them to hang together, and it is here that Fisher's steely authority with this material pays dividends. The first act of the film is a perfect example of this skilfulness, as a young French teacher, Marianne, finds herself at Castle Meinster, where she meets the attractive, haunted young Baron and his elderly, eccentric mother. The audience is ineluctably drawn into the young woman's nervous investigation of the castle, an investigation which is heavy with Freudian overtones (exacerbated by the Baron's peculiar, semi-incestuous relationship with his mother and an unusual family set-up). The production design here – with its mysterious and atmospheric castle, which is more compendious than the usual modest-sized Hammer set – is utilised by Fisher in the most thoughtful and creative of fashions. We are also witnessing a generational shift from the weakened Baroness (literally weakened through loss of blood) to her malign offspring, and it is ironic that the seductive Baron appears to offer a source of comfort and safety to the worried young woman when he is the source of the greatest danger. But perhaps the final testament to the strength of *The Brides of Dracula* is an unquantifiable one: why is it that these particular elements, wielded in a fashion not radically unfamiliar from other Hammer product, created a film which stays with the viewer considerably longer than many other films from this period?

By the time he directed the fourth film in Hammer's Frankenstein sequence in 1967, Terence Fisher would have been able to observe (had he taken an interest) a variety of younger directors whose approach to the horror genre was different from his own: edgier, more concerned with the contemporary scene and with perhaps a bleaker and more nihilistic view of the world (Michael Reeves, in his all-too-abbreviated body of work, is the exemplar here). As such, when one looks at the unorthodox strategies employed in *Frankenstein Created Woman*, it's tempting to speculate that Fisher might have been chafing at an approach that may have served him well in the past, but was in danger of becoming ossified. Was he concerned with such issues? The truth about Fisher's attitude to his work is probably more straightforward. Largely speaking, he took on the scripts that he was assigned – on some occasions, he was able to infuse them with more invention and vision than they had actually possessed, while at other times he found it impossible to transcend the limitations of the original, quotidian material. And if the fourth Hammer Frankenstein film takes on some startling new aspects – such as a provocative approach to gender – this is probably as much due to the screenplay of Anthony Hinds (writing under his 'John Elder' *nom de plume*) as any contribution that Fisher might have made, which is not to say that another filmmaker could have realised this curious, off-kilter piece with quite the screwed-down intensity that Fisher provides it with.

The pressure was on Fisher to exceed the preceding, underachieving entry in the Frankenstein cycle, *The Evil of Frankenstein* (1964), directed in lacklustre fashion by Freddie Francis and saddled with a particularly uninteresting, characterless monster. The same could not be said for the new film in which the dynamics of sexuality and personal power are explored in constantly surprising fashion.

In *Frankenstein Created Woman*, when one of the Baron's assistants, Hans (played by the handsome but bland Robert Morris), is executed for a murder of which he is innocent, his grief-stricken lover Christina takes her own life. The Baron – in a particularly perverse experiment – transplants the essence of Hans' soul into the revivified body of the young girl, creating the same kind of jarring interface between male and female sexuality that is to be found in Roy Ward Baker's *Dr Jekyll and Sister Hyde* (1971), but with even more complex results. In Christina's body, the vengeful Hans sets about pursuing and entrapping the three men who actually committed the murder for which he was originally executed. What is particularly interesting about this scenario is that for once the Baron is removed from his customary position as a proactive personality responsible for the thrust of the narrative; here, he is only able to look on as his creation wreaks havoc before ending his/her own life. This new presentation of the Baron's character is allied to a slight softening of the ruthlessness (and willingness to kill) which we have been shown in the earlier films. What's more, his examination of concepts such as the human soul – a far more evanescent notion than the blood-and-tissue components of his previous creations – suggests that he has acquired a more philosophical, speculative nature. Whatever achievements he may have brought about in the field of medical science (and we are reminded that they are striking achievements, particularly in the nineteenth century), he has hitherto been less concerned with notions of the soul and psyche, although his elevation into such rarefied realms actually has the same sanguinary, fatal results as his earlier experiments: wholesale death and destruction following. Cushing, as ever, is able to display his character's cutting-edge intelligence and innate sense of superiority to everyone around him (notably a prosecutor at a trial, with Frankenstein clearly feeling himself to be at a higher stage of evolutionary development compared to those around him). There is perhaps a less Manichaean view of human nature present here than in other films in the cycle, with a sense of possible amelioration for the human condition (although, despite this, the end result is inevitably disastrous, which, of course, it has to be, given the narrative imperatives of any Frankenstein film). But it is the humanity of the creature in the film – the eponymous 'Frankenstein created woman' – who presents the most curious figure in the whole cycle: an innkeeper's daughter, Christina, played by Susan Denberg. Much was made in the film's advertising of the physical appeal of the actress, who had appeared nude in a variety of men's magazines. The most famous still from the film showed the actress on Frankenstein's operating table, bare-midriffed, her breasts and groin covered by the briefest of bandage-like cloth. Denberg brought to the part a surprising degree of nuance and shading, marking her out from the many female Hammer stars clearly chosen for their pulchritude rather than their thespian abilities.

Denberg's character, Christina, initially suffers from looks that have been marred by scarring, and she is also lame. Christina was humiliated by the three men responsible for the death of her father, and after her suicide, Frankenstein's revivification has transformed her into something both physically attractive and utterly ruthless in her pursuit of murderous revenge. Fisher forces us into complicity with Christina's actions (she is, after all, the victim of three drunken thugs, as is her murdered father) and the ambiguity of the film's attitude towards her results in a shifting of emphasis from that usually placed upon the Baron by Fisher, whereby we are never quite sure quite what our attitudes to Frankenstein's behaviour should be: distaste or a guilty, furtive admiration.

But what really intrigues in the film is the shifting morass of sexuality which the Christina creature (after her resurrection) represents. She is now, of course, a hermaphroditic figure, and the two warring aspects of his/her personality are presented in a more ambiguous fashion than in Roy Ward Baker's spin on a female Hyde (although the film avoids the perverse confluence of female and male sexual desire in one figure, something tackled provocatively – if jokily – by Baker). Christina, however, is not always in thrall to the personality of the murdered Hans, who takes possession of her at different times. Before killing her victims, Christina is presented as a sensual and seductive figure (as so often in Hammer's films, the fluid spilled in a sexual consummation will be blood), and the sound of the dead Hans' voice issuing from this delicate female form is a particularly surrealistic and disturbing effect. The Baron's final attempts to persuade Christina (after the completion of her killings, influenced from beyond the grave) are curiously sympathetic as he tries to tell her who she really is, but at this point Christina already knows, making her inevitable death a genuinely tragic occurrence. It is one of the points in the Hammer Frankenstein sequence when we are prompted to have strikingly divided opinions about the Baron, and it is interesting to speculate on whether the foregrounding of *anima* as opposed to *animus* for one of the few times in the sequence is the reason for the film's particular resonance. The presentation in *Frankenstein Created Woman* of male sexuality (notably in the taunting attitude of the drunken males) has a distinctly feminist edge and would not look out of place in a separatist novel of the 1970s (or for that matter in Stieg Larsson's *The Girl with the Dragon Tattoo*, where male sexuality is pitilessly – and repeatedly – presented as something negative and destructive). It is significant that this first appearance of a major female transformation is accompanied by a strange new theme – the transmutation of a soul. But Christina remains essentially a victim: when she is proactive in her behaviour, it is at the behest of the murderous male for whom she is a host. Her destruction is poignant but, in the context of the narrative, inevitable.

T.S. Eliot suggested the world might end not with a bang but a whimper – as did one of the key Hammer cycles. The Indian summer offering *Frankenstein and the Monster from Hell* (1973) reminded viewers of the comfortable (if now unthreatening) virtues of the Hammer product, even with the creative fires burning at a distinctly low ebb. For all its infelicities (from Terence Fisher's rather tired resumption of the directorial reins to Peter Cushing's cadaverous appearance and unlikely bouffant hairstyle), the film did at least boast some virtues; it is stylish filmmaking, delivered with at least some of the old commitment. Most poignantly, however, this was the final pairing of Hammer's finest director (Terence Fisher) and actor (Peter Cushing) – a fact all too apparent at the time of the film's release. While the earlier glories are only fitfully present (and the eponymous monster, as played by the brawny Dave Prowse, lacks any distinctive character, unlike Lee's inaugural assumption), there are nostalgic pleasures to be had here.

5
Beyond the Aristocracy

The blue-blooded Baron and the Count may have been the Trojan horses for Hammer's inexorable ascendancy, but soon it became necessary to plunder other sources for material, both literary and filmic. Universal Studios continued to be a lodestone, and Peter Cushing and Christopher Lee were once again opponents in a new version of the Karl Freund/Boris Karloff classic, *The Mummy* (1959), helmed by Terence Fisher. Lee is once again at the centre of an erotic obsession, but on this occasion it is him who lives in thrall to another person. Lee's Egyptian high priest has become obsessed with the Queen – a passion which results in him having his tongue severed with a knife; he is then mummified to be buried with her in her sarcophagus. As so often in Hammer films, grotesque physical mutilation (while carrying sufficiently grim dramatic force within its own terms) has a secondary significance, sometimes involving the suggestion of emasculation, something that occurs in both in this film and in the little-seen *The Stranglers of Bombay* (directed by Fisher in 1959), another film which explicitly linked violence and torture with sexuality. A famous still from the film shows the actor Guy Rolfe spread-eagled on the ground, staked out by members of the Thuggee cult, while the actress Marie Devereux (whose generous cleavage was often utilised by directors in this era) displays her embonpoint while tantalisingly pouring away water within the sight of the tormented Rolfe.

The murdered Egyptian priest will be reanimated as the eponymous mummy later in the film, but the threat of Lee's monster in this film is an asexual one, unlike that of Dracula (although, of course, the latter is not interested in ordinary sexual congress). In seeking the reincarnation of the Egyptian princess for whom he was tortured and for whom he died, the priest/mummy becomes a motivated killing machine – the threat to women here is focused, and audiences might have been aware, on a subconscious level, that the only remaining life in the creature was reduced to a series of primeval impulses (with the sexual impulse conspicuously absent). The Egyptologist played by Peter Cushing is to discover that the life force moving the creature is not affected by the loss of other vital organs and a blast from a shotgun through its chest (a rupture prominently played out in the ads, which showed a torch beam shining through the hole in the chest of the mummy); similarly, a metal spear driven though its body gives no pause to the ambulatory creature. Its consummation can only reside in a final return to the earth, its from-beyond-the-grave mission unaccomplished.

Cutting-room floors throughout the world have often held fragments of Hammer films, ruthlessly expunged by the censors – fragments which (if they still exist) are now being restored, much to the benefit of these half-century-plus-old classics. This wash-and-rinse process was particularly advantageous in the case of Terence Fisher's attempt to revive another of the great Universal Studios monster franchises with *The Curse of the Werewolf* (1961). This film arrived at an awkward moment for Hammer, when the establishment disgust with the studio's product (which inevitably was inversely proportional to the public's wholehearted embrace of the films) meant that censorship customarily removed several key details and, moreover, pre-censorship took its toll (the film's scripts were invariably submitted to the BBFC, arriving back blue-pencilled with often-hilarious suggestions as to how elements that might disturb viewers should be removed). That Fisher's film (even before the recent restoration of censored elements) still carries a considerable charge today is not only a testament to the mixture of unassuming professionalism and Michael Powell-style romantic impulse that characterised Fisher's work, but is also due to a particularly fortunate piece of casting, with the late Oliver Reed moved up from supporting parts for the company to an important central role, which he attacks with customary ferocity (even, it has to be admitted, in non-lycanthropic state). The cadaverous actor Richard Wordsworth had already made an important contribution to Hammer iconography by appearing as the doomed astronaut in the studio's first horror/science fiction outing, *The Quatermass Xperiment* (1955), undergoing a grotesque transformation as he was infected by an alien presence brought back from a space mission. His transformation in *The Curse of the Werewolf* is in the nature of the make-up applied to the actor as a spectacularly unprepossessing beggar at a banquet; the Wordsworth character, however, is to be indirectly responsible for the real transformation in the film – that of his son (the unlikely premise at the base of the film is that the brutal rape of a servant girl, played by the pneumatic Yvonne Romain, by the imprisoned beggar (the latter has now been reduced to virtually animal level in his filthy cell) could produce as their offspring the lycanthropic central character is a ludicrous notion, but functions perfectly adequately as a plot engine here).

The narrative of *The Curse of the Werewolf* devolves on the tragic central character played by Reed. Leon is blighted with a lycanthropy which has strong sexual undertones, heavily emphasised by Reed's charismatic (if overwrought) performance. During the credit sequence, Fisher utilises the actor's eyes (in werewolf make-up) in extreme close-up, darting to the left and right, blinking and shedding tears – it is one of the most effective openings to any Hammer film and it is considerably finessed by one of the most impressive scores ever written for Hammer by British classical composer Benjamin Frankel. While James Bernard was the signature composer for the company and produced (again and again) plangently effective soundtracks for the variety of monsters and killers whose flesh-ripping activities he underscored, his speciality was the repetition of jagged dissonant motifs – admittedly effective, but inevitably beginning to sound rather like each other from film to film (particularly so in the composer's arresting *Dracula* leitmotif, which he utilised in several appearances for the Count). Benjamin Frankel's score for *The Curse of the Werewolf*, however, was considerably more complex than those of Bernard, and utilised subtleties and felicities of orchestration that would have been regarded as too nuanced for the more straightforwardly dramatic Bernard. Frankel's score is notable for its then-novel use of serial technique (which is music based upon all 12 notes of the chromatic scale and utilised in a series of variations); he had use this compositional approach in his First Symphony, and its ambitious employment here is of inestimable value to Terence Fisher's film.

But is Oliver Reed's twitching, hyper-tense reading of the tortured Leon an asset to the film or a weakness? Over the years, critics have disagreed, some calling the performance crass and obvious, but the truth is not so straightforward. The actor's un-English, Latin appearance and repeated filmic struggles with the demands of his characters' troubled psyches became a trademark of his early career, and although Terence Fisher's film would appear to call for precisely this kind of performance from Reed, it's hard to imagine another young actor of the period making such a strong impression in the relatively underwritten part. What's more, Roy Ashton's exceedingly effective make-up (given a relatively brief amount of screen time) was more striking than that created for such actors as Lon Chaney Jr. in *The Wolf Man* (1941) and utilised Reed's own physiognomy (notably his perpetually furrowed brow and flaring nostrils) to allow the actor's personality to remain visible even when he has become a snarling homicidal beast.

A potential salvation for Leon lies in the virginal Christina (played by Catherine Feller), the daughter of the man he works for, but there is no real sense in which it appears that Leon will be able to shake off his tragic destiny. His ultimate death at the hands of a sympathetic but stern father figure is nevertheless moving, and although the character could not be considered to be developed in any serious fashion, as a play on an archetype, it has considerable potency.

It is instructive to observe the change in attitude to the copious bloodletting and prodigious body count of the Hammer corpus (and no pun is intended in the latter noun). After the horrified disapproval that greeted the early films, there was a gradual (and perhaps inevitable) softening of attitude as the once-vilified films gradually became an ineluctable part of the national consciousness. In fact, the earlier films (particularly those made before the BBFC decided to apply the metaphorical blue pencil more enthusiastically) treated the violence in a more edgy and destabilising fashion, but it wasn't just the restraint placed on the more sanguinary scenes which brought about this change of attitude. The flesh-ripping mayhem in Hammer films had always been lent an air of unreality by the fact of the mittel-European settings and the distancing effect of period costume. Moreover, the various foreign languages (theoretically) being spoken were further homogenised (and domesticated) by the precisely enunciated dialogue (wherever the films were set, the norm was a very English received pronunciation, with such impeccably spoken actors as Peter Cushing encapsulating the status quo). For audiences watching the sudden violent deaths in these vibrantly coloured films and the blood spilling on the backdrops of Bernard Robinson's sumptuous production designs, the experience was rather like the careful enacting of a ritual – a ritual in its own way much like those enacted by the characters in the films themselves – cf. the revivification of Dracula performed by a depraved nobleman (and hypocritical Victorian businessmen in search of new sensations) in Peter Sasdy's *Taste the Blood of Dracula* (1970). The various discrete components of the films were choreographed with immense skill, and the feeling of arch self-parody which was to creep in with such lamentable misfires as Jimmy Sangster's *The Horror of Frankenstein* (also 1970) was wisely kept at bay – although a more acceptable playfulness might be noted in the sense that Hammer's talented filmmakers were assuming the role of mischievous uncles holding us all in thrall by a menace-filled ghost story, which was undoubtedly part of the ethos of the company. In addition, the element of the supernatural that allowed audiences to thrill to the driving of stakes into vampiric chests (and the satisfying welling-up of blood) further distanced Hammer films from the real world, allowing us all to smile at our complicity in this tried-and-true process. Audiences responded enthusiastically to the dynamically staged ferocity of the studio's product and would mentally tick off the various components as they appeared in the narratives of predators stalking their prey, pouncing and being bloodily dispatched. The fact that the films were once considered absolutely beyond the pale (and dismissed as horror pornography) began to seem ever more distant – a fact confirmed by the interviews given by the studio's two key players, Peter Cushing and Christopher Lee, who, as mentioned earlier, would lament (in conservative fashion) the graphic violence of horror films of the 1970s and described the kind of films they made as essentially fairy tales – thereby conveniently forgetting just how outraged the moral guardians had been over Lee's Frankenstein creature clasping a hand to his face as blood jetted from a gunshot wound.

Almost everyone connected with *The Gorgon* (1964) was prepared to admit – in rueful retrospection – that a key element of the film was simply not up to scratch, and the disappointment of audiences had seriously hurt the film's prospects. It was, in fact, the vision of the titular monster – the same syndrome, in effect, which had sabotaged another Hammer project, the distinctly non-frightening devil dog in *The Hound of the Baskervilles*, which had similarly drawn audiences' attention away from the excellences to be found elsewhere in the film (notably, in both films, the nonpareil acting). If this seems a touch unfair given the limited screen time these creatures were given, it was nevertheless short-sighted of Hammer executives not to see that cheeseparing and haste in this crucial respect would not be forgiven by audiences, not least because the build-up to the appearances of the eponymous monsters was so appetite-whettingly staged. But the compromise goes deeper than that, given the iconographic value of these particular ghastly apparitions.

The setting chosen for the Hammer Gorgon (Megaera rather than the better-known Medusa) to wreak her petrifying havoc on those unlucky enough to cross her path was a Teutonic Europe, some distance from the historical antecedents of the mythological Greek monster. As ever, Terence Fisher was aware that he could rely on the copper-bottomed production design of the inventive Bernard Robinson and that the public would cut him some slack for his performers. But the fires were burning lower than usual: while Christopher Lee's performance (for once in a sympathetic savant role) seems less engaged than usual, Peter Cushing as ever invested his character (a university professor) with the understated authority that was the actor's stock in trade and which lent such verisimilitude to so many of the films he appeared in. Neither, however, invested their role with quite the customary authority.

But the film has one other key asset – another actor quite as reliable Cushing: the luminous Barbara Shelley, lending to her role (as always for Hammer) a plausible inner life that granted a flesh and blood reality to her crinolined, corset-wearing heroine. In most of their films, Hammer's head honchos Michael Carreras and Anthony Hinds were canny enough to promote the pretty, innocuous blondes who invariably served as juvenile-leads-for-the-menacing, but both men were also well aware that an actress of Shelley's calibre was required for key female roles, such as the one she played in *The Gorgon* (and it should be noted that there is an assumption here that the reader will be familiar with the film and not disturbed by revelations). Shelley's reined-in, self-conscious character is (as contemporary viewers of the film no doubt guessed) capable of transforming herself into the snake-headed monstrosity whose gaze can transform her victims into stone, and viewers – then and now – might speculate on how much more effective the film's tentative mythological charge might have been had the actress herself been permitted to play the eponymous Gorgon (the part was in fact played, to no great effect, by the actress Prudence Hyman). The fact that the creature's face is merely that of a middle-aged woman with sinister lighting and a head full of immobile plastic snakes might be compensated for had we been allowed to see Shelley as Megaera. But while the film's incidental pleasures are many (staging, *mise-en-scène*, acting), it isn't just the fact that Fisher seems less galvanised by the project than usual – it is the writing (by John Gilling) which has not conjured any creative spin for the scenario. The interpolation of the Gorgon legend into a potentially militaristic Prussian setting is not fruitful, and even popular entertainment film such as this might have done something with the confluence of a society dedicated to war and a central character whose image is nothing less than the face of death, but that was not on the agenda here. Part of the problem is that Fisher and Gilling don't quite know what to do with their petrifying Greek monster, other than conform to what E.M. Forster once dismissively said of several Dickens characters: simply appear in order to do the action is expected of them and then retire, with no particular development. The various quadrilles executed here by the characters between castle, asylum and other settings have a formal rigour, but insufficient eerie charge, though Fisher's restrained but expressive romantic instincts infuse the material through the often startling visuals, full of lustrous colour and atmospheric lighting effects. All of this hardly makes up for the fact that Barbara Shelley, Hammer's most accomplished actress, isn't really a given enough to get her teeth into (although to some degree that is dictated by the exigencies of the narrative, which has to withhold certain facts).

Still leaving aside the Baron and the Count, another film which endured something of a lacklustre reception on its first appearance was Don Sharp's *Kiss of the Vampire* (1963), an idiosyncratic entry touching the customary bases, but with a subtly different identity from that of most of its stablemates, in which Dr Ravna, an aristocratic bloodsucker, organises bacchanalias at his estate and holds the surrounding countryside in the grip of fear, with only a strong-minded authority figure as his nemesis. As with the torment endured by Peter Cushing's character in *The Brides of Dracula*, a punishing, almost masochistic self-torture is required to extirpate the bite of the undead (here it is an incision on the wrist so that vampiric contamination may be burned away in similar fashion). The channelling of the erotic element here is (as in Robert Young's *Vampire Circus* (1972)) located within a seductive, vampiric brother and sister who cast an ineluctable spell over a naïve young bride. The blue-blooded monster Dr Ravna is here played by the capable Noel Willman as a supercilious authoritarian figure, with none of the romantic appeal that Christopher Lee brought to such parts, but it is a decision which renders Ravna's clash with his puritan opponent a meeting of cheerless equals. Interestingly, the score for *Kiss of the Vampire* (by the studio's signature composer James Bernard) appears to belong to another film, one of a more delirious inclination, utilising (as it does) late romantic orchestrations in the fashion of a slightly more dissonant Rachmaninov.

In the twenty-first century, it's hard to realise just how popular the writer Dennis Wheatley was. His success was something of a phenomenon and he achieved a virtual superstar status before such things were a regular occurrence for writers; he was (to some degree) a J.K. Rowling *avant la lettre*, and relished his celebrity. Wheatley's novels were mostly in the adventure field, but if he is remembered today (and there are many readers for whom his name would mean very little), it is for his supernatural outings – and of these, by far the most significant was his 1934 Gothic adventure *The Devil Rides Out*. Wheatley would preface his books with portentous, slightly hilarious warnings about the dangers of indulging in supernatural practices (such as those he wrote about) and suggested steering well clear of evil black magic cults (like the one that his aristocratic hero, the Duc de Richleau, tackles in his most famous book – and, frankly, something that was not likely to be on the radar of most of his readers), but this was of a part with the writer's own unerring instinct for self-promotion. Wheatley was well aware that the 'verisimilitude' imparted by these spurious warnings no doubt helped the popularity of his work. Read today, the book still functions strongly on a basic storytelling level (Wheatley undoubtedly possessed a glittering eye which could hold the reader), but the crudeness and lack of sophistication of his writing has dated badly (leaving aside the racial elements which would hardly conform to current standards – not to mention the rabid anti-communism, though the latter is not a feature of *The Devil Rides Out*).

When Hammer decided to film the latter novel in 1968, the writer's name still carried a commercial charge, although his literary star had seriously waned. It was to be the first in a series of adaptations of Wheatley, but (in similar fashion to the proposed series of Conan Doyle adaptations that Hammer's *The Hound of the Baskervilles* was designed to initiate), the film led to no further sequels, apart from a 1976 adaptation of Wheatley's *To the Devil a Daughter*, and this remains one of the great might-have-beens in the studio's history, not least because of the casting of the Duc de Richleau, played by one of the studio's great assets, Christopher Lee, who perfectly incarnates the combination of romantic energy and cool intellect in the face of unspeakable evil. The film also represented the last time Lee worked with the studio's signature director, Terence Fisher, who turned in one of his most authoritative jobs (sabotaged only by some unfinished special effects – a recent Blu-ray edition was controversially received despite providing a version of the film with more sophisticated effects work, finessed with modern technology).

The conflict (usually at one remove) between two charismatic and powerful figures, the Duc de Richleau and the sinister cult leader Mocata, is one of the unalloyed pleasures of the film, particularly as the cult leader is played by another great character actor of the day, Charles Gray (before the latter began to turn in performances which were virtual caricatures of his best work), and there is the same sense of the well-equipped savant up against an utterly ruthless and implacable enemy – but with the versatile Lee playing the former this time rather than the latter, thereby reversing the dynamic of his relationship with Peter Cushing in *Dracula*. Once again (as in earlier Fisher/Lee films), there are other less experienced, younger figures – to some degree, potential cannon fodder – who are caught in the clash of these two authoritarian figures and whose destruction is guaranteed if they do not allow themselves to be guided by possessors of superior knowledge. (In narrative terms of course, these younger figures exist in order to be rescued by the savant hero, who is thereby permitted to demonstrate expertise and exigent decision-making.) Fisher's approach (as so often in his career) is to treat the material in an absolutely straightforward, stylistically unfussy fashion, allowing his narrative to make its maximum effect without any directorial flourishes – the precise approach, in fact, which occasioned (at the time) a dismissal of the director as a rather dull, stolid filmmaker, but who is now perceived more sympathetically as a formal classicist who knows precisely when to trust the *mise-en-scène* he has fashioned with such skill. The aforementioned maladroit special effects (such as a spectral horse and rider which invade a country house and a disappointing demon in a cheap-looking mask glimpsed at a black magic ritual) are less effective than the scenes in which Fisher allows his actors to produce their effects with perfectly honed dialogue and nuanced performance, such as the sequence in which the evil cultist hypnotises a female character in order to draw back into his web one of his disciples, the character Simon (played by Patrick Mower) who has been rescued from the cult by de Richleau. Scenes like this – and the various mini-lectures delivered by Lee on the precise capabilities and level of threat of his devil-worshipping enemies – are extremely effective, and while the more dated elements of Wheatley's narrative are subtly excised, there are resonances which in the twenty-first century seem ever more pertinent, such as the terrifying hold that cults have over the disciples they have wrenched from a former life (and the now well-known attempts to brainwash cultists and remove all influence of former friends and family). But while Fisher's technique remains as unshowy as ever, he is even able to incorporate into his sinister narrative a certain energetic romantic impulse – the film, with its handsome vintage cars, sumptuous production design and exciting chases, functions on this more straightforward level quite as effectively as it does in conveying a sense of insidious evil (the tense traversal of a now-deserted site of a black magic ritual by de Richleau, finding evidence of devil worship, is as subtly disturbing a scene as any of the conspicuous bloodletting to be found elsewhere in Hammer products).

The contribution of American screenwriter Richard Matheson should not be underestimated; in some ways, he was the perfect fit for Fisher's vision, always foregrounding the uncluttered imperatives of the narrative but allowing characterisation to grow out of situation. In many ways, his admirable screenplay is an improvement over the lively and eventful but baggy original novel. As ever with Fisher, the treatments of elements of the supernatural (such as the spirit of a dead woman performing a crucial function in the defeat of evil at the end of the film) are treated in an unspectacular fashion which allows them to make their effects with quiet authority.

The Devil Rides Out also has some interesting sidelines on gender within its characters: the women in the film are by no means simply there to provide figures to be endangered, and the centrality of the young woman Tanith (played by Nike Arrighi) even takes on board notions of power and responsibility that transcended mere generic requirements.

A Hammer film that suffered from censorship excisions was *The Two Faces of Dr Jekyll* (1960), which was an ambitious attempt by the studio to do something different with Robert Louis Stevenson's imperishable original. In the twenty-first century, when such riffs on Stevenson's story are commonplace (Hammer itself was to attempt another such filigree with Roy Ward Baker's *Dr Jekyll and Sister Hyde*), a certain historical perspective is needed to appreciate how radical the notion was in *The Two Faces of Dr Jekyll* (courtesy of the playwright Wolf Mankowitz) to reverse the polarity of the doctor's transmogrification from a physically unprepossessing, dull and repressed Jekyll to an outrageously handsome dandified Hyde (the Manichaean contrast of good versus evil remains located in Jekyll and his alter ego as usual), but Paul Massie's bright-eyed Hyde, glittering with manic intensity and sexual appeal, is quite some distance from, say, Frederick March's simian, crouched assumption of the role for Rouben Mamoulian in 1931, with flared nostrils and a mouth crammed full of misshapen teeth. Interestingly, even in the early 1960s, there was still a resonance to Stevenson's once-subversive notion that beneath the carapace of rectitude of the upper-middle-class Victorian gentleman was the urgent promptings of a ravening, murderous creature from the id, eager to embrace all the vices that his respectable alter ego would fastidiously reject. The evidence that this was still tricky territory was clear from the fact that Hammer was obliged to once again pre-censor the script and even endure some ruinous tampering after the film was finished. Because of this homogenising process, this remains (more than most Hammer films directed by Terence Fisher) a work in which it is necessary to try to discern the director and writer's original intentions underneath a heavily compromised surface; it is a measure of the filmmaker's accomplishments that such an excavation is worthwhile. As with several other Hammer films, a restoration of certain sequences has repaired some of the damage done to *The Two Faces of Dr Jekyll*, which made the film often seem (unlike its untrammelled monster antihero) a touch listless. It is further compromised by the fact that Paul Massie's dual roles – while serviceably played – remain one-dimensional and discrete entities; perhaps Fisher remembered the response to Victor Fleming's anodyne version of the story (with Spencer Tracy) which attempted to draw congruences between the dual identities of the central character by eliding the two characters (and playing down the physical monstrousness of Hyde), prompting the uncharitable response to Tracy's performance: 'Which one is he playing now?'

The actor Christopher Lee (as is well known) has never been unforthcoming when talking about his own versatility, but it's hard to argue with the actor's own generous self-assessment when one sees the impressive range of characterisations that he created, not least for the studio that made him famous, Hammer. A good example is Don Sharp's *Rasputin, the Mad Monk* (1966), which may transform the historical events into a brightly coloured action-packed variant on standard Hammer narratives, but showcases a charismatic and disturbing performance by Lee as the demented religious figure who held such way over the Russian royal family. As with *The Devil Rides Out*, the notion of a cultist attaining complete control of individuals who come to feel that there is something missing in their lives is ever more apropos, and while the film may be something of a comic-strip approach to history, its sheer energy has ensured that it is as fascinating today as when it was made.

Captain Kronos: Vampire Hunter (1974), with the TV writer Brian Clemens in the director's chair, showed the pitfalls of grafting currently trendy elements onto classical Gothic motifs. The proof is that this film (which is not without a certain gusto) now looks far more dated than other products utilising less fashionable elements. As Hammer began to wind down, it became easier to assess the various changes of direction the company had initiated to stay fresh. Clemens, writer of the self-mocking espionage parody *The Avengers*, was drafted in for this pre-*Buffy* tongue-in-cheek vampire outing with the beguiling (if inexpressive) Caroline Munro joining the stolid Horst Janson in would-be colourful derring-do, using some of the self-reflexive humour of the director's TV work to far less congenial effect (Janson, of flowing locks and athletic mien, may have looked the part, but lacked the knowing qualities of Clemens' portly TV hero, Patrick Macnee).

The 1970s remained a busy and productive period for the studio. Time has been kind to Robert Young's energetic and grisly *Vampire Circus*

(1972), and even merely workmanlike pieces have acquired a patina of quality (such as John Hough's *Twins of Evil* (1971), which boasts as its key selling point the frequently nude – and nubile – Collinson twins, non-actresses set against a heavyweight and an icily unsympathetic performance by the admirable Peter Cushing) and one film that – as its voluptuous star Ingrid Pitt admitted – could have been far more involving if its director had been prepared to render it in more energetic fashion: Peter Sasdy's *Countess Dracula* (1971), co-starring Sandor Elès (see Appendix: Interviews). But the last two films make their mark, with occasional felicities.

Among the many and varied attacks on the horror film genre over the years (such assaults are a cyclical pleasure for many), there are relatively few maledictions from the left pronounced on the conservatism of the genre in which the preservation (or restoration) of a natural order is imperative; hardly a radical notion. But attitudes from either right or left *contra* the genre may be simply because insufficient attention (of either a positive or negative kind) was brought to bear by the critical establishment. Similarly, more vituperation might be directed against the unenlightened attitude to mental health of the horror film (although this is hardly peculiar to the British entries in the field). And off-kilter – or deeply disturbed – mental states are a *sine qua non* for at least one strand of the horror film.

Hammer's inconsistent (but often highly accomplished) black-and-white psychological horror subgenre began with the sublimely chilling *Taste of Fear*, directed by Seth Holt in 1961. This film, with its vulnerable young heroine (Susan Strasberg) under extreme psychological strain, borrows from two prestigious exemplars (Clouzot's *Les Diaboliques* and Hitchcock's *Psycho*) the notion of mental illness (usually reluctantly described as schizophrenia) as being the source of disturbed or violent behaviour, but it is possible to be too po-faced about such matters. In 2012, Hollywood struggled with the difficulties of sourcing its evil – specifically, identifying the ethnicity of villains in films, so sensitive are both audiences and markets (Chinese villains, for instance, are now *hors de combat* when the potential for offence in that extremely lucrative market was noted). But films require villains just as they require conflict (similar attempts have been made to rescue such splendid Shakespearian villains as Richard III by the application of history), and while the use of disturbed mental states as the source of the drama in, say, the Hammer psychological sequence named above may not figure in any medical textbook, there is no denying that it supplies the requisite elements for the better films trading in horror and suspense.

Seth Holt's *Taste of Fear* is impressive, borrowing from Clouzot (out of Boileau and Narcejac), but with the director's casual mastery of the suspense form effortlessly elevating the film above most similar fare (later entries, such as those directed by Freddie Francis, *Paranoiac* (1963) and *Nightmare* (1964), are more fitfully successful, but have their virtues). Francis' career contains some other interesting films, such as the visually striking *The Skull* (1965, based on Robert Bloch's story 'The Skull of the Marquis de Sade') and the surprisingly ambitious *The Creeping Flesh* (1973), which, while ostensibly another vehicle for the always-reliable Peter Cushing and Christopher Lee (as in *The Skull*), has some interesting things to say about the nature of evil in the person of the Cushing character's repressed daughter (vividly played by Lorna Heilbron) who becomes a libidinous creature (rather in the fashion that a similar Victorian woman played by Barbara Shelley was liberated in Terence Fisher's *Dracula, Prince of Darkness*). Regarding the Hammer psychological cycle, the creative personnel begins to subtly shift in importance. As the profession of screenwriter began to obtain the recognition that was its due in the 1970s, certain films (it was now becoming apparent) might well owe their success – or lack of it – to the writer rather than the director. Certainly, for all his misfires (notably some maladroit attempts at direction), Hammer's most overworked scribe Jimmy Sangster enjoyed a more impressive CV than Hammer executive (and occasional director) Michael Carreras. If *Maniac* (1963) has much to offer (and, frankly, it doesn't), it is probably due more to its writer (Sangster) than its director (Carreras). Still ploughing the post-*Psycho* furrow, the scenario here shuffles a few gruesome notions in relatively familiar fashion, but occasionally a flourish of imagination surfaces (only to quickly turn evanescent). The Camargue scenery (shot impressively by Wilkie Cooper in monochrome widescreen) is the setting for a convoluted tale of rape and revenge with such elements as a glistening Citroen used to transport bodies rather as Charon's ferry did on the River Styx. The film's most memorable image is one of violent death by oxyacetylene torch (leading to a mendacious poster which suggested a far more gruesome affair than that which cinemagoers were actually offered).

Two non-Hammer offerings are instructive: Vernon Sewell's *House of Mystery* (1961) is proof of that director's quiet expertise, with a nicely quotidian approach to some of its more unlikely elements such as a very British séance (rendered persuasive by the playing of Colin Gordon and Molly Urquhart) and a satisfying wrapping-up of its unusual revelations. While the underwhelming *The Hands of Orlac* (Edmond T. Gréville, 1960) seemed designed as an object lesson in ill-advised remakes of classic material, Karl Freund's delirious and creative original from 1935 was offered no challenge whatsoever by this lacklustre remake. *The Hands of Orlac* wastes, as in so many films of the period, the actor Christopher Lee (as a doll master) and gives Mel Ferrer very little to do as a pianist apparently haunted by the acquisition of a murderer's hands.

6
The Sexual Impulse

The feminine strain in Gothic writing has always been significant, not least in the predominance of female practitioners, Mary Shelley, of course, being the exemplar, but also Charlotte Brontë's *Jane Eyre* and Jane Austen's parody of the subject, *Northanger Abbey*. While the latter book may ridicule the trappings of the macabre, it also performs something of a balancing act in allowing the flesh-creeping window-dressing to function on its own autonomous level – much as many of the films do, balancing parody and straight-faced engagement with the subject. Women Gothic writers have long (consciously or unconsciously) utilised a series of Freudian metaphors to express certain aspects of female sexuality (the dangerous journeys through damp corridors and tunnels hardly need any explanation in terms of the symbolism). But the buildings which are the essential settings of the Gothic – the castles and splendidly accoutred houses of old and decadent families – may also function as representations of the female psyche. And given the reliance on inheritance and heirdom in the genre (in an era in which any power that women might accrue would be through the death or beneficence of a male relative), it is interesting how often the very inheritances of the female protagonists represent a threat to those receiving them; the positive effects (such as the freeing of them from financial worries that inheritance grants them) are of little comfort. This kind of conclusion might be seen indirectly as a criticism of a patriarchal society by women lacking autonomy, but such considerations carry far less elemental power than the awakening of the sexual impulse in women – particularly in the pre-Freudian era, where the standard perception was that women endured rather than enjoyed sex as an onerous part of their marital duties. And the sexual impulse is a natural fit for the cinema;

the demands of the libido have always been one of the most potent weapons in the armoury of the medium – especially for the horror film. *The Vampire Lovers* (1970) represented for director Roy Ward Baker something of a consolation prize in terms of it being an adaptation of J. Sheridan Le Fanu's 'Carmilla'. The director had originally planned a version of the author's *Uncle Silas* (to be written by the man who almost single-handedly created the modern espionage novel, Eric Ambler, who was also a leading British screenwriter). But while that project was stillborn, Hammer executives came to Baker with the suggestion that he film Le Fanu's influential vampiric novella. The resulting film was to create a certain degree of controversy and its then-ground-breaking overt use of sexuality, lesbianism and female nudity was to introduce a new ethos for Hammer (always keen to push the envelope in terms of the acceptable: its motto remained 'épater le bourgeois'). This new frankness in terms of sexual material was to remain the company's status quo till its final days. Earlier versions of Le Fanu's story had included an uncredited attempt by Carl Dreyer, and a later 1960 colour version (until recently impossible to see) directed by Roger Vadim, *Blood and Roses/Et Mourir de Plaisir*, which had its virtues in terms of visual style, although censorship had not yet relaxed to the extent that the erotic interaction between Vadim's beautiful stars Elsa Martinelli and his then-wife Annette Vadim (née Stroyberg) could be presented in the graphic fashion that Baker was to utilise in his unblushing version.

The Hammer Films studios had long represented a striking compromise between art and commerce. From its earliest days, the studio had made no secret of the fact that its deepest ethos was to make money, but this cheerfully realistic agenda was (fortunately) at the service of giving some considerable film artists their head, proving that a suitably commercial product resulted. This was an ethos maintained with the very talented Baker (though, according to the director, some pressure was applied to foreground the sexual elements). It is clear that Baker was prepared to give his paymasters what they wanted in terms of copious nudity and uninhibited sexual couplings, but his integrity as a filmmaker was never in doubt, and the strategies of Le Fanu's delicate tale are never ignored. Perhaps this dichotomy in the film may be read more clearly in the twenty-first century; certainly, at the time of the film's release, its lurid sensationalism was perceived as its defining characteristic, and tongue-clucking noises from moralists (along with BBFC disapproval) were inevitably accompanied by healthy box office receipts. Cinemagoers relished the fact that Hammer had found a new way to pleasurably shock its audiences, as it had once done with Terence Fisher's *The Curse of Frankenstein*.

Baker's achievement is particularly notable when the film is compared with the remaining two parts of what would become the 'Carmilla' trilogy, *Lust for a Vampire* (1971) and the same year's *Twins of Evil*, both of which replicated the graphic sexuality of the first film but with none of Baker's cinéaste instincts. Ingrid Pitt's unbuttoned (in every sense) performance as the polymorphously sexual Camilla became a defining image of Hammer – an image in which she was to cheerfully trade in several successive films, including the lacklustre *Countless Dracula*. The strong, assertive female figure she came to represent (while almost invariably malign) was nevertheless a sharp contrast to the decorative, vulnerable beauties of the earlier Hammer films, though perhaps Barbara Shelley should be excluded from this observation, as the actress repeatedly made the most of the slender material she was given, rising above her willowy fellow female stars.

The more indulgent attitude to nudity of the 1970s allowed the female sexual encounters in *The Vampire Lovers* to escape too much negative attention from the censor, but such aspects now seem less like modish flirtations with a more liberal era's eroticism than an attempt to engage with the rule-defying undertones of the original Gothic novels (though a new twenty-first-century puritanism may channel a different kind of moral disapprobation through accusations of sexism, etc.). The film's heady conflation of the erotic and the horrific suggested a strong congruence with the Gothic dissidence that had given birth to the film, notably the notion of the fatal woman and the endemic corruption of the aristocracy. Carmilla is – in both her vampirism and her blue-blooded antecedents – a distaff Dracula, and Ingrid Pitt (see Appendix: Interviews), while lacking Christopher Lee's reined-in charisma, still made a talismanic figure out of her voluptuous female monster. The use of iconic Hammer actors such as Peter Cushing to play a general whose daughter is one of the first victims of Carmilla establishes the parameters for audiences and cements such expectations by a (for the time) shocking decapitation. Baker's film makes much of a contrast between ages-old corruption (albeit in the spectacular body of the youthful-appearing Carmilla, although, in fact, Pitt was too mature for the part) and immensely vulnerable innocents (as in the figure of Emma, played by Madeline Smith). The latter is a particularly ingenious piece of casting, with the actress offering an almost comic vision of unspoiled innocence which is contrasted with her unabashedly displayed full-figured body; while the latter might be seen as a simple acknowledgement of box office imperatives, it can be speculated that Baker was suggesting that the Sapphic seduction we witness is not so much a violation as an inevitable conjoining of two elements – experience and innocence – in two women who are not quite so different as they might first appear.

As viewers, we are invited to enjoy the ruthlessness with which the single-minded Carmilla seduces almost everyone in her path, including the young girl's governess (played by Kate O'Mara) and even a servant who attempts to save the luckless young girl. The parallels between the once-innocent Emma and her vampiric seducer – a motif taken from the conclusion of the Le Fanu story – is chosen by Roy Ward Baker as a suitable conclusion for his version of the story (the staging of the final scenes, with the vampire laid out in a coffin and the young girl in a bed, are apposite, and perhaps the most telling element of Baker's take on the story is the almost hypnotic pull he allows his seductive monster to have over the rest of the cast – and over the viewers).

The director's subsequent work for the company included the lively (if ultimately dispiriting) *Scars of Dracula* (1970), which is a strictly by-the-numbers addition to a faltering cycle; Christopher Lee's impatience with the title role may be read in even the few scenes he is allowed in the film.

Roy Ward Baker had enjoyed a successful career in television, but was keen to return to the cinema and accepted Anthony Nelson Keys' invitation to direct the company's third adaptation of Nigel Kneale's astonishingly successful television science-fiction serials built around the British rocket scientist Quatermass. In fact, Baker's contribution, *Quatermass and the Pit* (1967), as well as being the best of Hammer's three adaptations, belongs in a study of British Gothic cinema such as this as it is the most conspicuous example of the dramatist Kneale's intelligent utilisation of Gothic themes (a recurrent motif in his work, though usually channelled through science-fiction narratives; even his famous supernatural drama *The Stone Tape* was granted persuasive pseudoscientific trappings). Despite the fact that Baker's skills as a director were continuing to be honed even through genre material, the critical consensus was that his career had taken an unfortunate commercial turn, with his more personal work behind him. This was not, in fact, the case, as *Quatermass and the Pit* comprehensively proves. The Gothic notion takes a literally subterranean form in the film when (during an excavation for London Underground), workmen come across skeletons when a wall is broken through in the Hobbs End station (the reference being a satanic one – the sinister appearance of the Martians later in the piece is in fact devil-like and is shown to have created the universal blueprint from which humanity created its images of demons).

Baker's engagement with more straightforwardly Gothic material (apart from the highly profitable *The Vampire Lovers*) was to follow in the unsuccessful *Scars of Dracula*. However, within a year, the director was to produce one of his most interesting and resonant films (with powerful sexual undertones) for the company with yet another spin on motifs from Robert Louis Stevenson, the cheekily named *Dr Jekyll and Sister Hyde* (1971). It was clear that Hammer was not prepared to learn anything from La Rochefoucauld's maxim that 'those who do not learn from the mistakes of history are doomed to repeat them', as it was once again attempting a fairly radical spin on the Jekyll and Hyde transmogrification – with added sex – which it had tried (with compromised results) in the earlier *The Two Faces of Dr Jekyll*. But that film's then-novel premise – a dull and unattractive Jekyll and a satanically charismatic Hyde – did not offer the possibilities contained in the outrageous scenario here, in which the doctor's transformation actually includes a sex change as performed by the actor Ralph Bates and the actress Martine Beswick. Moreover, the censorship problems that bedevilled the earlier film were less in evidence here, so the edgy material could be approached with a more adult frankness than had been permitted in the constrained Terence Fisher/Wolf Mankowitz spin on the notions of duality and the inherent evil in even the best of us.

The Baker film appeared in the same year as Peter Sasdy's highly effective *Hands of the Ripper* (with its flesh-transfixing hatpins; the film is discussed below) and both sported with relish the new tolerance for graphic and bloody violence; the restrictions placed on earlier Hammer films now seemed largely a thing of the past. Interestingly, both films utilised as a narrative motif the Whitechapel killings by 'Saucy Jack', but Baker was obliged to turn his murderous female protagonist into something other than Jekyll's alter ego – she becomes a surrogate Jack the Ripper, in fact.

Baker's film begins with a series of graphically shocking images – a close shot of the eye of a rabbit about to be carved by a butcher intercut with a woman followed by a sinister-looking man looking exactly like a nearby poster for a murderer who is clearly the Ripper. In a very short time, we are once again shown the poster, this time splattered with the blood of the murdered woman, intercut with the knife-wielding of the butcher. This juxtaposition of human and animal carnage is a familiar one (and allows a degree of explicitness in terms of the slicing of a piece of game, which might not be permissible with a human victim), but also suggests the sheer physicality of the film that is to follow, which is very much concerned with what happens to human bodies – although, ironically, the most shocking image is possibly that of a woman we know to be a man in transformed state caressing (with an erotic fascination) his newly acquired breasts (Martine Beswick is able to convince us that a male sexual consciousness is now in a female body). The gender shift in Baker's film, however, is fraught and dangerous, with hideous consequences for everyone involved; unlike such films as Hitchcock's *Psycho*, which holds out a possibility of human redemption amidst the carnage, Baker's film offers no such amelioration.

The screenplay for the film is by Brian Clemens, also responsible for scripts for TV series that Baker worked on, such as the tongue-in-cheek *The Avengers*, and the writer's speciality is quirky and not-too-serious plotting (as in the misfiring *Captain Kronos*). Clemens' involvement poses the following question: who incorporated the more intriguing gender-based ideas into the film? Nothing in the rest of Clemens' work shows this taste for the more outré. The aggressive woman that Dr Jekyll becomes is not only (it is suggested) sexually voracious but all too ready to sublimate her sexual instincts into acts of homicide – a temptress, in fact, who is a literal femme fatale. Because this female Hyde is not bound by the constraints under which most Victorian women of her class laboured, she is much more prepared to behave in an instinctual fashion – a fashion which of course suggests masculine behaviour and a readiness to break with the rules of society. But that readiness is not characteristic of the men in this film, who are motivated by a combination of lust and timidity – a fatal flaw that is perhaps the reason for their destruction.

One luckless victim is a scientist engaged in tracking down the killer prowling London's streets and is, ultimately, an example of a man who thinks with his genitals and pays a bloody price for his indulgence. There is also in the Hyde character a proto-feminist slant, leaving aside her contempt for the sex she has abandoned (the latter an element that would have chimed with the anti-male ethos of such unsparing feminist writers as Marilyn French and, later, Andrea Dworkin). As an audience, we are invited to enjoy Hyde's readiness to behave in a fashion totally contrary to that expected of women in this era – not so much the killing by phallic knife as the energetic rejection of society's expectations concerning female mores. The relaxed censorship of the day for the Baker film allows Hyde to mentally and physically explore the difference between the experience of sex for men and women, as he/she is able to describe the experiences for both, But the complexity of the sexual approach goes even further: when in the male Jekyll identity (with his personalities at war), the protagonist finds himself sexually attracted to men and even has to check himself from making a small sexual advance to a man. How would the BBFC have dealt with this in the early days of Hammer?

Given that detractors of the studio could point to the endless parade of female pulchritude as a defining characteristic of Hammer (which continued – and greatly expanded – on its predecessor Gainsborough Pictures' generosity with exposed cleavage), it's notable that the female sexuality in the film, while resulting, praying-mantis-like, in the death of the male partner, is shown as a strangely liberating force; the opposite impulse, in fact, of the men in the film, who are in thrall in a negative way to their erotic impulses. The modern, sexually liberated aspects of the female Hyde are pointed up by the presence in the film of virginal, sexually dormant women of the respectable classes and the-ever available prostitutes who were the hidden aspect of Victorian society (Dickens' Nancy in *Oliver Twist* is the *locus classicus* here; the writer can only suggest her profession to his easily shocked Victorian readers). Stevenson's notion of a war between a hypocritical rectitude and the more pressing demands of Eros finds a powerful expression in the version presented in Baker's film, particularly as the film moves towards its inevitably violent climax, and the casting of Ralph Bates and Martine Beswick in this regard is particularly fruitful. It is something of a cause for regret that neither actor was ever really able to otherwise explore their unorthodox skills, spending most of their careers shoehorned into one-dimensional parts; Beswick, in a couple of Bond films, is merely called upon to display her impressive, scantily clad body, while in the Baker film, she shows herself as an actress capable of finding a variety of nuances in a part which could so easily have lent itself to lip-smacking indulgence. One element which gave pause to audiences was the understated element of self-parody, but it is this which now appears knowing in the best sense; as well as confronting the implications of a shifting of sexual identity, Baker is well aware of the possible pitfalls of the subject descending into the ludicrous and copes with this by building in an awareness of such dangers.

The film was not markedly commercially successful, proving that Stevenson was not a particularly profitable source of narrative for the company, in the same way that Conan Doyle had similarly not furnished the goldmine that Hammer was expecting (although in that case, the projected series of Sherlock Holmes films was terminated). One wonders why the advertising campaign did not attract more viewers with its excited come-on tagline: 'WARNING! The Sexual Transformation of a Man into a Woman Will Actually Take Place Before Your Very Eyes!' No doubt, if an uncompromising director in the twenty-first century were tackling the subject – someone such as Lars Von Trier, say, or Gaspar Noë – an unblushing close-up of the transformation of male into female genitals could be shown, something that was not a possibility in 1971.

Further work in the Gothic genre for Baker was to involve the lacklustre *And Now the Screaming Starts!* in 1973 and a satisfying and inventive Amicus portmanteau film, *Asylum*, in the same year. The principal point of interest in many adaptations of the Jack the Ripper story often runs along the lines of a jazz musician improvising on the structure of a 32-bar song from the standard repertoire. Generally speaking, there have to be common points of reference, i.e. fragments of the original tune should surface in order that the inventions and diversions are set in an 'anchoring' context so that their ingenuity in deviating from the norm may be admired. Similarly, a variety of concepts are generally invoked with Ripper-derived material: how to conceal the identity of the killer from the audience; how to make him sufficiently interesting (a simple psychopathic monster would be unchallenging, so the killer is generally a member of the professions or even of the aristocracy); and how to present the familiar scenes of bloodletting and evisceration in a fashion we haven't quite seen before.

What makes Peter Sasdy's contribution to this extensive sub-genre for Hammer, *Hands of the Ripper* (1971), one of the more valuable entries in the genre is its often radical approach to these familiar notions, as well as its readiness to tackle new areas, including sexuality. There is a particularly pronounced Freudianism in the film (and not just in the sense that the writer L.W. Davidson is aware of such texts as *The Interpretation of Dreams*), along with a nuanced examination of patriarchy – the film is in fact centrally about the daughter of Jack the Ripper. And the fact that such concepts are treated responsibly within the context of a lurid and graphically violent Hammer film (which tips its hat to all the commercial requirements of the genre) makes the achievement all the more accomplished.

As with so many Hammer films, the casting here is particularly valuable, with the company – as ever – able to call upon the services of the very best of the British acting profession, giving a patina of quality to the material, however threadbare it may be at times (although not in the case of this film). The film's virtues are enhanced by the presence of the always-impressive Eric Porter as Dr John Pritchard, who grants a home to a disturbed young girl Anna (played by the equally excellent Angharad Rees). But Pritchard discovers that he has a new responsibility, which is to cover up the grim evidence of the sexually motivated bloody murders committed by the young girl at intervals. Pritchard begins to investigate Anna's traumatic past, and the central all-damaging incident in which the girl saw her mother savagely killed by her father – the latter, we learn, was no less than Jack the Ripper. The film delivers the requisite quota of gruesomeness: one murder, in which hatpins are driven into the eye of a luckless female victim, succeeds in presenting one of the more unnerving images of the film, even though in effect no physical damage was initially shown in the censored version (since restored) – rather, blood streams through the fingers of the victim who has suffered this terrible injury to the eye, as gruesome here as it was when used by Arthur Crabtree in *Horrors of the Black Museum*. But the real darkness at the heart of the film concerns the psychological damage done by parents to their offspring – and even male attempts to refashion women into an acceptable image (itself redolent of the similarly doomed activities of James Stewart's character in Hitchcock's *Vertigo*). In *Hands of the Ripper*, Pritchard undertakes the task of creating a simulacra of his late wife using the seemingly pliable young girl who is his charge – she is to adopt the submissive attitude characteristic of the Victorian era, but (as we are well aware from filmic example where such territory is concerned) certain impulses are not to be quietly shuttered away. Freud's notion of the 'return of the repressed' is an ineluctable force here, and the linking of sexuality with violence is emblematic, if specious (other problematical areas of sexuality are drawn into the mix, such as the prostitute 'Long Liz' as played by Lynda Baron, who, despite the sex she is obliged to have with men for her livelihood, actually prefers lesbian sex with young women, as does, perhaps, the housemaid Dolly played by Marjie Lawrence) unwittingly makes the act of bathing the young Anna into an erotic activity. Both women, Liz and Dolly, are to pay a heavy price for these ventures into sexually forbidden waters, but that is not to say that the film has a negative attitude to anything other than heterosexual sex – it is sex per se that is dangerous in the disturbed central character, and the awakening of the sexual impulse for her can only lead to bloody murder. There are, however, other layers of an examination of character here: while the Pritchard character initially appears to be benevolent and altruistic, we are shown that he is as prone to compulsion and psychological disarray as those he would attempt to correct. What's more, he is uncomfortably aware of the multiple layers of personality which make people behave as they do (this, of course, in an era when such discussions were relatively novel in Victorian society – the film features a conversation between Pritchard and another male character, the corrupt Dysart (played by Derek Godfrey), which shows a level of sophistication not often found within generic horror films). The film allows itself to accept the convention of visual pressure points as the harbingers of violent retribution (it is the glittering reflection of light on glass objects combined with potentially sexual situations which take the disturbed Anna back to her childhood and unleash the forces of chaos within her). Interestingly, the various murders and ruptures of flesh in the film have an appropriately phallic quality, from the stabbing of Anna's mother in a pre-credits sequence to an impaling with a poker and the slashing of a throat with a piece of broken glass (not to mention the aforementioned stabbing in the eye with hatpins).

The film may take place (as it tells us) some 15 years after the death of the Ripper (although of course that date is not known to history), but the film remains almost a discourse on legacies, not least the legacy of religion, which offers no consolation here (or even as a convenient method dispatch for the monster, as is so often the case in Hammer films). The climax in the Whispering Gallery of St Paul's Cathedral in London, which brings about the death of the two principal characters, has a striking visual component to its orchestration, but provides no sense of a spiritual element; the cosy pieties of an earlier generation of horror films were a world away by 1971. And while the film plays fast and loose with the actual facts of the case (Victoria still appears to be on the throne, despite this being somewhat anachronistic in the context of the film), these touches serve in a more contextual fashion – the character of the prostitute Long Liz appears to be based on that of Elizabeth Stride, who actually died at the hands of the real Ripper, as opposed to his offspring here. Perhaps most interesting, however, is the Pygmalion-like attempt to remould the heroine, which is handled in complex fashion, taking on board both sexual and sociopolitical elements. If the fact that an attempt to rescue a damaged individual is doomed to failure because of deep psychological damage hardly suggests a world in which the amelioration of a damaged human character is possible, it should not be forgotten that in the context of the Gothic horror film, there are constant sacrifices that must be made.

Sexuality – of the adolescent variety – was at the heart of another influential British film. At the time of its original release in 1984, Neil Jordan's *The Company of Wolves* was generally considered to be unlike any other film in the fantasy genre that the viewer might have encountered. And to some degree, this was true – the innovative qualities of this unusual, ambitious film could not be gainsaid. But, in fact, mixed into Jordan's rich stew were a variety of familiar elements, sampled by the cinéaste director, as familiar with film language as the modern literary tradition of which he was part. The film is a smorgasbord of ingredients gathered from Joe Dante's unconventional werewolf epic *The Howling* (1981); its visual style owing a great deal to Michael Powell's delirious colour extravaganzas of the 1950s (clearly a crucial part of Jordan's filmic DNA); Charles Laughton's masterly and atmospheric and uncommercial one-shot as a director, *Night of the Hunter* (1955), is in here as well, as is Jean Cocteau's surrealistic *La Belle et la Bête* (1946). But Jordan's visually sumptuous movie is more than just the sum of its polyglot influences. Written with the late (and much-respected) fabulist Angela Carter and based on their exploration of the (sometimes sexual) undercurrents of fairy stories (a notion also provocatively treated in the 1986 musical by Stephen Sondheim and James Lapine, *Into the Woods*), *The Company of Wolves* presents with some panache a Freudian world of brutal, iridescent imagery, with Little Red Riding Hood at the centre of its complex myth-spinning. The film's framework consists of an Alice-like dream, with the naïve heroine (Sarah Patterson) on the point of sexual awakening creating a fairy-tale world while lying in a twentieth-century bedroom. Along with the poetic writing and direction by the talented Jordan and Carter (who shared a similar gravitas as novelists), technical effects such as Chris Tucker's spectacular wolf transformations made a considerable impact in their day (notably the actor Steven Rea's alarming transmogrification, all glistening, flayed skin and splitting muscles). But these sequences are not treated in the fashion of such directors as John Landis or Joe Dante (i.e. as audience-pleasing set pieces); rather, they are integrated into the whole 'fabulous' (in the literal sense of the word) scenario. Those looking for a straightforward linear narrative found it unsatisfying, but viewers with a taste for something more challenging were pleased with Jordan's ambitious film, which was considerably finessed by George Fenton's unusually orchestrated score, producing exactly the right colourful musical palette for the storybook visuals.

7
The Rivals: On Hammer's Coat-Tails

The till-ringing success of Hammer Films led other studios to enthusiastically emulate the studio's money-making ethos and lurid ad campaigns. In a similar fashion to the way in which the noun 'Penguin' became synonymous with paperbacks at a certain period, so 'Hammer Horror' became a generic description (and remains so to this day), whether or not a particular film was produced by that company. Such confusion would hardly have been a cause for concern among the company's rivals, who did their very best to emulate (and replicate) as many aspects of the Hammer template as they could.

These rivals also cannily attempted to utilise the same creative approach – and many of the same personnel, including the cheerfully unpretentious writer Jimmy Sangster and velvet-voiced actors Christopher Lee and Peter Cushing – to produce a product which was initially indistinguishable from the original creative template (and is still routinely described as Hammer product to this day), but which on examination has its own marked individual identity (notably the Robert Baker/ Monty Berman productions, such as the lurid and overtly Hammer-style *Blood of the Vampire*). But any consideration of other producers and production companies hitching their wagons to Hammer's star has to begin with a discussion of the once-notorious, now-cherished Sadean trilogy of films produced by Anglo-Amalgamated (Michael Powell's *Peeping Tom*, Arthur Crabtree's *Horrors of the Black Museum* and Sidney Hayers' *Circus of Horrors*) – three films sharing a colourful, sardonic relish for modern-day Grand Guignol cruelty and a glossy late-1950s eroticism, but differing wildly in their individual levels of achievement (though the two lesser films in the trilogy are undoubtedly guilty pleasures).

Long perceived as an unofficial trilogy (although actually united only by the film company that distributed them), the three Anglo-Amalgamated films of the late 1950s and early 1960s came to define a sleek, poster-coloured alternative to the refulgent period-set dramas of market leader Hammer. What the Anglo-Amalgamated films shared with that company's product, however, was a full-throttle, sanguinary approach to their hideous set pieces, but with their contemporary settings giving them a more dangerous edge, less distanced by nineteenth-century milieux. All three films occasioned a degree of nervousness in the censors about their enthusiastic indulgence in flesh-creeping effects, but vary massively in terms of their individual achievement.

One film is the work of a journeyman filmmaker, *Horrors of the Black Museum* (1957, directed by Arthur Crabtree); one is by a British stylist of real achievement who never quite fulfilled his original promise, *Circus of Horrors* (1960, directed by Sidney Hayers) and the third (made in the same year as the Hayers film) is generally considered to have sabotaged the career of one of the British cinema's two greatest directors (the other being Alfred Hitchcock), Michael Powell's richly textured *Peeping Tom*. The range of achievement and vision (and the last word is not used lightly in the context of the Powell film, which has a complex level of symbolism and resonance concerning vision and seeing) is a considerable achievement, far more ambitious in its reach than its stablemates. But all three share vivid contemporary settings, a sharp eye for the mores of the time (including a variety of specific observations of British society – catchpenny publishing and empty celebrity, for instance, in *Horrors of the Black Museum*), and a predilection for violent lacerating death shown in unsparing detail.

While its milieux and locales are undoubtedly English, the cheerfully garish *Circus of Horrors* is pitched at a heightened, Italianate operatic level, particularly the opening, with the forceful score of composer Franz Reizenstein underlining the lurid activity at a Puccini-esque pitch. A voluptuous woman dressed only in diaphanous gown and lingerie (and shot revealingly from below, her face hidden) rushes dementedly about her house smashing mirrors, hysterically screaming the name 'Rossiter!' (we're later to learn that he is the monomaniacal plastic surgeon who becomes the *éminence grise* behind the eponymous 'circus of horrors'). Only at the end of the scene do we see the woman's face, which is a grotesque and mutilated wreck – she is one of Rossiter's failures, her hideous face the result of one of his surgical techniques that has gone wrong. Throughout the film, the woman's ugliness is to be echoed by a variety of other specimens presented for Rossiter's knife (his highly unlikely speciality is to give new faces to a variety of strikingly built women who then become a performers in the circus he has hijacked; it is never quite explained how these transformed women acquire the necessary athletic skills for a job that customarily takes a lifetime of training). *Circus of Horrors* also features a catalogue of gruesome deaths, in which various people (both male and female) attempt to contravene Rossiter and pay a heavy price – and all of this is played out in the kind of circus scenario which invites the audience into a guilty complicity with the bloody mayhem we are presented with on the screen. This, of course, is precisely the thing which ordinary circuses tempt us with and then, finally, avoid. The real skill in the circus is the avoidance of death, but this is not on Hayers' agenda: the film gives us the mutilation and mayhem that we guiltily crave. Perhaps the most iconic image in the film (which echoes the similar bloodletting via spiked binoculars in Arthur Crabtree's film) is the large knife bloodily piercing the neck of a half-naked female human target on a spinning wheel. It's an image which would hardly raise an eyebrow today, but which – for the time – was remarkably graphic.

The operatic metaphor mentioned earlier is further compounded by the performance of the physically striking but limited German actor Anton Diffring, who was usually handed sinister Nazis to play, but here was given free rein with the vain and monstrous abuser of women (and murderer of men) at the centre of the narrative. Had Peter Cushing or Christopher Lee been given the part, they would have been more likely to have played it with their customary icy menace, but Diffring – charismatic but relatively one-dimensional and rarely an actor attracted to the nuanced moment of characterisation – is encouraged by Hayers to pitch his performance at a just-below-fortissimo level, which in fact precisely matches the dramaturgy that the director is striving for throughout. In fact, Hayers' film is highly adroit at evoking in the spectator precisely those impulses that must would been found in the observers of Newgate hangings – all of us, that is, who are prepared to watch a film with the title *Circus of Horrors* – but we are allowed a degree of absolution here. Everyone – actors, director and audience – are partners in a contract: this is a game of charades and it's played with maximum skill here. The parameters of horror cinema are, to some degree, being re-codified even as we watch, even though the ingredients are ages old.

Interestingly, Sidney Hayers' most conspicuously successful contribution to horror cinema is not as enjoyably a poster-coloured outing as his circus film, but the much more subtle and allusive *Night of the Eagle* (1962, after Fritz Leiber), a film which achieves its effects in a far less direct fashion (it is discussed in Chapter 8).

Arthur Crabtree's often enjoyably ludicrous *Horrors of the Black Museum* is the closest of the three to a straightforward exploitation film, replete with illogical plotting and featuring a minor character who endures a totally meretricious Jekyll-and-Hyde style transformation into a ghastly-visaged killer in a film already overloaded with grotesque elements, such as a highly unlikely portable guillotine (to be installed above the beds of nubile starlets). It was produced by American huckster/ showman Herman Cohen (of *I Was a Teenage Werewolf* fame), whose skills lay in the creation of crowd-pleasing concepts rather than any more nuanced attitude to filmmaking, but the film still managed to produce one of the indelible Gothic images of the day, mentioned above. In modern-day London, two young women receive a pair of binoculars through the post, and as one of them adjusts the setting (off-camera), we hear a horrendous scream accompanied by a loud dissonant chord courtesy of the composer Gerard Schurmann. There is a cut to the luckless girl sprawled on the floor, her hands clasped to her eyes with blood running between her fingers, and on the floor a pair of binoculars with bloodied spikes which have sprung from the apparatus. In fact, the gruesome object itself had allegedly appeared in the real-life Black Museum at Scotland Yard and figured in an early murder case, but it's used here to produce what is essentially a highly effective Sadean moment. Interestingly, it is the kind of conflation of the Grand Guignol effect with the notions of vision and seeing that is so central to the Michael Powell film, although Crabtree is not the director to explore such areas (and Cohen, with an eye on the cash register, would quickly have put paid to such artistic aspirations). But perhaps he would have been right – although Powell's film is now seen as one of British cinema's key masterpieces, the moral outrage and critical opprobrium that fell upon *Peeping Tom* did the director's career no favours. The erotic impulse (or a dark perversion of it) is key to the psychology of his protagonist of *Peeping Tom*, the shy, vulnerable murderer Mark, and the character's sympathetic treatment by Powell may be one of the reasons why that film was so roundly detested by the press when it appeared in 1960. The hysterical denunciations directed against the film effectively stalled its director's carer, though he was able to make a few films (of no great distinction) in his later years. Ultimately, modern filmmakers such as Martin Scorsese and Francis Ford Coppola began to extol Powell's now-neglected virtues and recognise his single horror film as a masterpiece.

Scorsese and Coppola have both talked about Powell's influence on their own work, particularly his astonishing facility for colour photography and cinematography. This visual facility, however, was always at the service of a romantic, humanist (and sometimes pantheistic) view of humanity – a view that was key to his work. The relationship between anti-hero Mark and his appalling father (played, significantly, by Powell himself) is suggested as the reason for his murderous behaviour, along with the twisting out of shape of a healthy sexual instinct, now able to find release only in murder. Critics in 1960 lamented the fact that the director had deserted the romanticism of his earlier work, in which surrealism, mysticism and a rich colouristic palette coexisted with an intense response to the English countryside. *Peeping Tom* was, of course, very different – deeply urban, with its now-quaint vision of corner shops selling discreet pornography and studios renting out nude models for amateur photographers.

Powell had flirted with the macabre in such films as *The Thief of Baghdad* and *Black Narcissus* (the latter shot through with thwarted erotic impulses), but a certain romantic libertarianism was recognised as his principal arena. *Peeping Tom*, focusing on a damaged young photographer who shoots films of women while killing them, was something new and disturbing for the director. This rich and resonant film tackled the voyeuristic interaction of viewer and film with a complexity not seen even in similar work by Alfred Hitchcock (notably *Rear Window*). Critics of the day, however, dismissed it with such adjectives as 'stinking', 'depraved' and 'evil'. The critics may have been unhappy with the fact that Powell provocatively engages with the viewer, confronting us with our own voyeurism – via point-of-view shots, we become Mark as he murders a prostitute. And cinema itself is the conduit for our most stygian impulses, given full rein in a darkened auditorium. In *Peeping Tom*, our gaze becomes a metaphor for the psychopathic hero's murderous impulses.

The outrage at the time over the film's violence now seems absurd, but critics were equally upset by Powell's attempt to attempt to understand the psychologically deformed Mark (brilliantly – and subtly – played by the young German actor Carl Boehm), whose foreignness is set against the quintessential Englishness of the piece. The vision of an England of under-the-counter lingerie porn corner shops and camera-for-hire studies of naked models is worlds away from such classic Powell films as *I Know Where I'm Going!* and *The Life and Death of Colonel Blimp*.

Finally, the most radical element of the film is Powell's aforementioned observation that voyeurism is common to all of us: the process of experiencing a film in a cinema makes us all complicit and our final participation invites us to watch as Mark impales himself on his own camera tripod – a despairing final action that is the only way to shut off the film's (and our) murderous gaze.

Despite their sensational, catchpenny advertising, *Grip of the Strangler* and *Corridors of Blood* (both 1958 and both directed by Robert Day), with Vera Day's ample cleavage prominently displayed, in fact enshrine two of Boris Karloff's most subtle and intelligent performances, a world away from the homicidal madmen that the advertising suggests. The British actor was now in his seventh decade and had undertaken a series of unrewarding roles, but the enterprising producer Richard Gordon was a countryman and a fan, and was able to work with him in this intriguing duo of British films (pre-sold on the basis of the actor's name, which was still potent despite his increasing age). *Grip of the Strangler* focuses on the philanthropist James Rankin (Karloff), who is researching the case of a dead killer from 20 years earlier, the 'Haymarket Strangler'. Rankin is convinced that the accused man was innocent and exhumes the body of the suspect, Edward Styles. But in the open coffin, there is the missing murder weapon, which is a surgeon's scalpel, and in touching the implement, his own features twist into the distorted face of a killer. The murders of the Haymarket Strangler are to begin again. The desperate conflict within the central character (whose family life and reputation are inevitably destroyed) clearly appealed to the actor, tired of one-dimensional bogeymen, and (though too old for the part) demonstrated precisely why his career had a longevity denied to that of his less talented rival Bela Lugosi. The physicality of the part remains constantly surprising. What is also surprising is the level of thoughtfulness to be found in what could simply have been an exploitative script – and, along with its companion piece, *Corridors of Blood* (which deals responsibly with the discovery of anaesthetic, but livens things up with a miscast Christopher Lee as 'Resurrection Joe'), the film remains a testament to the ageing actor's abilities. The film works best when taking on a familiar target, the intransigence of authority. However, *Grip of the Strangler* is also fairly sophisticated in investigating the parameters of obsession within its right-thinking hero, flirting with self-inflicted insanity in pursuit of his altruistic dream: to disprove the maxim of his colleagues at the hospital that 'pain and in life are inseparable'. Such things apart, Day is particularly skilful at conjuring up the atmosphere of the London slums of 1840, with a particularly colourful Seven Dials (thronging with prostitutes, pickpockets and drunks, with nary a chic wine bar in sight), but perhaps the real revelation here is the way in which Karloff, an actor perfectly at ease with more mimetic performances, conveys a subtle and understated life in his obsessed character.

Aficionados of the Gothic just don't know how lucky they are these days. Everything – or almost everything – is readily available: the seminal original source novels, the many films (handsomely spruced up on DVD and Blu-ray), reprints of once-despised, now esteemed, censor-baiting comics and magazines, and (perhaps best of all in the latter arena) the innumerable reprints of the greatest of all horror comics companies, Al Feldstein and Bill Gaines' literately written, beautifully illustrated 1950s EC Comics (the most recent of many incarnations include deluxe full-colour, large-size bound volumes of the seminal flagship titles *Tales from the Crypt, The Haunt of Fear* and *The Vault of Horror* – all three books heavily channelling classic Gothic motifs, sometimes in period settings, sometimes in contemporary guise, cross-hatched and feathered by the best comics draughtsmen in the field).

In Britain in the 1950s, shocked questions had been asked about horror comics in Parliament (after Scottish schoolchildren pursued a 'Gorbals Vampire' through a graveyard, supposedly inspired by an American comic) and a mini-version of the Senate censorship scare that had neutered the American comics industry had taken place in England, which was more sedate, but effectively banishing (by the early 1960s) the gloriously grisly titles that many readers had enjoyed. But even the most draconian censorship was not able to completely cut off the source of subversive material, try as it might, and although schoolchildren had to make do with more homogenised post-code reprints (admittedly, not really a hardship, as the inventive 'Silver Age' of comics was in its first flush of invention via DC Comics), those who knew how to look in dark corners for such things (as many of us do) could find the odd horror tale which somehow sneaked into the British 68-page shilling reprints series, such as L. Miller's *Mystic* and *Spellbound* titles. These concise macabre pieces (which, of course, we now know to be reprints from the Atlas horror lines before Stan Lee and Martin Goodman made their real fortune with superhero material) were very distinctive. They usually boasted introductory blocks of text set in white against a strik-ing black background, which whetted appetites for the grisly delights to follow. These 'come-on' panels were similar (youthful enthusiasts quickly realised) to the gleefully hair-raising introductions given by the grotesque hosts of the EC Comics line – the Crypt Keeper, the Vault Keeper and the Old Witch – although there was no accompany-ing drawing of some monstrous-looking host grinning malevolently at the reader in the Atlas riffs on the EC formula. The tone was similar (editor/writer Stan Lee was clearly inspired by the decrepit horror hosts of Feldstein and Gaines), but everything was slightly less literate: phrases such as 'how are you' were invariably rendered as 'how are ya' (a typical EC strapline might be 'the old man sat amidst unremoved human excrement' – strong stuff for the time, but better written). And many of the Atlas stories were less inspired filigrees on Gothic ideas done with more panache in the EC titles. But, caveats aside, these reprints of 1950s horror material were, for the most part (from either Atlas or the market leaders, EC), kinetically enjoyable.

The EC titles (in which the scions of Frankenstein, Dracula and co. regularly made dutiful appearances) often made up in sheer gusto what they lacked in finesse (though the latter quality was also to be found), and from the middle period to the end of the line (say, 1952–4) – just before the Comics Code sanitised the whole industry – the stories often matched those of more respectable literary figures for sheer inventiveness and gruesome gusto. And the artwork! What a cadre of talents. There was the brilliant clean-lined draughtsmanship of Johnny Craig, with his dramatic compositions; the pleasingly old-fashioned (but highly distinctive) Jack Kamen; the moody photo-realist George Evans; and the spidery, gothic curlicues of EC's eccentric master Graham Ingels. In Ingels' strips, nobody, but nobody had a mouth of even teeth; all sported what Americans think all Brits possess: mouthfuls of misshapen molars.

EC's brand of the Gothic had an important cinematic progeny in the UK, a key rival for Hammer – a boyishly enthusiastic American producer relocated to London. My own conversations with Milton Subotsky (the ideas man behind Amicus; his partner Max J. Rosenberg was the hard-headed money man, responsible for raising finance with a knack for commercial titles for the duo's films) made it clear to me that the EC comics mentioned above were a primary source of inspiration for him, along with the seminal British horror film *Dead of Night*, which similarly dealt with short, sting-in-the-tail episodes of the disturbing and horrific. It might be said that these were the two key influences behind Subotsky's work. Personally, the amiable Subotsky struck me as a rather naïve, unworldly figure and, as someone who might now be regarded as a slightly geekish fan, keen to transmit (via his films) his massive enthusiasm for the horror material he so revered. In fact, Subotsky (as a young man) had originally offered a treatment of *Frankenstein* to Hammer Films, one discarded when the studio decided to take its own approach.

But Subotsky finally found other fish to fry. In many ways, the modestly budgeted *The City of the Dead* (1960) was a calling-card movie for the producer and was a harbinger of the successful career in British horror he was subsequently to have. The film is very English, despite its putative New England setting. The town of Whitewood which has been labouring under a curse for three centuries after a woman called

Elizabeth Selwyn has cast her imprecations upon the village that burnt her at the stake. The original script was written as a television pilot for Boris Karloff by George Baxt (whose hand was to be found in several accomplished screenplays of the day) and although the actual production of the film was apparently fraught, its lean and effective dramaturgy convinces, despite the economical (and inauthentic) settings; there is even the surprise killing-off of the heroine (*Psycho, avant la lettre*), while Christopher Lee's sepulchral presence adds gravitas to what is essentially a cameo part (the film's US poster, where it was renamed *Horror Hotel*, showed a dramatic but totally mendacious spread of rotted, monstrous visages – nowhere to be seen in the film – drawn by EC Comics' star artist Jack Davis). The director John Moxey makes a virtue of the limited budget by utilising the paucity of resources with maximum imagination, often invoking the subtlety of the Val Lewton supernatural films of the 1940s. Sorcery was also the subject of another successful British film, Don Sharp's *Witchcraft* (1964), which similarly made the most of its modest resources, although problems with the prodigious alcoholic consumption of its star Lon Chaney occasioned a variety of script rewrites (his scenes were always shot in the early afternoon, the actor's preferred time period before his concentration slipped). The film's linking of its supernatural activities with actual witchcraft practices was specious, but *Witchcraft* benefited from the presence of the sultry Welsh actress Yvette Rees, whose looks echoed the dark beauty of British-born (but relocated to Italy) actress Barbara Steele.

The notion (referenced elsewhere in this book) hopefully propounded by Peter Cushing and Christopher Lee that their films were more innocent, less shocking examples of the horror genre than the field subsequently became known for is perhaps true of one particular film that the duo made together. It was a film that both launched the Amicus portmanteau series of short tales of the macabre and demonstrated (if such a demonstration were needed) that the mere presence of Cushing and Lee, while providing admirable box-office clout, could elevate material – however threadbare – to a more rarefied level. *Dr Terror's House of Horrors* (1965), very mild indeed by today's standards (and often maladroit), is perhaps the first demonstration of Milton Subotsky's slight squeamishness when it came to producing his own versions of the horror material that he loved so well. The female victim of a werewolf in this film, for instance, has the merest suggestion of blood upon her neck, and this is a film made several years after the Hammer revolution had rendered earlier visualisations of such material thin and bloodless. The same is true of the various highly derivative stories contained within the anthology (all generically titled 'Werewolf', 'Disembodied Hand', etc., and credited solely to Subotsky as screenwriter; disingenuously, as they are all heavily indebted to other writers – the best segment, in which the supercilious art critic played by Christopher Lee is pursued by the severed hand of an artist for whose death he is responsible – is a version of Robert Florey's 1946 film *The Beast with Five Fingers*). But creaky though the various episodes look today (and, if the truth be told, they looked a touch antediluvian even when the film was first made) and compromised by the presence of non-actors from musical field, the disc jockey Alan Freeman (crushingly wooden) and the comedian/musician Roy Castle (by contrast, irritatingly antic), the film is, as mentioned earlier, comprehensively redeemed by the presence of the two actors who became the key figures in British horror. Christopher Lee's appalling art critic – who gets his just deserts in satisfyingly gruesome fashion – is another demonstration of the actor's considerable authority, particularly in unpleasant characters (and with an ability to suggest weakness beneath a confident exterior), while Cushing subtly enjoys himself as the eponymous dispenser of grim fates, seen only shuffling tarot cards in a railway carriage which looks like no rolling stock that ever travelled upon British Railways; with his unlikely bushy eyebrows, cod German accent and rather delicate underplaying, Cushing has the viewer hanging on his every word.

Despite its reluctance to deliver the blood-boltered goods to its contemporary audience, the film (flatly but capably directed by Freddie Francis) did remarkably well and inaugurated the long-running series of Amicus anthology films, most of which were to be much more accomplished than this tyro effort as the company grew in confidence.

There is, however, one important element to the film which makes it significant in terms of the development of Gothic themes in British cinema. Although several traditional horror scenarios are given inventive spins (including the old standbys of vampires and werewolves), the contemporary setting was (and is) startling. The effect of this is ironically pointed up by the fact that (for budgetary reasons) the production design grants a particularly impoverished and soulless look to the modest British settings (although one segment – graced by the then-unstarry presence of a young Donald Sutherland, more naturalistic in his playing than anyone else in the film – is putatively set in New England, it never for a second looks like anywhere but Great Britain). Rather than weakening the film, the locales demonstrate the durability of the Gothic myths even when set down in quotidian and unatmospheric settings such as those that the viewer is shown here.

If aficionados of the Gothic film give any thought to the second Amicus anthology, *Torture Garden* (1967), they often struggle to remember any one of the various segments apart from the last one, which is actually memorable (even though in a narrative sense it falls completely to pieces at the climactic conflagration). This is 'The Man Who Collected Poe' and is the only one of the episodes here by which director Freddie Francis appeared to be inspired. Like the rest of the film, the episode is adapted by Robert Bloch from his own short story, though the writer's association with Milton Subotsky was to bear more interesting fruit in a later anthology film, *Asylum* (1972). The Poe-related story involves an encounter between two nigh-obsessed collectors of material relating to the greatest American writer of the Gothic story, and the contrast between Jack Palance's twitching, monomaniac collector and the more reserved (but, as it transpires, equally obsessive) Poe aficionado played by Peter Cushing is fascinatingly handled by Francis – particularly the revelation that (after Cushing's bludgeoning murder by Palance) the dead man was the ultimate Poe collector, having collected no less than the writer himself, brought back from the dead and kept, covered in cobwebs, in a subterranean lair, turning out new pieces with titles such as 'The House of the Worm' and 'The Further Adventures of Arthur Gordon Pym'. The glimpse of these apocryphal manuscripts is one of the pleasures of the film – what if there were undiscovered Poe stories languishing in a cellar somewhere? But when the now-demented Palance character brings about the destruction of the writer he is obsessed by, along with the definitive collection of Poe's work and even himself (Palance is seen smiling in the middle of a raging fire), audiences were confused. The sequence makes absolutely no sense, given the previous behaviour of the character, and it was no surprise to learn from Robert Bloch that last-minute alterations (apparently by Freddie Francis himself) were responsible for this nonsensical conclusion. Nevertheless, this half-hour conclusion to *Torture Garden* renders the film an interesting addition to the Gothic cinema genre – but only just.

Roy Ward Baker's *Asylum* (1972), from a selection of stories written by Robert Bloch, was one of the biggest hits on Amicus' balance sheets, and for those with memories long enough, its cinema showings were a genuinely kinetic affair, prompting repeated physical responses in the audience (in pre-*Exorcist* days) that showed its makers had their finger on the pulse of the British Gothic genre (not least involving still-sentient severed body parts wrapped in brown paper). More than most other entries in the field, the film is concerned with notions of storytelling, as evinced in the wraparound story (the investigation of a group of patients in an asylum to discover the truth about them). While the outward accoutrements show the comfortable aspects of British society, we quickly learn that nothing here is to be taken at face value, and even the comforts of domesticity and happy marriage are not to be trusted. The character Barbara (played by Charlotte Rampling) in one story ('Lucy Comes to Stay') has returned to her home after spending time in a sanatorium, but discovers that her brother has hired a nurse to supervise her on a day-to-day basis. For her, the house is not a comforting place and she is to experience savagery far more lethal than that which had originally occasioned her incarceration. If the most successful episode remains that starring Richard Todd dealing with hideously twitching, carefully packaged human limbs in a freezer (mentioned above), it still has time for quieter pleasures. While the requisite Grand Guignol moments were checked off, other, more subtle, strategies were at work. Given the success of the film, one might speculate why Milton Subotsky could greenlight such misconceived projects as *I, Monster* (1971, a wholly redundant version of the Jekyll & Hyde story, wasting Christopher Lee) and the truly woeful *The Deadly Bees* (1967, showing that a low-budget version of *The Swarm* could be just as disastrous as Irwin Allen's prodigally expensive flop). Other films in the Amicus filmography, such as *The Psychopath* (1966), suggested that the writer Robert Bloch was merely recycling (less effectively) material he had tackled before, but on balance, the company's successes comprehensively outweigh its failures, such as the discreetly effective *The House that Dripped Blood* (directed by Peter Duffel in 1971), which demonstrated that suggestion could be as effective as copious ghastliness (despite the come-on title, the film is conspicuously bloodless).

After negotiation with the initially reluctant head of the EC Comics Company, Bill Gaines (now publishing only the satirical *MAD Magazine* after the anti-comics hysteria had obliterated his profitable line of horror books), Subotsky added to his catalogue of portmanteau films (which he had inaugurated, in emulation of *Dead of Night*, with *Dr Terror's House of Horrors*, discussed above) the lively *Tales from the Crypt* (1972), utilising the reliable talents of *Dr Terror's* director Freddie Francis, a mainstay of the Amicus and Hammer studios. The adaptations of the original Feldstein/Gaines stories (by Subotsky himself) were typically utilitarian rather than inspired (characterisation of necessity being decidedly economical), but that was precisely what was required in finding filmic correlatives for these cannily constructed short horror tales (written by Al Feldstein, Gaines and Johnny Craig). The use of the imposing figure of Sir Ralph Richardson as the hooded storytelling host the Crypt Keeper was something of a surprise to those expecting the sardonic ghoul of the comics, but gave a patina of respectability to what might otherwise seem catchpenny.

Once the British-relocated stories got underway with an expertly edited version of Johnny Craig's 'And All Through the House' (featuring an increasingly hysterical Joan Collins pursued by a psychopathic Santa Claus), it was already clear that Francis had the measure of the tales, even utilising the striking panel design of the original artist/ writer artist Craig as a ready-made storyboard for the film. As with all Amicus anthologies, some tales are more serviceable than others (and nothing after the Joan Collins episode delivers the same visceral punch), but most viewers felt that justice had been done to the source material (including Bill Gaines himself, although with some reservations). *Dead of Night* it wasn't (Freddie Francis was no Cavalcanti), but *Tales from the Crypt* was a sizeable commercial hit for Amicus.

The success of the film guaranteed a follow-up, and Roy Ward Baker (who had already made two films for the company) was hired by Subotsky for *The Vault of Horror* (1973), an adaptation of further stories from the EC heyday using the title of another flagship comic of the group. Baker, however, seemed curiously constrained in this follow-up effort, and the success of the first film was not replicated; as a result, a third anthology (to be named after the company's other horror title, *The Haunt of Fear*) was never made. The celebrated shock endings of the film were delivered with a certain panache, as were the linking sections (in which five luckless characters discover that they are eternally trapped in a cemetery, doomed to live over the events that brought about their demise for eternity – a sort of horror comics version of Jean-Paul Sartre's *Huis Clos/No Exit*). Subotsky had always prided himself (rather curiously) on the fact that these films utilised comparatively little gruesomeness, and the often tongue-in-cheek tone of the original comics was echoed in such sections as the first episode, 'Midnight Mess' (the titles were usually outrageous puns, the import of which became apparent at the end of the piece), in which Daniel Massey murders his sister (his real-life sister, in fact: the actress Anna Massey) for a family inheritance, only to wind up in a restaurant serving disgusting fare (and whose patrons – in the shock ending – turn out to be vampires). The final image of Massey hoisted upside down with a tap driven into his neck to provide the blood-drinkers' preferred alternative to wine perfectly caught the tone of the original comics, but quickly proved too gruesome for TV networks, which substituted a curious and confusing still onto the climax of the episode (a particularly maladroit form of censorship). Similar cack-handed surgery was performed on the later episode featuring Terry Thomas and Glynis Johns, where the latter drives a hammer into the former's forehead; this was similarly freeze-framed. But if all of this makes the film sound like good, macabre fun, such enjoyment was to be had only fitfully, and the characters (unlike those in the earlier *Tales from the Crypt*) clearly existed only as set-ups for the gruesome punchlines. The final editing duties on the film were performed by Subotsky himself, and not to the advantage of Baker's work.

The brevity of the entries in the Amicus anthology films performs the function of craving the audience's indulgence, along the lines of 'if you're not very impressed by this episode, there's another one coming along shortly'. But one of the very best and most accomplished entries in the whole sequence takes its time, and elevates the episode (and, *inter alia*, the film itself) above most other films in the cycle. *From Beyond the Grave* (1974) features what is in essence a mini playlet ('An Act of Kindness'), in which style, characterisation and dialogue are reminiscent in their demotic observation of such writers as Harold Pinter. A former military man in a loveless marriage encounters a shabby match-seller, also ex-army. A bond is formed between the two men, and we quickly realise that the character played by Ian Bannen is self-deluding about his own military achievements (he steals a medal from the antiques dealer played by Peter Cushing in order to impress his new friend). The latter is beautifully played by Donald Pleasence as a man from the lower ranks whose every utterance is a kind of banal cliché, but who generously offers hospitality to the unhappy Bannen character and even – it is suggested – offers the sexual favours of his very strange daughter, played by Pleasence's own daughter Angela. Apart from the exquisitely playing of the two men and the idiomatic dialogue they are given, as well as the telling points about the British and class, perhaps the most striking thing about the episode is the use of Angela Pleasence as a sort of unconventional femme fatale. The actress, with her lank hair and lack of make-up, is so radically different from the kind of nubile temptress who might have been given the part that the effectiveness of the piece is immeasurably enhanced, and when the Bannen and Angela Pleasence characters actually have sex, the audience is invited to feel sympathy and liking for this odd couple, even though there is not the slightest attempt to make the young woman anything other than strange and disturbed. The demands of the narrative ensure that her character inexorably leads the military man into the realms of death and horror, but even the shifting of gears with this revelation is well handled by director Kevin Connor (the excellent screenplay is by Raymond Christodoulou, from stories by Ronald Chetwynd-Hayes). The other episodes in the film are far less individual, even borrowing a 'haunted mirror' concept from *Dead of Night*.

The independent company Compton/Tekli was responsible for James Hill's *A Study in Terror* (1965), one of the most ingenious entries in the increasingly populous Sherlock Holmes vs. Jack the Ripper subgenre, with what now looks like a remarkable cast (Judi Dench and Anthony Quayle in small parts), while John Neville makes a solid, energetic Holmes (regrettably, however, Donald Houston settled on Basil Rathbone's companion Nigel Bruce as his model for Watson – only Bruce can get away with this level of dim-witted bluster). It is the late 1800s: Jack the Ripper is terrorising London's East End and murdering prostitutes. The only clue Sherlock Holmes has to work on is a mysterious box sent to 221B Baker Street. The box contains a selection of surgical instruments and bears the crest of a well-placed family . . . only the scalpel is missing. The smorgasbord of graphic 1960s violence, a revisionist take on Holmes and some ingenious plotting more than make up for the missteps here.

Another company attempting to rival Hammer and make its name synonymous with cinematic terror (unsuccessfully in the event) was the British film production company Tigon. The company was founded by the energetic Tony Tenser, an enterprising producer (with a solid, hard-as-nails commercial instinct) who encouraged the directors he hired to push the barriers of acceptable taste beyond their limits. His battles with the censors became as notorious as his maxim: only two things are guaranteed to sell a film – sex and horror. While Tenser's career as a British film producer has several highlights, there are some notable blots on his escutcheon – the Tigon portfolio included three indifferent films, *The Body Stealers* (1969), *The Beast in the Cellar* (1970) and *Virgin Witch* (1972), an interesting (if compromised) misfire, *The Haunted House of Horror* (1969) and three which achieved cult status, *Blood on Satan's Claw* (1971), Polanski's *Repulsion* (1965) and the late Michael Reeves' massively accomplished *Witchfinder General* (1968), a film whose significance in the British Gothic genre cannot be overestimated.

The maladroit *The Beast in the Cellar* squandered the usually reliable (though signally not on this occasion) Beryl Reid and Flora Robson as a pair of elderly spinsters cloistering their demented brother in seclusion for 30 years until he (inevitably) escapes and begins a bloody rampage.

James Kelly's direction, never rising above the quotidian, fails to engage with his material in any productive fashion.

There are, however, shards of flickering interest in another Tigon film which now resembles something of a harbinger of the latter-day menaced teenagers/slasher film, Michael Armstrong's *The Haunted House of Horror* (1969), which was notably gory for its day and in which the ghost of another, more intriguing film may be seen imprinted on the DNA of the concept. A polyglot multinational cast is headed by minor American pop star Frankie Avalon (playing a teenager at 30), with a slew of second-string British actors later to make their mark in TV sitcoms (including Richard O'Sullivan) and another minor pop singer, the UK's Mark Wynter (whose version of 'Venus in Blue Jeans' may have been running through the minds of the audience as he is bloodily slaughtered in the film's most memorable set piece). As a group of youthful revellers are stalked and dispatched by an unseen knife-wielding psychopath, the talented Armstrong's instincts sometimes guide him in interesting directions (his original concept was apparently more surrealistic and non-linear, and the film was tampered with), although miscasting (such as the uncharismatic Julian Barnes – not the novelist – in a key part originally intended for David Bowie) compromises his vision. The final tense confrontation with the soon-to-be-unmasked murderer (in which a phallic knife rises slowly between two survivors, with the audience uncertain as to who is holding it) suggests the more imaginative film that this might have been.

The undistinguished *Virgin Witch* in 1972 (featuring nubile real-life siblings Ann and Vicki Michelle) added no lustre to Tigon's reputation, with journeyman director Ray Austin proving a better stunt coordinator (his real métier) than director in a torpid tale of two sisters who are lured to an orgiastic Satanic ritual in which they are inducted into a witches' coven. A much more ambitious and interesting entry in the Tigon filmography was a film which was initially received coolly but has steadily achieved more status over the years. The director Piers Haggard produced a career *chef d'oeuvre* with *Blood on Satan's Claw* (1971), with the reliable middle-aged character actor Patrick Wymark set against a youthful Linda Hayden (as so often in her career, seen naked), the latter channelling a dangerous sexuality. Haggard's skill was to marry an almost Hardy-esque response to the English countryside (possibly influenced by the director Michael Powell's similarly evocative use of an Arcadian Albion) to a nasty supernatural menace – a menace which spreads from one manifestation to an almost endemic level. Haggard's film sees a seventeeth-century English village caught up in a fever of demonic hysteria after the discovery of a deformed skull in a local field. But accomplished though Haggard's intelligently made film is, there is no gainsaying which film was to be Tigon's chef achievement as a film production company – and one of the definitive British Gothic films.

It is rare indeed for a film nominally in the horror genre to be applauded by mainstream critics as a minor classic (Clouzot's *Les Diaboliques* being the obvious winner in this area), but Roman Polanski's first film in English, *Repulsion* (1965) was rightly recognised as a subtle, intelligent and terrifying portrait of a young girl's descent into schizophrenia and murder (Polanski had acquired much critical goodwill for such arthouse successes as *Knife in the Water* three years earlier and was a canny hiring by the astute producer Tony Tenser). One of *Repulsion*'s most striking aspects is the expatriate Polish director's vision of modern London, with its beauty parlours populated by raddled matrons, and unpleasant, sexually threatening workmen catcalling passing women. Catherine Deneuve's playing, all neurasthenic tics and alienated dead emotional responses, as the young Belgian girl in Earls Court (whose frustrated sexuality leads to a descent into psychopathic behaviour in her sister's flat) is superbly understated in its beneath-the-surface shadings, and Polanski treats the incidental details of her madness (a putrefying rabbit left on a plate, the simultaneous attraction/repulsion of a man's vest – that of her sister's lover – left in the bathroom) with as much unsettling attention as the frighteningly violent assaults with razor and candlestick. The bloody razor-death of the Patrick Wymark character, for instance, is particularly disturbing, with the use of sound quite as unsettling as the shocking imagery. The world into which Deneuve's character withdraws in *Repulsion* might be seen to be not dissimilar from that in which many of us are living, however far from psychosis our own mental states may be. And Polanski conveys more acutely than any previous film what the experience of going slowly mad must be like – there is nothing here that resembles the ludicrously accelerated, heavily telegraphed progression of most such films. The world of the young girl, Carol, has an isolation that places it almost outside of time, though with a reality that is physical and specific (as suggested by the variety of sometimes nauseating physical detail) and with a total avoidance of any crass verbalisation of the subject. Perhaps the real insight of the film lies in the final shots of Carol (whose various bloody killings have now come to light) being regarded as something almost inhuman by her neighbours, but it is her consciousness that the viewer feels themself most thoroughly inside. The brutal hallucinations involving rape have further forced us to identify with the vulnerability of the young girl, even though she is the one who ruptures human flesh, with everything from a pair of nail clippers in the beauty parlour in which she works to the murderous razor she ultimately wields.

Throughout the history of the cinema, stories of legendary and bitter clashes between stars and directors are legion, but one of the most famous is that between a young doomed British director and a veteran Hollywood star working in the UK. The bitterness of the relationship has been much chronicled, but while most such clashes allow for a range of opinions on who was right and who was wrong, that is not the case with *Witchfinder General* (or, to give it its full on-screen title, *Matthew Hopkins: Witchfinder General*). The star was the charismatic (but frequently mannered) American Vincent Price, whose career stretched from such classic film noir as *Laura* to his reign as the king of horror in 1950s films such as *House of Wax* (1953) and *House on Haunted Hill* (1959), and the young director was the massively talented, ill-fated Michael Reeves, whose lifestyle was to cut short one of the most promising careers in the cinema. And in the acrid disagreements over the actor's performance, it was the young man who was to be proved right in his view – despite Price's pitched battles with him over the tenor of his performance, the film enshrines the very best work Price did for the cinema (pitched much less melodramatically than his customary performance and to infinitely greater effect). Reeves was not to live to make another film, but with *Witchfinder General*, he made one of the most fully achieved pieces in British Gothic cinema.

England in the year 1645 is a country in barely controlled chaos, with the authorities barely able to keep control of civil disorder. The Civil War, however, has created career opportunities for certain ruthless individuals, including the lawyer Matthew Hopkins, who now styles himself as a 'witchfinder'. Through the counties of East Anglia and Suffolk (assisted by his sadistic henchman John Stearne), he plays upon the superstitious belief of the locals to draw (under torture) confessions from the hapless women – and sometimes men – accused of witchcraft before meting out lethal summary justice. This is the basic premise of *Witchfinder General*, a co-production of American International Pictures and the British company Tigon. The source for the screenplay was a novel written two years earlier by Ronald Bassett, and American actor Price, the most significant star in the genre from the US, was cast as the sinister Hopkins; Price's authority was such that he could play a British character such as Hopkins with virtually no attempt to finesse his incongruous American accent. For Price, it appeared to be simply another money-making exercise with the actor (as so often) on autopilot (although both audiences and Price himself were well aware that full value was always delivered in any film he made, however ramshackle the structure); he could pocket his salary and add more items to his highly impressive collection of fine art (like another perennial Hollywood specialist in villainous parts, Edward G. Robinson, Price was a highly educated aesthete whose knowledge of paintings was so considerable that he could lecture on the subject). But the actor was quickly disabused of the idea that this was simply another Vincent Price vehicle on which he could coast when he was introduced to the prickly young director (no respecter of reputations) who was to helm *Witchfinder General*: Michael Reeves.

Set against the ruthless Hopkins is a determined Cromwellian soldier, Richard Marshall, played by the actor Ian Ogilvy (a friend of Michael Reeves who appeared in all of the director's films: the partially successful *Revenge of the Blood Beast* (1966) with the expat British Queen of the Italian horror film, Barbara Steele, and the much more interesting *The Sorcerers* (1967), with an elderly Boris Karloff in a complex and intriguing tale of mind control). But the last collaboration of actor Ogilvy and director Reeves was to be their unsurpassed magnum opus.

After an act of bravery leads to promotion, Marshall is granted leave and journeys to the village of Brandeston for a meeting with his lover Sara (played by the luminous Hilary Dwyer), who lives with her clergyman uncle John Lowes (Rupert Davies). Subsequently, on his way back to his platoon, Marshall has a fateful encounter with two men who are to destroy everything he holds dear when he gives directions to Hopkins and Stearne (played by Robert Russell). The two threatening visitors are en route to investigate Sara's uncle, whom viewers have already seen as a humane and likeable man, if stiffly constrained by his religious calling. But Lowes is to fall victim to Hopkins and Stearne, and will undergo the most hideous tortures – tortures visited on many individuals throughout the film, in which the levels of violence and bloodshed grow ever more operatic. The film's opening image in which an accused 'witch' is dragged to a hideous death (not dissimilar to a scene in Ingmar Bergman's *The Seventh Seal* (1957)) has already alerted audiences that this is a serious and uncompromising picture; what's more, those expecting the usual knowing, self-referential performance from Vincent Price are in for a shock.

The division of character traits between Hopkins and his brutal enforcer (who clearly feel contempt for each other, despite their symbiotic relationship) might initially be read in Freudian terms as (respectively) controlling superego and rampant id, but such an analogy is only superficially appropriate. While the icy, repressed Hopkins functions as an authoritarian intellect and the thuggish Stearne is there to perform acts of appalling savagery (for instance, 'pricking' with a knife the innocent priest Lowes), both men are essentially representations of chaotic evil. When Sara attempts to save her uncle from painful torture, Hopkins agrees but forces her to have sex with him. And when Stearne subsequently learns of this sexual encounter, he opportunistically takes advantage of Hopkins' travelling to a neighbouring village to investigate another case, and rapes the girl. On his return, an enraged Hopkins commissions the death of the accused, including Sara's uncle. Marshall learns what is happening and swears revenge. But much is to happen before that bloody settling of scores takes place. And when Marshall wields an axe against the witchfinder (in a climactic scene with more visceral impact than virtually anything that had been seen in British horror cinema before), there is only a peripheral sense of justice being done – and a heavy price is paid by everyone involved, not least the unlucky Sara, who is driven mad by the appalling events she has been forced to experience.

There are so many remarkable things about *Witchfinder General* that it is difficult to know where to start in identifying its innovations. There is initially the sense that this period horror film was located some distance from the style perfected by Hammer, with a far greater attention to realism and authentic historical detail and with the supernatural firmly at bay – there are no witches in this film, despite the torture and murder of people accused of the art. Moreover, few films have addressed notions of evil and responsibility in quite as rigorous and coherent a fashion, particularly as Reeves was able to coax from the reluctant Price his most restrained and terrifying performance as a man given the power of life and death over innocents and abusing it; Hopkins is not just a picture of hypocritical religion, but every demagogue and dictator who finds that he is above any culpability for his actions. In addition, Reeves is not interested in the simple imperatives of uncomplicated dramatic involvement with his characters. By the end of the film, we may be utterly desperate for the Marshall character to both save the life of Sara and wreak revenge against the two monsters at the heart of the film (which he does by blinding the hideous Stearne and violently attacking Hopkins before the latter is killed in an act of mercy by another soldier; 'You took him from me!' Marshall shouts in frustration), but there is not the exhilarating sense of release that we are customarily granted in such scenarios. The world that Reeves shows us is not precisely Manichaean in its opposition of good and evil; we are presented with a more complicated and compromised universe which is to some degree a product of the ethos of the 1960s; amelioration of the evils of society is not casually granted, and the good is tainted by the bad. Evil may be punished in this film (unlike the corresponding characters in its best-known imitation, Michael Armstrong's *Mark of the Devil* (1970)), but the virtuous are damaged or destroyed by the actions they are forced to undertake. There is nothing comforting about *Witchfinder General*.

On encountering Reeves' remarkable work, the critical fraternity quickly acknowledged that the young director had created a modern film classic – one that his premature death (from an overdose of drugs) ensured would never be followed up. Subsequent responses to the film have long enshrined it in this classic status, and recent restorations of the swingeing censorship cuts that the BBFC imposed upon the film have, if anything, proved just how radical a piece of cinema this was even before such attempts to vitiate its power (however, Reeves himself was not happy with the topless serving wenches, now restored to some versions of the film). Needless to say, there have been dissenting voices, and a film which is so unrelenting in its treatment of violence (not to mention its bleak and uningratiating tone) has occasioned remarks to the effect that the loss of innocence and racked-up levels of atrocity after Reeves' film have led to the Sadean spectacle of such franchises as the so-called 'torture porn' movies (the *Saw* and *Hostel* films), but while Reeves may have been a progenitor of the sometimes difficult-to-watch mayhem of such successors, his attitude was clearly more responsible and intelligent. While the events of *Witchfinder General* have a grim and bloody fascination, we are not encouraged to enjoy the film on a simple level of a spectacle of dread.

Reeves himself was a fascinating figure: handsome, charismatic and intelligent, he was the right man at the right time to deliver his three remarkably interesting (if sometimes compromised) films – and his youthful death has subsequently linked him to such *poètes maudits* as Keats and Coleridge (with both of whom he shared a truly dark vision of the Gothic). Certainly, the Gothic romanticism of the young director had a congruence with that of an earlier era. His obsession with cinema – and in particular the American director Don Siegel – marks him out as an early example of the 'film geek-turned filmmaker' (now enshrined in the public imagination with such directors as Quentin Tarantino). This writer spoke to Don Siegel on one of his visits to London, and Siegel talked sadly and admiringly of the enthusiastic young Englishman who had turned up on his doorstep in the USA and offered his services. The two were of course very different kinds of filmmakers, and Reeves' idol showed little interest in the Gothic (although in a related area, he was to produce one of the great films combining science fiction and terror in

Invasion of the Body Snatchers (1956)), but Siegel told me that he regarded *Witchfinder General* as one of the most accomplished and disturbing films ever produced in the UK.

Reeves was clearly not a man at ease in his own skin, and suffered from depression, dealing with the latter via an ill-advised mixture of alcohol and barbiturates; when I spoke to the writer Iain Sinclair, who knew Reeves, he mentioned to me the young director's prodigious use of a variety of pills including Valium and Lithium. 'I don't think Mike saw himself as part of the British Gothic tradition and I'm not sure how much he knew about that', said Sinclair. 'His main man was the American director Don Siegel. Gothic was a great way for someone with private means and serious aspirations to get straight into feature films as a very young man. Italy, then exploitation crossover in London, then the great vultures of AIP and Vincent Price. The Suffolk landscape of witch-hunting became for him a form of English Western, with revenger motifs. He wouldn't have been looking much at Carl Dreyer and Ingmar Bergman. I think, if he'd been able to push on, he'd have become a very competent journeyman professional, taking on whatever projects came to hand. He'd been discussing *Bonnie and Clyde*-ish apolitical shoot-ups for the Ireland of Michael Collins. But the success of *Witchfinder* might have condemned him to the Gothic for years to come which might have contributed to the tensions at the end of his life.'

Sinclair continued: 'I couldn't be sure (I wasn't close to him, just a friend of a friend, with an interest in cinema) about the death/suicide. There were a number of personal crises, fall-outs with his girlfriend, and with his writer Tom Baker; something of the atmosphere of *The Sorcerers*, in fact. And in the end, what happened fed the mystique. There are elements of the Powell of *Peeping Tom* and the Hitchcock of *Frenzy*. He was of his time and able to operate in a way that would now be impossible. And interesting for that.'

There are those, including Vincent Price, who did in fact describe the filmmaker's death as suicide, but the cause of death on the coroner's report is given as 'accidental'. Is the despairing *Witchfinder General* a true reflection of the young man's bleak *weltanschauung*? Or was he aware that the film was simply an achievement that he would not be able to top? (His next assignment, *The Oblong Box*, again with Vincent Price, was completed by the director Gordon Hessler and was singularly unimpressive, but it is difficult to see what Reeves might have made of this intractable material.)

The mention of Vincent Price above prompts one of the most discussed elements of this memorable film: the actor's unique approach to the part in the context of his other work. Is the achievement of Price in the film to the actor's credit or due to the unbending coercion of his director, desperate to avoid the self-parody that Price so often traded in? When Price began to appear in such American horror films as *The Tingler* and *House on Haunted Hill*, his approach had been to utilise his charisma and the timbre of his highly musical speaking voice while incorporating elements of knowingness (as opposed to parody), particularly in the films he made for the director William Castle. It's a truism that when the mesmerising Price was on-screen, other actors stood very little chance of attracting the audience's attention, and one of the achievements of Reeves (in his bitter disputes with Price over his performance, constantly attempting to damp down the elements of parody and melodrama) is not only to remind one what a considerable screen actor Price was before the self-mockery of such films as Douglas Hickox's *Theatre of Blood* (1973) took centre stage, but just how well he could interact with his fellow actors. The scenes with Ogilvy and Dwyer in this film allow the younger actors to be considerably more than simply feeds for the veteran performer, and everyone is shown to the very best advantage. Price, famously, was particularly resistant to what he considered the young upstart director's attempts to bully him into a different kind of performance from those he was accustomed to giving (the clash between the two is entertainingly described in a radio play, Matthew Broughton's *Vincent Price and the Horror of the English Blood Beast* (2010)). Price was ultimately forced to admit that his young director had been right and knew exactly what he wanted from his star, which was not the kind of tongue-in-cheek performance he had so often been encouraged to give. Sadly, Price was never again to match his achievement in this film.

Since his death, whether accidental or otherwise, Michael Reeves has become emblematic of a certain kind of self-destructive nihilism, a view of him that is actually somewhat reductive. Despite the fact that his films appear to offer a bleak world view, they nevertheless posit certain possibilities in human existence, even though these possibilities are frustrated or unexplored in his films. And the achievement of his earlier films is patchy: *Revenge of the Blood Beast*, the film in which he began to explore the possibilities of the Gothic genre, also deals with witchcraft, but in this case, it is the real thing. Reeves seemed unconscious of the particular kind of fatal beauty possessed by the British Rank starlet-turned-Italian horror queen Barbara Steele and uses her idiosyncratic erotic appeal far less interestingly than such Italian directors as Riccardo Freda (apart from anything else, Steele wears grotesquely dated fashions of the day which do her far less justice than the period gowns she wears in most of her films). If *Revenge of the Blood Beast* is remembered for anything today, it is for the bloody attack by the witch with a sickle before throwing it away so that it lands across a hammer (the film is set in Transylvania).

The Sorcerers, made in 1967, is far more intriguing, with its particularly fruitful use of a sympathetic Boris Karloff, who is forced into self-destruction by his ruthless wife (excellently played by Catherine Lacey). The couple utilise the inventor's device to mentally control (at long distance) a young antiques dealer played by Ian Ogilvy, allowing them to vicariously experience the things that happen to him, from sex to murder. As the Karloff character's wife descends into madness and sadism, the consequences of the characters' actions are brought home to them in the most forceful (and ultimately fatal) of fashions, prefiguring certain notions in *Witchfinder General*, although the film is compromised by its restricted budget and unrealistic shooting schedule. But the vicarious nature of the cinematic experience is touched upon by the director, if without the rigour of Powell's *Peeping Tom*.

By the time of his signature film, Reeves had become accustomed to exhausting himself in attempting to fulfil the vision that so enthused him, and the forcefulness with which he realised this vision (in the teeth of an unsympathetic response from the film's producers – subsequently, of course, revised – and the positively hostile one from its unhappy star) almost suggests that he knew that *Witchfinder General* would be his final fling of the dice. Whilst the adjective 'nauseating' was routinely evoked to describe the film on its first appearance (along with accusations of gratuitous sadism), it quickly became apparent to perceptive critics that the film's virtues were many and varied, including an astonishingly vivid and intelligent use of the English countryside. Despite its gruelling horrors, this is a film whose subtle and alert response to the English locales recalls both the composer Ralph Vaughan Williams and the writer Thomas Hardy (and the latter comparison is not so unlikely as it might initially seem: Hardy utilised elements of English Gothic in such stories as 'The Withered Arm' and 'Barbara of the House of Grebe'). This vision of England was further enhanced by Paul Ferris' beautiful score, and as much as the ruinous censorship cuts, the replacement of the score by a hideous synthesised one on some American prints (for copyright reasons) was a particularly barbaric act. (The film was speciously renamed *Edgar Allan Poe's The Conqueror Worm* to fool American audiences into thinking that it was part of the profitable Poe cycle inaugurated by Roger Corman.) But in its complex response to landscape, history and character, along with its utter commitment and gravity of intent, the film's reputation is now secure. The terrifying final sequence in which the youthful protagonists are chained to a wall as Hopkins begins to heat a metal cross to torture them has an irresistible power: the viewer, already placed in a notably uncivilised period of history, is now inhabiting the dark psyches of the three central characters, all moving in the same nightmare world. The orgy of retributional violence that follows has Marshall finally able to meet the savagery of his oppressors with equal bloodthirstiness. But the last sounds that the viewer is left with are the keening cries of a distraught, disturbed Sara, even as Ferris' score offers a romantic resolution at odds with what we are seeing on the screen. Unlike, say, the films of Michelangelo Antonioni, where we are invited to respond coolly and objectively to the images we are presented with, Reeves' agenda is to involve us on every level, leaving us both shaken up and exhausted by the experience of the film. Watching *Witchfinder General* today, perhaps the most overriding final impression is a keen sense of loss – not just the loss of everything important to the sympathetic central characters, but the loss to British cinema of one of its most challenging and provocative talents.

The success of *Witchfinder General* spawned a variety of sequels from the rivals of Hammer, most famously (and most notoriously) the much-banned, spectacularly gruesome *Mark of the Devil* (1970), with its tongue-rippings and other horrors. The British director Michael Armstrong was a friend of the late lamented Reeves, but Armstrong's film, made in tribute to Reeves' masterpiece (and, unsurprisingly, with a view to replicating its box office success), while photocopying the narrative of *Witchfinder*, demonstrated its divergence from the brilliantly personal vision of Reeves, substituting a brusque efficiency (not to mention a lack of understanding of one crucial aspect: that the crushing brutality of the earlier film functioned organically, rather than simply being ladled on for exploitation reasons). Despite the much-publicised grisly detail of the tortures and horrors in Armstrong's film (tongues torn out by the roots, feet crushed in iron boots, burnings, etc.), Reeves' picture of a Cromwellian England in the grip of a witch-hunting fervour is a much more disturbing experience, as the grim events happen to fully realised, often sympathetic characters rather than papier-mâché victims-for-the-disposal-of.

But such unflattering comparisons are not entirely to be made at Armstrong's expense. His maladroitly post-synced protagonists are a problem (the film is an international co-production, the classic 'Euro-pudding', involving Austrian money via the producer Adrian Hoven – an actor in the film – who Armstrong felt had compromised his intentions), with only Herbert Lom in the Vincent Price role of witchfinder delivering a (for him) relatively restrained performance. The other actors, including a miscast Udo Kier (bringing an inappropriately fey quality to what might be described as the Ian Ogilvy juvenile lead role), do not register on any level – Olivera Vuco, in anachronistic make-up, is particularly unprepossessing, and unlike the situation in Reeves' film, the clash of personalities (once again: middle-aged authoritarian figure, endangered young couple) sounds no particular resonance. Particularly damaging is the fact that Armstrong eschews Reeves' cathartic bloodbath at the end of the film for a very unsatisfactory resolution (a then-modish point about evil going unpunished in the real world might have been the intention, but the final effect is one of clumsy, acutely frustrating dramaturgy). The only level on which the film really works is on a kind of grim parade of Grand Guignol horrors, and this spectacle, while having a certain gruesome fascination (the use of real-life torture instruments to bloodily remove tongues, for instance) don't disturb in context as the texture of the film is unpersuasive (not least for its crass scoring). It goes without saying that those of a squeamish disposition might find the film disturbing, but such individuals are unlikely to be committing themselves to Armstrong's efforts in any case.

8
Nights of the Demon: The English Supernatural Story and Film

There are other, durable strands to the English Gothic film than merely those dealing in sanguinary, violent excess; the crucial influence of the English ghost story tradition on British cinema continues to this day, re-discovered by successive generations. Any attention paid to this particular strain of (often monochrome) film, featuring more subtle atmospheric narrative devices as opposed to the more graphic blood-letting of the colour rivals, must examine the influence of M.R. James on British cinema (notably in what is generally considered to be the finest single Gothic film ever made in this country, Jacques Tourneur's *Night of the Demon*) and must also take on board a detailed celebration of the another great British horror film, Ealing's portmanteau classic *Dead of Night* (with its celebrated Michael Redgrave ventriloquist dummy sequence), along with later offshoots of this trend, including *The Innocents* (after Henry James), *The Haunting* and *Night of the Eagle*.

The glorious multi-director *Dead of Night* (1945) is not quite the only British horror film made in the 1940s, but it so nearly qualifies that all other rivals for the title seem footling. On its original cinema showing, the film created something of a minor sensation – it should be remembered that such fare was rare indeed on British screens in this era, and audiences hungry for a dose of the macabre or the supernatural had to be grateful for all the crumbs they were thrown. The fact that such an unsettling piece of work – surrealistic and nightmarish on the deepest level – was a product of the comfortably bourgeois Ealing Studios, famous for its affectionate and indulgent pictures of a certain version of British life, is perhaps part of the film's appeal. The presence of the actors Naunton Wayne and Basil Radford (so memorable – and hilarious – as the cricket-obsessed Englishmen in Hitchcock's *The Lady Vanishes*) perhaps lends an air of cosy complacency to the piece, but their episode should be seen in context; the 'golfing' story is basically a *jeu d'esprit*, an attempt to lighten the mood between darker sequences. And the darkest episode – which is also not without a deeply sardonic humour – is one of the great glories of British Gothic cinema: the ventriloquist's dummy episode directed by the maverick Brazilian auteur Cavalcanti and starring Michael Redgrave as a man obsessed with his wooden alter ego (Redgrave, of course, was an actor well acquainted with psychological conflict in his own troubled life, which he often channelled into his work). The subversive nature of this deeply creepy episode should not be underestimated, and the murderous, independently minded dummy at war with its putative master has been much imitated since (cf. Lindsay Shonteff's *Devil Doll* (1964)). It is perhaps only within the context of a portmanteau ghost story film that such an unyielding picture of psychosis and obsession could be presented. It goes without saying that the force of the episode is often due to the quietly monomaniac playing of Redgrave; if the actor considered this performance to be a lightweight assignment sandwiched between his more serious work, that was to seriously underestimate the truthfulness of his performance – a performance all the more impressive given that its levels of psychological observation were more at the service of raising the hackles on the viewer's neck (a function the film can still effortlessly maintain over 60 years later) than offering a plausible picture of psychosis.

Dead of Night takes on board a variety of interesting psychological issues, such as the stripping away of layers of psychological deceit in the innocence of the dream state, and even incorporates an examination of the British tendency to 'pull together' to obtain a common goal, which might be said to be what happens with the very disparate group of individuals that the architect played by Mervyn Johns meets at the house at which he finds himself in his recurrent dream. Are we shown in these very different types (young, older, spontaneous, stuffy) a microcosm of British society (even though the real agenda is, of course, to provide a variety of narrators)? And speaking of this last aspect, the film also provides an early example of the unreliable narrator – at least one of the stories we are told is, quite self-consciously, a lie.

In fact, although *Dead of Night* is generally regarded as a compendium of ghost stories, the various episodes at times move beyond this category – the throwaway Wayne and Radford piece (which is different from all the other pieces in the film in that it is related as a wind-up joke rather than a true story by its narrator) is very different from the subtly unsettling story of a ghost child that appears at a children's party. Apart from the ventriloquist episode, it is now generally considered that the other key sequence is the one involving a supernaturally charged mirror that maintains a terrible hold over its owner. Directed by the other key auteur associated with the film, Robert Hamer, 'The Haunted Mirror' incorporates subtle points about the shifting nature of identity (how culpable, in the final analysis, is the husband transformed into a murderous figure by the mystical mirror?). Along with such added value, the straightforward exigencies of chilling the audience's blood are finessed by the quirkily orchestrated score by a displaced member of *Les Six*, Georges Auric, a stalwart of British sound stages at this time.

Of the various might-have-been careers in the British cinema, few are more poignant than that of the neglected Thorold Dickinson, whose slim body of work (including the impressive *Secret People* (1952)) suggests that, had he had the opportunities, he might have been a director to rival such better-known names as Michael Powell. And it is interesting to speculate how the latter filmmaker might have handled one of the UK's strangest and most haunting ventures into the Gothic, the 1949 adaptation of Pushkin's *The Queen of Spades*. An obsessed, resentful army man played by Anton Walbrook enters into a Faustian pact to learn the secret of winning at cards from a baleful elderly countess played by Edith Evans; Walbrook's character is delivered by the actor with all the overwrought romanticism that the part demands (rendering it, in the process, very un-English). But as the narrative descends into supernatural dread (and the Walbrook character is haunted by the malign spirit – and dead eyes – of the woman whose death he is responsible for), Dickinson finds an aesthetic approach which fine-tunes the minatory atmosphere, and the ever-more-demented progress of the narrative is further enhanced by a score by Georges Auric, one that is as plangent and unsettling as the one he produced for *Dead of Night*.

Ten years after *Dead of Night*, Ealing Studios was once again to dip its toes into the supernatural field – not a favourite genre of the level-headed studio executive Michael Balcon – with the diverting *The Night My Number Came Up* (directed by Leslie Norman in 1955), which dealt with issues of predestination and dreams effectively enough, but signally lacked the sheer poetry of its eminent predecessor.

While many people agree that Jacques Tourneur's *Night of the Demon* (1957) is unique in its multiple achievements, there is a debate that rages about the film to this day, even among those who would place the film securely in the pantheon. The famous image of the gigantic eponymous demon itself (much reproduced) has made it well known even to those who have never seen the film: a hideous bestial visage with flaring nostrils, horns, pointed ears and basilisk eyes, its open maw crammed with vicious fangs. And this monstrosity was a problem – not just for the critical establishment (who saw it as an emblematic, debased example of a certain kind of popular culture), but for the auteur director on whose film this iconically unpleasant image was imposed (and who was keen to keep his film's supernatural manifestations off-screen). The film's producer, Hal Chester, was certainly no Val Lewton in terms of taste and influence (Chester was undoubtedly closer to such fairground hucksters as Herman Cohen of *Horrors of the Black Museum* fame), but the director's loathing of the tampering to which he felt Chester subjected the film also needs to be examined (and certainly not taken at face value). Tourneur was wrong (as this discussion will attempt to prove) to suggest that his producer's crassness in adding explicit shots of the gigantic, horned demon discussed above (which the director was reluctant to show) had ruined his film.

Traditionally, the serious press (both in broadsheets and magazines) has treated films utilising Gothic horror themes with an aloof combination of derision and distaste. The critical climate has changed recently (with more iconoclastic writers casting their nets wider than the standard literary or filmic canon) and has become less allergic to genre. It might be said that there is a more serious attempt to examine such subjects on their own merits, even though there is still a basic assumption that this material is automatically suspect and has to establish its worth in a way that more respectable subjects are not obliged to do. The heavyweight literary antecedents cut no ice here, as it is considered that the popular cinema has often cheapened and tarnished such legacies. The corollary of this is the fact that the 'quality' bar for genre product is set much higher, and horror films, which may offer considerable rewards but are still perceived as endemically flawed works, are invariably judged from a jaundiced viewpoint. This negative perception kicks in before any secondary attempt is made to perceive the virtues of such films – and it frequently occasions a simple dismissal of the Gothic as a now-debased genre. Certainly, many horror films which appeared as a corollary of Britain's long fascination with the macabre are obliged to suffer from a variety of compromises (mostly because of commercial imperatives), even though the actual level of accomplishment is often considerably greater than that of more mainstream establishment fare.

A good example of this qualified response is that accorded to *Night of the Demon*. As a work of art, it undoubtedly has its flaws – and many viewers (even admirers of the film) might consider the imported American actor Dana Andrews to be one of these. But a lively defence might be made of his work in Tourneur's adaptation of M.R. James' story 'Casting the Runes'. Film aficionados might be aware of the actor's well-known alcoholism, fully developed by 1957, which often compromised his work and dulled the sharp edge that his performances had sported in his younger days (notably as the obsessed detective in Otto Preminger's definitive film noir *Laura* (1944)), but such problems are not really evident in his performance in the Tourneur film. Admittedly, it is hard to accept him in the profession he is given in the film – the academic, Dr John Holden – as the actor was far more at ease playing tough-guy heroes or no-nonsense reporters. But Andrews is always professional (if limited) and fulfils the function that is required of him in the film (not least being an American name utilised in order to sell a British film such as this in the USA, where it was re-titled *Curse of the Demon*) and the virtues of the film lie elsewhere than in its slightly dull hero. There are so many aspects of *Night of the Demon* which are simply nonpareil (not least the most fully rounded, nuanced villain in any British horror film) that its cult status is unchallenged – and Tourneur, very much a genre filmmaker, is undoubtedly a better director than many contemporaries who specialised in more ostensibly serious subjects. The son of celebrated filmmaker Maurice Tourneur, he had made his mark in the subtle, intelligent supernatural films produced by the urbane and civilised Val Lewton in the 1940s, and his oblique and subtle approach to eldritch subjects chimed with his producer in such poetic pieces as *Cat People* (1942) and, a year later, *I Walked with a Zombie*; the famous description of the latter film as 'Jane Eyre in the West Indies' is not a wry dismissal (as it might sound), but the suggestion of the level of ambition for producer and director.

Made over a decade later in Britain, *Night of the Demon* is a valedictory work for the director in the Gothic genre, and one wonders if he was aware of the fact that he would not work in this field again. Certainly, this would account for the rigorous effort on his part to make this his magnum opus and infuse it with every facet of his considerable skills. In this endeavour, he accomplished his goal triumphantly. Even though he regarded the film as irredeemably compromised, the unique status of the film is assured.

Time, audience taste and the vagaries of critical fashion have a way of turning previously held judgements head over heels – and that's certainly true where films are concerned. In 1933, a now-forgotten film of Noel Coward's *Cavalcade* collected more Academy Awards than a contemporaneous film about a giant ape falling to its death from the

Empire State Building, now rather better remembered than the more upmarket Coward adaptation. The house magazine of the British Film Institute, the prestigious *Sight & Sound*, thought so little of horror films that it routinely ignored them. But short-sightedness in these areas has a way of being corrected by time, and that has certainly been the case with *Night of the Demon*, sniffily received on its first appearance (when it played in the UK as the supporting feature on a double bill with the Hammer film *The Revenge of Frankenstein*). There was some praise, but it was largely muted, and the film enjoyed the further indignity of being cut by ten crucial minutes by its producers for its American release. But this once-under-regarded piece of work is now esteemed for its intelligent, subtle and atmospheric approach to material that could so easily have received a catchpenny, obvious rendering.

Dr John Holden finds himself in a terrifying drawn-out battle with a malign (but civilised) opponent, Karswell, whose mastery of the uncanny allows him to dispatch a cat that becomes a leopard along with other terrifying manifestations (such as a rapidly travelling, gigantic ball of fire) and – both invisible and all-too-visible – the eponymous demon which makes its appearances both at the beginning and the end of the film. With the focused command of the medium that he learned under producer Val Lewton, Tourneur is able to manipulate audience expectations with an audacity that was not to be seen until some five or so years later, when Alfred Hitchcock similarly orchestrated a subtle manipulation of audience nerves with *The Birds*.

But while to some degree the film is a vindication of the auteur theory (any examination of Tourneur's career quickly demonstrates how consistent his achievement was over the years, and his contribution to *Night of the Demon* is inestimable and unarguable), the film (despite its French director and imported American star) is quintessentially English in its exploration of the Gothic, not least because of the writers involved in its creation.

M.R. James' short story 'Casting the Runes', which originally appeared in the collection *More Ghost Stories* in 1911, has enjoyed several stylish adaptations over the years (none, however, to match the Tourneur film in sheer accomplishment). The villain here is the enigmatic Karswell, a practitioner of the black arts who has a particularly human weakness – an intense dislike of not being taken seriously. His victims include the author of an excoriating review of Karswell's *The History of Witchcraft* – and a bad review for this author results in something a little more serious than a complaining letter to the literary editor. The character of Karswell in Tourneur's film is one of the key reasons for the success of the piece, as we shall see. The eponymous process of casting the runes is a description of the magician's skill at placing curses in long-distance fashion: symbols on parchment that, when passed to the luckless recipient, bring about their violent death (in the story, the victim has fallen to his death from a tree after attempting to escape from some unnamed animal – and readers were to learn that this is no ordinary beast). Locating the story in a specific locale was one of James' specialities, and the fact that the runic symbols are insinuated into the victim's papers at the British Museum both establishes the Englishness of the tale and finesses the literary cachet (the device is to be maintained in the film).

But the second English writer whose contribution to *Night of the Demon* is incalculable is scriptwriter Charles Bennett, a favourite scribe of Alfred Hitchcock's who was able to combine superbly written dialogue with perfectly engineered narratives – skills which are fully on display in his work for the film. Some, however, may be intrigued or puzzled by the name of the undistinguished Hal E. Chester on the credits as co-writer. Chester is now seen as a business-oriented (rather than creative) producer whose earlier work included the lowbrow *Joe Palooka* series and whose eye was firmly on the box office takings of the film rather than its artistic success. In fact, it appears that Chester's name appeared on the credits as co-writer only when Charles Bennett requested that his own be removed – clearly, like Tourneur, he had come to believe that he was working on a deeply compromised piece and was not proud of his contribution. Retrospectively, of course, this may now be seen as a particularly wrongheaded decision, as he was not the first writer to underestimate the growing cult reputation of a film which he decided had traduced his work: the novelist Richard Matheson was similarly brusquely dismissive of Jack Arnold's film of his *The Shrinking Man* (as *The Incredible Shrinking Man* (1957)), until he realised the high esteem in which the film is now regarded and retrospectively upgraded his own view of it.

Bennett's screenplays for Hitchcock had included the latter's first talking picture, *Blackmail* (1929) and the original *The Man Who Knew Too Much* (1934), as well as the first and best version of *The 39 Steps* (1935). Bennett was also to work for Hitchcock during his Hollywood period on *Foreign Correspondent* (1940), always bringing to his work the same impeccable craftsmanship. But perhaps further giving the lie to the auteur theory which always prioritised the contribution of the director, further progenitors might be adduced to explain the film's success. Other creative personnel included the composer Clifton Parker, whose score is now justly celebrated, and the production designer Ken Adam (later famous for his innovative work for Stanley Kubrick and the producers of the James Bond films). Finally, there is the beautifully wrought cinematography of Ted Scaife, instantly establishing his authority in the opening shot by means of a windswept Stonehenge, suggesting both the Englishness of the subject and the continuing influence of ancient mystical forces.

Tourneur's carefully honed techniques of establishing unease in the minds of the audience by nuance and suggestion (as demonstrated in such films as *Cat People*) are demonstrated here at full stretch. We know we are in the hands of a master from the first shot, with the headlights of a car jutting out from between the trees on a benighted country road. The driver, Harrington (played by Maurice Denham), is clearly in a frantic, disturbed state, heading towards the country pile Lufford Hall. He pleads with the avuncular (and not at all sinister) Dr Julian Karswell, played by Niall MacGinnis, who, despite his amiable demeanour, is in fact a Satanist with real and fatal powers. The casting of the versatile MacGinnis is one of the film's masterstrokes (along with the writing of Charles Bennett). MacGinnis' Karswell is some considerable distance from practitioners of the black arts like that played by Charles Gray in *The Devil Rides Out*; his manner is always deferential and apologetic, never threatening or hectoring in the way that one might expect from a clearly established villain. He has set in train the events which will bring about the death of the Harrington character and notes regretfully that nothing can be done. It is this unorthodox reading of the character (along with surprising touches, such as his masquerading as a friendly magician at a children's party and the fact that he appears to be something of a mother's boy – rather like the equally homicidal Robert Walker character in Hitchcock's *Strangers on a Train*) that renders him perhaps the most thoroughly chilling (and plausible) nemesis in any film of the supernatural.

Harrington allows himself to believe that the curse has been lifted, but as he arrives home, the treetops near his house are agitated by unnatural smoky clouds and an electrical disturbance which forms into the towering basilisk monstrosity of the title. The terrified Harrington drives his car into a telegraph pole and as the severed power line crackles and dances, a gigantic claw reaches down for him and the demon's massive hoof slams down beside his car. So utterly successful is this operatic orchestration of suspense and so effective is the melding of Tourneur's filmic technique and the sight of the monster that many an admirer of the film has been moved to disagree with the director's assertion that the creature should never have been seen. It is, however, not seen again until the film's equally unnerving climax alongside a moving train, when the creature once again brings about a violent and hideous death.

Controversy continues to this day over who added the much-commented-on shots of the demon. Tourneur originally claimed that he wanted (under duress) to utilise only a handful of frames showing the creature, but it now appears that he had something to do with the shooting of the sequence. Certainly, Charles Bennett's original screenplay describes the appearance of the rampaging monster on both occasions, but (customarily) the most creative film directors rarely regard the screenplay as sacrosanct.

The nigh-inevitable 'meeting cute' scene on a plane between the Holden character and the niece of the late victim of Karswell (well played by the English actress Peggy Cummins in one of her two cult movies – the other was Joseph H. Lewis' *Gun Crazy* in 1950) is discreetly done, as is the film's romantic interest in general, but this inevitable component is clearly not what got the director's creative juices flowing. Holden's investigations into the activities of the Satanist cult led by Karswell are handled with total verisimilitude, and such details as a fluttering piece of parchment that appears to have a life of its own nicely finesse the increasing sense of supernatural dread. Holden, of course, remains as obstinately sceptical as the Peter Wyngarde character is later to do in *Night of the Eagle*, even in the face of unarguable evidence. But he is similarly to pay a heavy price for his refusal to accept the reality of what is happening to him. Even the bizarre fireball that he is chased by in the woods is dismissed by him as some trick that the Satanist has set up, and the film appears to be making some points *inter alia*: a repudiation of the evidence of one's own eyes (or, by extension, the existential truth of unarguable evidence) is a recipe for the destruction of the personality, which we suspect may happen to Holden as it did to the terrified (and doomed) Harrington at the beginning of the film, forced to accept the existence of the uncanny before his violent death.

One of the film's great set pieces is the Halloween party given by Karswell at his country house as a treat for the children of the village. A reading of the film in the twenty-first century – when paedophilia appears to be endemic – might lend itself to a darker retrospective reading of Karswell's motives, but the film actually does not support this. Karswell is a complex character and he appears to be genuinely possessed of an altruistic nature, giving the impression that he cares for the children he deals with (though the viewer may find themselves remembering how good – apparently – Adolf Hitler was with children). But as a demonstration to Holden of his occult powers, Karswell calls up a terrifying windstorm which destroys the good spirits of the party (whipping chairs and tables into the air) and has the children running in panic. A superb shot of MacGinnis in grotesque clown make-up smiling in melancholy fashion at the evidence of his abilities is one of the most unsettling images in the film.

The variety of small-scale incidents that follow are handled by Tourneur with customary authority, leading inexorably towards the film's pulse-raising climax set on a train, the final duel between Holden and Karswell (and involving once again the passing of the fatal runes), as Karswell, now an unimpressive figure, overweight, unthreatening and scrabbling for the fatal parchment before the inevitable appearance of the demon, meets his end at the claws of the monstrosity. Even though the creature when seen in longshot (a man in a suit tearing a Karswell doll to pieces) does not match the highly impressive mock-up of the creature's head and shoulders, the effect is not vitiated. If the final effect of the film appears to carry a plea for belief in the existence of the supernatural, that is an inevitable corollary of the genre – and aficionados will always point out (whatever their personal beliefs) that films or books which attempt to explain away the occult by natural causes or trickery are invariably betraying the essence of the genre. We, the viewers, are readily prepared to believe in the supernatural for the duration of the work we are watching, just as we willingly accept – for a couple of hours – the existence of the gods in the tragedies of Euripides and Sophocles.

Just why do some films work so well? Anyone who has seen Sidney Hayers' *Night of the Eagle* in a cinema with an audience will be well aware that this is one of the most efficiently made, tense and effective British supernatural films ever made, with nary a misstep (except perhaps some less-than-convincing shots of the eponymous eagle at the film's climax, including the visible cord that pulls the bird – a real one – towards the terrified hero). But the sheer expertise of the film is breathtaking and it is not surprising that some journalists have rushed to praise the impeccable direction of Hayers – as, indeed, they should. But like all the best films, *Night of the Eagle* (re-titled *Burn, Witch, Burn* in the USA) is the result of a concatenation of elements: Hayers' direction, of course; an impeccably written script by American masters of the supernatural short story Richard Matheson and Charles Beaumont (and finessed by the highly professional George Baxt, who had worked with Hayers before on the memorable *Circus of Horrors*), and based on the novel *Conjure Wife* (1943) by Fritz Leiber (whose speciality was locating the supernatural in quotidian modern-day settings, as in his remarkable short story 'Smoke Ghost'); crisp and effective cinematography by Reginald Wyler; and impeccable editing by Ralph Sheldon. Then there is the powerfully effective score by the distinguished British symphonist William Alwyn (who, like his fellow English composer Malcolm Arnold, proved highly adroit at film scoring). And finally, of course, there is the impeccable casting of the film: Peter Wyngarde (still a serious and solid actor before growing a Zapata moustache and donning the ludicrous, now-dated garb of TV's Jason King), suggesting the cool, soon-to-be-punctured rationality of his slightly pompous academic, Norman Taylor, in the face of the inexplicable – in this, as in so much else in the film, reminiscent of the Dana Andrews character in *Night of the Demon*. *Night of the Eagle* also showcases a career-best performance for the American actress Janet Blair (under-used elsewhere) as his wife Tansy (and before we continue with this discussion, it should be pointed out that the reader should be familiar with the film to avoid spoilers), who is dabbling in witchcraft to advance his career as a lecturer at a local college and, what's more, to protect against unspecified evil influences (and this is the second spoiler), the source of which is Flora Carr (played by Margaret Johnston), the envious wife of a fellow lecturer, The latter actress is perhaps the film's ace in the hole – for narrative reasons, misdirection means that she must be presented as a sardonic, mischievous onlooker throughout the film (another jealous college wife played by Kathleen Byron is the red herring here) and she is particularly effective in an acidulous bridge game, wryly weighing up all the bitchy undercurrents flowing between the academics and their wives. But when Flora's malign influence is exposed at the climax of the film, as she faces off Norman Taylor at night in her college office, Hayers wisely gives the actress her head (with spectacular results). The scene in which she verbally menaces an increasingly distraught Taylor, bringing about the burning of his house and the potential death of his wife, is powerfully done, and the tense latter section is another echo of Jacques Tourneur's very similar film. The decision to show the all-too-real eagle might be regarded as a miscalculation, but Hayers and editor Ralph Sheldon's cutting is brisk enough to keep our cynicism at bay.

The relocation of the American College of Fritz Leiber's original novel to Britain allows for some acridly observed byplay on the politics of the groves of academe in the UK – and here Matheson and Beaumont's adroit screenplay is more than· just a set-up for the blood-chilling business that is the film's real agenda; the social politics are quite as nuanced and sharply observed as the descriptions of this world to be found in the work of such novelists as Malcolm Bradbury and David Lodge. In fact, such is the plausibility granted to the scenes involving the Wyngarde character, his wife and his colleagues that the film's underpinning of reality is unshakeable, so that when the supernatural events begin to occur, they are grounded in a recognisable milieu.

But there is a question which admirers of the film have happily debated – does, in fact, anything supernatural happen in *Night of the Eagle*? Or are we shown a landscape of the mind? The answer would appear to be the latter – the burning of Norman Taylor's house, for example, can only have a supernatural impetus (unless we see a cat's overturning of an oil burner as a unlikely coincidence), but there are two key signifiers here: statues in the grounds of the college are damaged by the gigantic eagle which attacks Taylor, his jacket is ripped to shreds by its claws; and the massive bird smashes its way through the wooden doors of the college. After the Margaret Johnston character has been distracted from her murderous endeavours, all of these things revert to their earlier condition: undamaged statues, untorn coat, intact doors. But Taylor's character has accidentally erased from a blackboard something he had chalked earlier, 'I do not believe' – the word 'not' has been removed. The limits of scepticism have been tested.

Sidney Hayers, like Jacques Tourneur, was never really able to capitalise on the achievement of his middle career. Both directors ended up in television, gainfully employed, but hardly able to utilise the wellsprings of creativity which were clearly in their gift when forced to earn a crust by turning out unambitious, formulaic TV product. On the strength of the taut effective crime film *Payroll* (which I examined in the companion volume to this book, *British Crime Film*), the colourful and excessive *Circus of Horrors* and this supremely effective black-and-white chiller *Night of the Eagle*, Hayers' career might have – had it been nourished – acquired the reputation that was enjoyed by many a more acclaimed (if less talented) director. But is it necessary (*pace* the auteur theory) to also spread the achievement of this film in the direction of its talented screenwriters? Do we credit Matheson and Beaumont (and even Baxt) for the possible dual reading of. the narrative which was adumbrated above: supernatural manifestations or psychic attack by hypnosis? And *Night of the Eagle* should be viewed in the context of its then-modern 1960s settings when the supernatural would have been far less easy to accept for cynical audiences (period-set horror films allowing the viewer to cut more slack for the implausible, and the distancing accoutrements of the past – with their fairy-tale associations – making the contract of suspension of disbelief between filmmaker and viewer easily fulfilled). But regarding the illusion of plausibility, Hayers never puts a foot wrong – we are shown the trappings of witchcraft (fetishes, bones, the dead spider in a jar which is the first object that alerts Taylor to the fact that his wife has taken her earlier encounter with witchcraft in Jamaica very seriously), but we are not actually shown a great deal of the mechanics of weaving spells and so forth, which would undoubtedly have stretched the credulity of the audience. A good example of this grounding of the uncanny in the quotidian is the final scene in which – in the middle of a conversation with the malign Margaret Johnston character – the latter produces a deck of tarot cards and casually constructs a simulacra of the house; she then causes a conflagration (or does she?) by burning the cards. So plausibly handled is this scene that the audience is perfectly prepared to accept why Norman Taylor – by now (one would have thought) disabused of his scepticism about the inexplicable – simply lets her proceed, with dangerous results. Ironically, Wyngarde's greatest fame arrived (as mentioned earlier) with his hilariously mannered Jason King character, all luxuriant moustache and permed hair – admittedly with a built-in parody factor, but it is virtually unwatchable today except as a historical artefact.

It's interesting that the charges of sexual harassment brought against Norman Taylor by an infatuated younger female student (almost certainly under the long-distance influence of the Johnston character) seems a very modern career-destroying occurrence even in the early twenty-first century, when such things are the stuff of newspaper headlines on an almost daily basis. Finally, though, the real achievement of the film is the transplanting of the Gothic ethos into a contemporary setting with truly pulse-raising (and persuasive) results. As a pulsing, sinister noise is emitted from a telephone and Taylor prepares to open his front door to something nameless and unspeakable that is scratching outside, it would be a very strong-minded viewer who is not with the Janet Blair character as she struggles to save her unwitting husband's life by tearing loose the telephone cord.

Hayers, unlike Tourneur, had not been part of the Val Lewton stable producing the classic series of supernatural film in the 1940s, but certainly drew upon the indirect, subtle approach to the uncanny which had been the hallmark of Lewton's productions, while also (along with Richard Matheson and Charles Beaumont) drawing on the ambiguity regarding the central occult threat, in which the suggestion is maintained that the terrors produced were those of the mind, a product of the psyche as much as any malign entity. The Taylor character's smug examination of neurosis in front of his students also chimes with the possibility that his wife's behaviour is the product of sexual psychosis; certainly, Tansy's behaviour is often very irrational-seeming, but the couple's sex life is not really touched upon in the film. And it is a measure of Hayers' craftsmanship that Norman's suggestion that many women (with their penchant for strange rituals) belong in asylums does not come across as a dated piece of 1960s sexism, but as a comment on the restricted vision of the Taylor character – one of his many restrictions that are to be sorely tested during the course of the film. The proto-feminist slant here is pointed up by the fact that Taylor's destruction of his wife's witching apparatus – which clearly leaves her utterly bereft – suggests a lack of respect for her and has an almost immediate concomitant effect when everything that has been satisfactory and successful in his life begins to turn sour (including, for instance, that accusation of rape brought against him by a student). And it is perhaps these complex elements which cement the reality of the narrative – that and the fact that there is a palpable sense of intelligence at work in *Night of the Eagle* informing virtually every level of the piece, something that is hardly a pre-requisite of most films in the genre. The everyday settings and carefully detailed, unreliable protagonists are also a contributing factor to the success of the film, particularly when contrasted with the curious fetishistic objects (including the dead spider in a jar which comes to frightening, scuttling life when it is thrown in a fire). The film was tampered with for its American release, being saddled with a hokey, hucksterish narration which nevertheless did not diminish the film's considerable charge, in which no familiar object can be trusted – even a tape recorder, when tampered with by hostile forces, can be minatory and lethal.

There are inevitably ambitious filmmakers who wish to test the parameters of commercial cinema while still pleasing their more bottom-line-oriented producers who are suspicious of the unorthodox. But the Gothic film – more than most popular genres – actually allows such experimentalism (it even, it might be observed, encourages it, given that the paraphernalia of the genre is so overfamiliar that something novel is required to elicit an audience response). But, accordingly, there is a risk of key narrative imperatives being neglected in the search for something unusual – and this is a risk that Jack Clayton takes at times in his adaptation of Henry James' 'The Turn of the Screw' (re-titled *The Innocents* (1961), from a screenplay by the surprising trio of Truman Capote, John Mortimer and William Archibald). However, Clayton (with the aid of the exquisite black-and-white cinematography of Freddie Francis, prior to the latter's directing career) is able to mix the various elements into a whole that functions both as a genuinely disturbing supernatural story or (for those who wish to adopt a more rational view) the projection of a frustrated woman's sexual neurosis onto her two innocent childish charges – bringing about the destruction of one of them.

The film is adapted from one of the greatest ghost stories in the English language written by the American Henry James, whose interest in the psychology of his characters was perhaps more pronounced than that of his great English namesake M.R. James. The latter's protagonists (economically but convincingly developed) exist in order to further the narrative, invariably some kind of terrifying confrontation with the supernatural (such as a supposed treasure discovered in a subterranean hiding place which terrifyingly reaches out to grasp the central character). James' ambiguous story deals with the legacy of sexual dissolution, which is (as in Oscar Wilde's *The Picture of Dorian Gray*) carefully unspecified – and perhaps made all the more resonant for that. The young governess (played with characteristic psychological truthfulness by Deborah Kerr, possibly a shade too mature for the role) to two lonely children, Miles and Flora, is replacing a dead woman, Miss Jessel, who engaged in some kind of murky sexual games with the film's second ghost, the sadistic gamekeeper Quint – with a suggestion that Miss Jessel's two youthful charges were somehow involved in these depraved activities. But when Miss Jessel and Quint (Peter Wyngarde) begin to make terrifying appearances to the increasingly distraught governess (in scenes which have been much imitated since – such as the dead Quint's face appearing suddenly and shockingly at a window), the governess' attempts to save the children from the continuing influence of the malign spirits leads to a disastrous outcome.

Do we witness the psychological study of one woman? The unsparing results may be read as the consequence of the projection of the governess' own psyche (her own repression is hinted at in her one charged encounter with her employer, played in charismatic but chilly fashion by Michael Redgrave). She is, it becomes apparent, possessed of the ability to save Miles from the baleful influence of the dead Quint (Miles is effectively played by the child actor Martin Stephens, who made one other extremely successful appearance in a film of the period, Wolf Rilla's excellent *Village of the Damned* (1960)), but at the expense of his (Miles') life. As viewers, we are invited to be complicit in her fears (we, like her, see the ghosts – but do they actually exist?). Thus, in Hitchcockian fashion, we are complicit in the guilt after the calamitous resolution of the conflict.

Clayton's attempts at finding a visual expression for the undercurrents of James' story are largely successful (another important collaborator is his composer, Georges Auric – once a member of *Les Six* – who utilises an economical orchestration of folk song material to underscore the subtle menace), though the director is obliged to lose the all-important framing device – the story of the governess in James' original is told at one remove; distanced even further from those to whom it is related in the novella so that the interpretation by the reader becomes paramount. As so often with Henry James, much is conveyed by suggestion and allusion rather than direct statement – inevitably, this strategy will not work in a film where we viewers are obliged to be shown what may be between the lines on the printed page. Clayton's (and Freddie Francis') exquisite use of widescreen photography is one of the film's felicities. Performances are impeccable (notably Megs Jenkins as the housekeeper, who is the conduit to all the grim events of the past), and Clayton, aware of the contemporary readings that we will impose upon the story, carefully balances this inevitable modern apprehension of the piece with the judicious use of period trappings. His talent as a filmmaker appeared fitfully (his CV boasts less successful efforts than *The Innocents*, such as a lifeless adaptation of *The Great Gatsby* in 1974), but his was a meticulous British talent. *The Innocents* has its flaws, but joins the select group of intelligent and oblique ghost stories made for the English cinema.

The Innocents enjoyed (if that's the right word) a sort of sequel a decade later. The basic idea of *The Nightcomers* (1971) was interesting and provocative – a prequel to Clayton's film in which we see how the ghostly presences in the film (the gardener Quint and the governess Miss Jessel) corrupt the two children Miles and Flora through murky S&M games. But the plusses of the film (Brando's eccentric performance as Quint, mesmerising despite an ill-advised 'Oirish' accent) and Jerry Fielding's rich and sinister score are undercut by inadequate playing from the children, Christopher Ellis and Verna Harvey (a comparison with Martin Stephens and Pamela Franklin in the original film is instructive), and Michael Winner gives no evidence of an interest in the subtle and effective approach of Clayton in the original film, allowing Brando his head rather than finessing the actor's more subtle instincts (the director was frank about his slightly craven reluctance to try to modulate the actor's performance). The more explicit, brutal treatment of the sexual encounters is justifiable (in relatively graphic fashion, the nude scenes involving Stephanie Beacham as a pneumatic Miss Jessel are some distance from Henry James, which is fair enough) and we see precisely what the malign lovers got up to (sexual activity only hinted at in Clayton's film), but it is not so much that greater expressiveness which moves the film further away from James and Clayton's universe than the director's lack of sympathy with the more indirect and allusive approach and evident lack of sympathy with the material, less malleable than his customary fare.

The Haunting (1963) is the work of another director (like fellow alumni Jacques Tourneur) trained in the school of Val Lawton's subtle, understated supernaturalism, and is a perfectly judged film version of Shirley Jackson's classic novel *The Haunting of Hill House*. Showcasing subtle performances by Julie Harris and Claire Bloom (with an understated lesbian subtext), the film (unlike its ill-advised Jan de Bont remake in 1999, which ladled on the special effects in lieu of atmosphere) trades in suggestion and nuance for its haunted house (famously – and radically – not showing a single physical manifestation of the occult). A viewing of both versions is an object lesson in the most intelligent approach to such material.

But haunted houses have had a somewhat chequered history in British film. Judging a work of art, it's sometimes necessary (or useful) to use the less fully realised piece as a way of appreciating (by contrast) how successful another venture treating the same material has been.

At first glance, Richard Marquand's *The Legacy* (1978) sports a variety of elements in common with the *Night of the Demon* and *Night of the Eagle* discussed above: supernatural curses (the plot devolving on the malign application of witchcraft); an ornate and baroque building as the setting at which demonic deaths take place; a brace of top-notch British character actors; and (for marquee value) imported American stars (albeit not of the first rank). But Marquand's compromised film is clear proof that the judicious assemblage of such elements is no guarantee of quality, and despite the professionalism with which the product is assembled, not a single one of the components listed above is able to compare – either individually or as part of the total fabric of the piece – with its inspired predecessors. Katharine Ross and Sam Elliott (the latter's luxuriant moustache, worthy of Frederic Nietzsche, is almost a star of the film in its own right) are young Americans lured to Britain to work (it appears) on an architectural project, but find themselves – after a car accident – stranded in the country pile of amiable aristocrat John Standing (whose pill-popping character is clearly very ill and vanishes from the film, until a surprising final reveal). His mansion is populated by a rather cynically chosen group of lambs for the sacrifice, well-heeled power players mostly played by British actors with a variety of unlikely accents. Lee Montague is a corrupt French businessman, Charles Gray an autocratic German war criminal, and the lead singer of The Who, a permed Roger Daltrey, is considerably stretched by having to play someone in the rock business. Almost without exception, none of the people involved add any lustre to their reputations: Ross and Elliott are pretty but relatively faceless, while the urbane Charles Gray has clearly passed the point when his sinister charismatic turns (as, for instance, the villainous Mocata in *The Devil Rides Out*) have shaded into caricature, and his mannered German accent in particular verges on self-parody. Ex-swimmer Marianne Broome appears to be there in order to die (in career synergy) in a swimming pool (Marquand utilises low-angle up-shots of her lithe body swimming long beyond any dramatic – or even erotic – justification). And Daltrey, before his character's table-top tracheotomy, reminds viewers how ill-advised the average rock star's move into the acting profession usually is.

Free of blame, perhaps, is the screenwriter Jimmy Sangster, whose efforts were apparently considerably tweaked by the producers (he had no actual involvement in the making of the film), so the reasons for the failure of the project must be firmly laid at the door of the director, the late Richard Marquand. Again and again, he appears to disregard the factors that made *Night of the Demon* and *Night of the Eagle* so successful – a poetic and finely honed approach to the supernatural manifestations is replaced by unconvincing gruesome deaths, often involving facial mutilation (the latter not, of course, without their place in the genre, but infinitely more effective when the prior orchestration of such set pieces is treated with intelligence). Marquand also forgets that the illogicality of the genre must be carefully finessed at all times, so that viewers are able to perform the act of suspension of disbelief, something most of us are keen to do even when we realise we are not in the presence of a genuinely creative piece. But while Marquand may not borrow from Jacques Tourneur or Sidney Hayers, he does lift notions from other directors: a taloned hand which appears suddenly from behind the curtain to grasp the heroine's arm is straight out of Dario Argento's *Suspiria* (made a year earlier), and the precise and methodical British nurse (played by the estimable Margaret Tyzack) who turns into a spitting, hissing monster in defence of her evil charge is a version of Billie Whitelaw's similar figure in Richard Donner's *The Omen* (1976).

While all of the foregoing may have certain common elements of English gothic, they were by no means representative of the whole territory, which had many mansions – as we shall see.

9
One-Shots and Short Runs: The Black Sheep of Gothic Cinema

Not every film in the British horror genre inaugurated long-running franchises and there are many one-off films which offer very different rewards via the variations possible within a series – perhaps because each of the individual films had to establish its own parameters – and explore them fully within the 105 minutes or so allotted to it; a certain fruitful concentration was inevitable. Even certain mini-series (if that is how one might consider three films) offer illumination here, such as the American versions of works by Edgar Allan Poe, transplanted from the USA and made in England (Roger Corman's intelligent adaptations *The Masque of the Red Death* (1964) and the same year's *The Tomb of Ligeia*, along with the earlier and less successful *The Premature Burial* in 1962), which complemented adaptations of Poe by British filmmakers such as Ernest Morris' *The Tell-Tale Heart* (1960). These one-offs include bizarre but somehow perversely watchable misfires such as Alfred Shaughnessy's *Cat Girl* (1957), Sidney J. Furie's *Doctor Blood's Coffin* (1961) and Lindsay Shonteff's *Dead of Night*-inspired *Devil Doll* (1964), along with some fully realised, imaginative pieces – all offering singular experiences rather than fleshing out elements of over-extended series – with, admittedly, some sense of exhaustion. And the mistakes that the directors of these cherishable *films maudits* make are often the sand in the oyster that produces the pearl. Regarding *Doctor Blood's Coffin*, perhaps more unlikely than the notion of the walking dead is the speed with which Dr Blood dispatches, unassisted, an operation involving the grafting of a heart in a tin mine, though audiences may not have been persuaded by Blood's expertise. *Doctor Blood's Coffin* was not the director's sole contribution to the Gothic genre. In a fitful career that included such memorable pieces of work as *The Ipcress File*, Sidney J. Furie would no doubt have preferred to draw a discreet veil over his woeful 1961 film *The Snake Woman*, a film that manages to fumble almost every potential source of frisson. Susan Travers plays a young woman whose herpetologist father applies a treatment of snake venom to his mentally challenged wife during their pregnancy, with disastrous shape-changing results for his daughter, all of this taking place in a village full of hysterical yokels who would not be out of place in a Universal film from the early 1930s. People are dying of snake-bites and Scotland Yard is soon on the case, dealing with something a little more outré than the usual line in crime. Travers' perfectly spoken snake girl possesses not an iota of menace, and the special effects trickery (what there is of it) would not be likely to deceive the most naïve viewer.

While many period-set British films of the late 1940s and early 1950s had utilised elements of the macabre and incorporated a pronounced sense of threat (a recurrent characteristic of Gainsborough films, which were precursors of much that was to follow in the Islington studio's then-audacious sexual undercurrents), the subsequent full-blooded (in every sense) embrace of the genre by multiple filmmakers in the UK was to have a peculiar force, marrying the interface of uptight British decorum with the chaos that results from an exposure to a corrupting or destructive foreign force. But whereas earlier films had located this threat from *terra incognita* specifically in the realm of the monstrous/ unacceptable, British Gothic cinema was all too well aware of the seductive attractions (often in libidinous form; a generous display of cleavage was usually a part of the package) with which hapless British protagonists were lured to their doom.

The Gothic cycle (which began in the late 1950s and continued at full strength for a decade before overfamiliarity sapped the vitality of the field) placed its menacing scenarios both in the past and in the present, with trappings of decorative antimacassar or glossy formica. It is instructive to notice the peculiar parabola through which these half-century-old films have passed. Audiences were initially intoxicated by the poster-colour grotesqueries on offer to them for the first time, which made most previous horror fare, however effective (notably the celebrated Ealing portmanteau film *Dead of Night*), seem somewhat anaemic. And the latter adjective has particular significance, given that Kensington Gore (as film blood is known) was splashed with a greater liberality in the new films than had ever been allowed before (in fact, after the first flowering of the genre, an initially lenient BBFC became far more prescriptive, and many of the subsequent films suffered swingeing censorship cuts). But the enthusiastic audience embrace of this new breed of Gothic film was to be matched by a critical revulsion on the part of the establishment, which now seems quaint indeed.

Terence Fisher shares with another British director a particularly cherishable characteristic: even his misfires, however flawed, generally sport elements that make them worthy of attention, and that is the case with two films that Fisher made in 1958, *The Hound of the Baskervilles* and the slightly inert *The Man Who Could Cheat Death* (both films appeared in cinemas a year later). Those who have seen the Conan Doyle adaptations after its initial cool reception might be forgiven for thinking that they are about to experience an underrated piece of vintage Hammer melodrama, firing on all cylinders, so impressive is the opening sequence here. Viewers are presented with details of the eponymous legend and a visualisation of the depraved Sir Hugo Baskerville, a decadent aristocrat whose pleasures involve orgies, hunting and the brutalisation the local peasants. Sir Hugo is responsible for the death of a recalcitrant young peasant girl after issuing the ruthless instruction to let loose his hounds. But his own death at the slavering jaws of an unseen hound follows, and the film proper begins. All this is delivered at full throttle, with every discrete element of Hammer's tried-and-trusted armoury of effects employed to maximum effect; even the rather limited performance of the actor (David Oxley) playing Sir Hugo works in the sense that it conveys an impression of pure, undiluted evil. For this sequence to work, we need to be distracted by no nuances of character. In fact, the fortissimo orchestration of effects here has an almost operatic quality, rather similar to the equally horrific opening scenes of Sidney Hayers' *Circus of Horrors*, and, like that film, nothing else in the subsequent narrative quite matches this opening for intensity (although Hayers cannot be accused of muffling his effects later in the film, as Fisher undoubtedly does with his distinctly underwhelming hound).

The foregrounding of the Gothic elements which are undoubtedly present in Doyle's original story are perfectly permissible and have parallels with earlier filmmakers' approaches to Doyle; the low-budget, atmospheric Universal series starring Basil Rathbone (and largely directed by Roy William Neill) frequently placed the more horrific elements – such as the deformed, back-breaking 'Hoxton Creeper' in *The Pearl of Death* – front and centre (not to mention Twentieth Century Fox's solid version of *The Hound*), and the presence of the inestimable Peter Cushing as Holmes would undoubtedly have set up a degree of audience expectation which inevitably had to be met. In Cushing, viewers were presented with an actor who could both finesse the horror tropes with which his name had become ineluctably associated, but also convey with maximum forcefulness the cool ratiocination which is the Great

Detective's most salient feature. Ironically, it is the casting of the equally iconic Christopher Lee as the latest endangered scion of the Baskerville family that registers less strongly, but the film succeeds for the most part as a reimagined version of Doyle's tale, leavened with an enthusiastic treatment of a recurrent Hammer theme: the destructive decadence of the aristocracy (a theme which perhaps find its most pure expression in John Gilling's *The Plague of the Zombies*). But it remains a cause for regret that the projected Hammer Holmes series was stillborn.

The Man Who Could Cheat Death (1959), a version of Barré Lyndon's play *The Man in Half Moon Street*, is compromised by a variety of factors, including the casting of its leading man, the efficient but always glacial German actor Anton Diffring, who, while able to convey the ruthless single-mindedness of the eponymous death-cheater Dr Bonner, provides his character with few other character facets (Bonner has retained a youthful appearance by a series of operations requiring the murder of donor victims). Another alienating aspect is the conspicuous absence of any warmth towards (or chemistry with) his inamorata, played by Hazel Court – and this, along with no attempt to suggest that Bonner has ever experienced any kind of *crise de conscience* over his murderous actions or has even thought of his elective condition in any examined fashion, makes the character somewhat one-dimensional. And this, finally, has the viewer regarding the whole enterprise in a relatively uninvolved fashion, despite the fascinating central premise.

It is interesting to speculate how effective the film might have been had the original casting choice, Peter Cushing, been available, and such thoughts are further prompted by the presence in *The Man Who Could Cheat Death* of the studio's other key actor, Christopher Lee, who would surely have been the most apposite casting for the character of Bonner. Terence Fisher's commitment to the project seems professional as ever but relatively neutral, and his contribution is further hamstrung by censorship interference. Despite the film's poster, which displayed Anton Diffring's face with different left and right sides, one handsome, one hideously decayed (rather in the fashion of one of the Dark Knight's nemesis, Two-Face), the film itself is singularly lacking in horror – and even in the final scenes, when the Diffring character's great age finally catches up with him and his face becomes a dripping, putrid nightmare, the effect is distinctly unchilling. It is interesting to speculate that had Fisher ever directed opera (as other film directors did, such as John Schlesinger, who successfully tackled the work of Richard Strauss), he might have had an interesting vision for Janacek's most Gothic opera, *The Makropolous Case*, which similarly ends with an ancient character who has cheated death – Elena Makropolous – finding her years speedily accumulating on her face to horrific effect.

The attitude to Britain's imperialist past as represented in Hammer films could not, it has to be admitted, be regarded as a balanced and enlightened one. But to criticise a film such as Terence Fisher's notorious, much-excoriated *The Stranglers of Bombay* (1959) for its one-dimensional presentation of India as a cultural residue of potential evil sent to plague the sympathetic British characters is not a realistic stance. For a start, the company made no bones about the fact that it was in the business of making exploitation films, and audiences did not approach their product for considered historical insights. It might also be argued that the murderous Thuggee cult was a historical fact and that the company was at liberty to utilise such material, although the approach remains very much in the territory of delivering the customary visceral shocks to the audience (via mutilation, dismemberment and – of course – strangulation, all performed with relish) rather than examining the interaction between two non-homogeneous cultures; inevitably, it is the less-than-judicious approach of Fisher's film (not to mention its now-frowned-upon use of non-Asian actors in key native roles) which has probably consolidated its neglect over the years. For quite some time, *The Stranglers of Bombay* was almost impossible to see, and then only in a heavily cut print. More recently, audiences have had a chance to assess Fisher's original, uncut vision. As with the other film he made in 1959, *The Mummy*, Fisher presents his British characters – while flawed – as representatives of a controlled and civilised order, in which foreign elements serve the function of threatening or destabilising this order. But there are defences to be made of his (and Hammer's) approach, not least in the fact that there is an implicit critique of British inflexibility and a certain inherent weakness of character which lays open the protagonist to possible destruction; this is not flag-waving imperialism of the kind that is to be seen in many British films up to and including the 1950s, but a more subtle examination of the variety of elements within the British character (which, Fisher and his colleagues imply, is to some degree always riding for a fall in its dealings with foreign nations). The fact that the foreigners in such films as *The Stranglers of Bombay* and *The Mummy* are presented in a relatively unambiguous, threatening fashion may not conform to current politically correct standards, but the film fulfils the narrative function of providing the nemesis which must be overcome in order for the central characters to survive. Viewed in this light and extending to Fisher and his colleagues a certain degree of understanding of the political attitudes of the day might allow for a more judicious approach to such often-despised films as *The Stranglers of Bombay*.

Fisher himself had no great opinion of the film, perhaps perceiving that it was by no means a fully realised piece (and certainly not in the way that much else of his work for the company is). There is a glancing treatment of the class issue which is a recurrent theme in Hammer movies – in this case, a supercilious commanding officer whose authority is clearly a gift of his background rather than his accomplishments, set against the more sympathetic protagonist played by Guy Rolfe (who is less secure socially, but is clearly the identification figure for the audience, precisely because of his quiet command of his own resources). The latter's personal authority is contrasted with the craven fear of his inefficient superior officer during a vicious assault by the natives.

The Mummy belongs in a chapter devoted to one-shots as its progeny are different breeds rather than direct sequels. The film conflates a variety of plot notions concerning this iconic monster figure from earlier films, but such a strategy is probably unavoidable given that both the screenwriters and the audience would have been conditioned to (respectively) deliver and expect certain recurring motifs. What is notable is the suggestion in this very British film that the English are given to ill-advised forays into dangerous territory, allied to a crass inability to respect information imparted by the natives they encounter. An instance of this is the Cushing character's disregard for the warning against opening the tomb of the Egyptian princess and thus unleashing chaos. And this destabilising chaos, ironically, is brought back to the British homeland when the mummy is transported to an Arcadian England – something that was also true of Bram Stoker's original novel of *Dracula* but which (for budgetary reasons) does not happen in the Hammer film adaptation, unlike the original Tod Browning version. One of the most famous scenes in the film is that of Lee's bandage-swathed creature violently smashing though bay windows into the house of the Egyptologist responsible for his disinterment. The mummy is ineffectually tackled by having a spear driven through his body – it is a scene similar to that in the same director's *The Revenge of Frankenstein*, suggesting that a heavy price must to be paid for incursions into certain realms; not so much the supernatural as alien, non-English territory to which the British protagonists bring a little understanding or sympathy.

Several of Terence Fisher's films qualify for the W.S. Gilbert description of 'things of shreds and patches' – films which have their virtues (often hidden), but which, generally speaking, only the cognoscenti have the time and patience to winkle out. A good example of this syndrome is one of the director's most egregious box office failures, the second remake of Gaston Leroux's *The Phantom of the Opera* in 1962. The film's commercial failure was a great disappointment for Fisher, less so the critical opprobrium heaped upon his head (he was becoming wryly used to the latter).

Inevitably, when a remake is attempted of a literary property which has already enjoyed a classic treatment (as Gaston Leroux's novel had with the celebrated Lon Chaney silent version in 1925), the definitive take on the work is usually used as a stick to beat any upstart pretenders with; in fact, the Hammer executives and Terence Fisher had no excuse for being unaware of the pitfalls here, as this syndrome had already taken effect with the glossy, lifeless colour remake in 1943, directed by Arthur Lubin. Made when the censorious Production Code was forcing any serious treatment of adult subjects to be suitable for the youngest children, Lubin's remake siphoned off a great deal of the story's horrific potential, rendering it an anodyne vehicle for Nelson Eddy. Eddy was the 1940s equivalent of such singers as Russell Watson today: perceived as an opera singer but having only the most glancing acquaintance with an actual opera – in fact, the copious musical extracts in the film (for rights reasons) are mostly a strange hybrid, with lyrics added, from Tchaikovsky's Fourth Symphony. But the Lubin film's pussyfooting avoidance of anything sinister or horrific (in comparison to the memorable horrors of, for instance, Lon Chaney's unmasking to show a hideous face with distended nostrils, grotesque teeth and bald pate) was compounded by the actor Claude Rains' reluctance to have any extensive facial make-up for the Phantom's scarring.

When it was announced that Hammer was to remake the property, with Herbert Lom as the eponymous Svengali for a terrified young singer, hopes were high that at least some of the original film's Grand Guignol charge would be channelled into the new version, but such was not to be the case. The fact that Lom's disfigurement (when it is finally revealed) turns out to be even less disturbing than Claude Rains' unthreatening appearance was perhaps a metaphor for the whole film, which (as so often with Hammer films of this period) suffered from the dead hand of censorship, removing all but a few moments of the grotesque. That said, however, Fisher is still able to infuse much of the film with the kind of foreboding atmosphere that had become his stock in trade, and Lom's performance has a certain tragic grandeur.

The presence of the Phantom in the film achieves some of the eldritch, incorporeal quality that had been lacking from the Rains version, and a decision concerning the music in the film showed a certain radical intelligence. Instead of the rejigged Tchaikovsky of the Lubin version, Hammer commissioned the composer Edwin Astley (famous for his tensely syncopated TV scores such as that for Patrick McGoohan's *Danger Man*) to compose fragments of an original opera based on the Joan of Arc story. Instead of the late romantic writing one might have expected, the style here was abrasive and dissonant (but with a powerful lyrical underpinning), rather in the manner of the composer Alban Berg (both of whose operas, 'Lulu' and 'Wozzek', had featured macabre elements, even down to the knife murders featured in Fisher's version of *The Phantom*). Making this the musical idiom as opposed to something more audience-friendly allows the film – for all its softening – to still carry something of Fisher's expertise in the Gothic, and his version of the Leroux tale is an honourable failure, worthy of some attention from the director's admirers. But the film's box office failure seemed to put the director's career into the doldrums and it was to be two more years before he worked again for the company which had become his home-from-home.

Regrettably, however, it was not the nadir of Fisher's career during these dark days. A doleful would-be comedy remake (thankfully, a one-shot) of James Whale's imperishable *The Old Dark House* (1932), re-titled *The Horror of It All* (1964), demonstrated the director's complete lack of sympathy with this broadly comic material, a world away from the more sophisticated pleasures of the Whale original (and saddled with the ano-dyne presence of an American visitor, the singer Pat Boone, best known for his devout Christian beliefs). Even a quirky cast of British eccentrics as the denizens of the sinister mansion were poorly used by the director. A trilogy of science-fiction films, *The Earth Dies Screaming, Island of Terror* and *Night of the Big Heat* (1964, 1966 and 1967, respectively), despite the director's avowed lack of sympathy with the science-fiction genre, were enlivened by the presence of Hammer regulars Christopher Lee and Peter Cushing, but showed Fisher working at a lower voltage than was his wont. *The Earth Dies Screaming* suggested possibilities that were not neces-sarily explored, with the film's crisp black-and-white photography of the living dead wreaking havoc, anticipating the later films of such directors as George Romero. But Fisher was to demonstrate that his creative bat-teries were only temporarily burning low when he produced one of the most accomplished and unusual of all Hammer films (and one of his own signature works): *Frankenstein Created Woman* in 1967, discussed earlier.

Blood of the Vampire, directed by Henry Cass in 1958, instantly sets out its stall with its memorable pre-credits sequence. 'Transylvania' (we are told): a burly, masked figure drives a stake into the heart of a body in a coffin; blood wells up as the credits roll (in a vivid day-glo font). We are unquestionably being told that this is to be the kind of delirious poster-coloured exercise in Gothic horror that dominated the genre in the 1950s – and, of course, it's a Hammer film, isn't it? After all, the scenario is by Jimmy Sangster, that company's principal scribe, and the film contains the kind of ghastly narrative material that the company gleefully traded in. What's more, Henry Cass' direction has the same unfussy, utilitarian style that Terence Fisher had honed for Hammer, though it lacks that director's rigour. But, in fact, this is a film produced by one of Hammer's ambitious rivals, Tempean Films, inaugurated in 1948 by the enterprising team of Robert S. Baker and Monty Berman. The duo (who were subsequently to enjoy considerable television success with far less confrontational material in such bland series as *The Saint*) had an eye for the profitable main chance and had already produced a science-fiction/horror outing inspired by the success of the Hammer *Quatermass* adaptation, Quentin Lawrence's *The Trollenberg Terror* (1958), which was renamed *The Crawling Eye* in the USA. Inspired by the commercial success of this film, Baker and Berman then produced a trilogy of mordant period horror films – all now difficult to see in their original, uncut forms – which gave the Bray-based company that had inspired them a run for its money. By hiring Sangster and instructing him to painstakingly emulate the elements which had worked so well for Hammer, the duo then cannily hired other highly professional crafts-men to deliver their trio of terror which (in their different ways) make a significant contribution to the Gothic cinema of the late 1950s and early 1960s. The films were the aforementioned *Blood of the Vampire*, *Jack the Ripper* (1959, co-directed by Baker and Berman themselves) and *The Flesh and the Fiends* (1960, directed by John Gilling). Although Gothic elements were creatively re-utilised by Baker and Berman, they appeared to be less interested in the supernatural than the company which had inspired them, and the 'monsters' in all three films were very much of the human variety – even the 'vampire' played by Donald Wolfit (in the barnstorming larger-than-life style of his theatrical actor-manager days) was suffering from a medical condition which required blood transfusions. There were no transformations into bats or other occult paraphernalia here, though audiences of the day clearly did not miss these things (or, if they did, were consoled by the other sanguinary delights on offer).

What is most distinctive about all three films is the pervasive atmos-phere of human corruption; the trio of films present in their various ways a truly Sadean universe in which the survival of the innocent (if it happens at all) is a lucky accident, and ruthless authoritarian figures use their positions without compunction to attain their various ends. In *Blood of the Vampire*, it is the single-minded Dr Callistratus using patients in his asylum as human blood banks; in *Jack the Ripper*, it is a variety of brusque authority figures whose attitude to their fellow man is pitiless and unsparing – not least the professional man, Sir David Rogers, who is revealed to be the knife-wielding Jack; while in the more sober but still satisfyingly melodramatic *The Flesh and the Fiends*, it is the Edinburgh doctor played by Peter Cushing (no stranger to such parts), who utilises a pair of depraved grave-robber-cum-murderers to supply cadavers for his medical school (the subject is the historical one treated by Dylan Thomas in his screenplay *The Doctor and the Devils*). Only the first of the three films is in colour and the lurid cinematography delineates the corrupt world on view in a fashion that renders it simultaneously fascinating and repulsive.

All three films present a bitter picture of nineteenth-century British society in which the more elevated social classes are perfectly happy to exploit those lower down the social scale. Not that there is any Ken Loach-style nobility afforded to all those in the taverns and backstreets from a different social strata. What is presented in all three films is the kind of depravity linked into the straitened circumstances of the working-class characters. But there remains (particularly in the Henry Cass film) the notion that the real exploitation – the kind which we are invited to disapprove of – is the prerogative of those powerful enough to manipulate and even destroy those below them.

Blood of the Vampire is interesting in several ways. Firstly, it is a more genuinely Sadean film than most other Hammer films it attempts to emulate; certain elements may be thrown in for mere grotesquery (notably Victor Maddern's deformed assistant to the evil Dr Callistratus, though his shaggy make-up, with one eye further down his face than the other, was well remembered by aficionados of the genre). And the film also gives viewers a rare chance to see the kind of performance that might have been central to the Gothic films of the 1950s had actors of the Bela Lugosi school (as opposed to the more subtle playing of Peter Cushing and Christopher Lee) found employment in such fare.

Donald Wolfit was perhaps one of the last great actor-managers, taking his productions of Shakespeare around the country (and managing the troupe as well as directing). Although his performances in numerous films of this period are distinctive and memorable (including, for instance, Jack Clayton's *Room at the Top*), his is an old-school acting style in which all gestures are writ large – and there is little attempt in *Blood of the Vampire* to adjust his broadly drawn kind of performance to the more intimate demands of the camera. Having said that, taken on its own terms (and Wolfit would have expected no less), his one-dimensional monster is still utterly watchable, though one doubts that the Hammer revolution would have had the longevity it did had such playing become the norm.

The film is set in nineteenth-century Carlstadt in an asylum for the criminally insane run by the ruthless Dr Callistratus and his deformed assistant Karl. Callistratus finds himself with a new inmate, John Pierre (played by Vincent Ball), who is incarcerated as a result of a travesty of justice, but finds his status changed when Callistratus suggests that he helps him work on research he is conducting into various blood types. But the young doctor realises that the older man is utilising inmates of the asylum (along with a cellar full of decorous female victims, clad in tattered flesh-revealing robes) to take his experiments into thoroughly illegal territory in order to prolong his own life. Pierre's girlfriend, played by the excellent Barbara Shelley (another Hammer alumnus borrowed by the producers in an attempt to replicate the success of that company), takes a job as a housekeeper for Callistratus. But she is, inevitably, to end up in his laboratory where the doctor's knife has been wielded numerous times to lethal effect. Unsurprisingly, Callistratus comes to a bloody and gruesome end at the fangs of the hounds used to control his prisoners – a death, in fact, not dissimilar to that of the equally ruthless Dr Genessier in Georges Franju's *Les Yeux sans Visage* (1960). All of this is dispatched with some exuberance, the cast perhaps taking its tone from the overbearing central performance by Wolfit, although Cass' approach to the material replicates Terence Fisher's straightforward presentation of the horrific happenings without, say, the delirious slightly surrealistic approach of such directors as Sidney Hayers in *Circus of Horrors*. The film was a considerable commercial success, although its critical standing has never been high. Ironically, much criticism of the film over the years has focused on its unsophisticated primary-colour palette, one of the elements (it might be thought) that was precisely matched to the grotesque material. Unlike the other films in the Baker and Berman canon, a variety of continental versions of these films were prepared for the more liberal foreign markets, with extra nudity and scenes of carnage (stills from these foreign versions appeared over the years, whetting the appetite of British viewers who had been protected from such corrupting material).

Nothing else in the director's career suggests the forcefulness which he brings to *Blood of the Vampire* (his other films include the workaday *The Crooked Sky* (1957)) and the concentration of a variety of unsettling visual details (such as the production design which often has the faux sumptuousness provided by Bernard Robinson for a variety of Hammer films) ensures that the narrative functions with total efficiency in delivering its parade of horrors. In some ways the film might be seen as an argument against the auteur theory: the rest of Cass' career suggests that it is the concatenation of elements here (screenplay, acting, cinematography, etc.) which makes the film work. The writer Jimmy Sangster was to some degree a bankable commodity, sometimes billed on posters as 'Jimmy "Frankenstein" Sangster' – a fairly unusual tactic in the days when writers of films were virtually invisible. Sangster's screenplay utilises several elements to be found in his writing for *The Revenge of Frankenstein*, but the Cass film was one that had a relatively small retrospective impact on him, and he admitted that he did not remember working on it.

The film experienced inevitable run-ins with the censor, as did (routinely) the product of the company that Baker and Berman were attempting to emulate. Cuts imposed included a shot of a human head in a glass jar and a variety of human organs, along with the trimming of a scene in which Callistratus extracts the blood from the jugular vein of one of his victims (the flow of red liquid was considered too shocking for English audiences). But Baker and Berman were well aware that the more easily shocked censorship boards in the UK would not pass certain details and added other elements which are only to be seen in, for instance, the French version, in which female characters in the dungeon scenes are shown with explicit nudity as opposed to the clothed versions shot for the English market. Similar dual versions featuring undressed, as opposed to dressed, actresses were shot for other films by the company, such as the brothel scenes in *The Flesh and the Fiends* – a still exists of the actress Billie Whitelaw, fully dressed, surrounded by naked actresses playing prostitutes – and even the orgy sequences of another Baker and Berman film, *The Hellfire Club*, were never seen in the UK (in fact, the film – in its British cut – appears to be one of the most anodyne produced by the company). Baker and Berman did not even bother showing the nude scenes to the British censor, as they knew they would simply not be passed. Interestingly, Baker is said to have looked upon the censor of the time, John Trevelyan, as something of an ally – a man who was to some extent protecting the filmmaker as much as the public and who preferred to work with filmmakers rather than simply applying swingeing cuts. It might be argued that more Draconian legislation would have been passed by a succession of governments had Trevelyan not wielded his scissors.

We will never really know 'the facts' about Jack the Ripper unless a dusty doctor's bag is found with bloodstained scalpels and a signed confession or a long-suppressed Scotland Yard document is released in which royalty is implicated in the grisly work of history's most famous serial killer. And, even then, Jack's identity will still be essentially unknowable. Which, of course, is precisely why we are so fascinated – even in the twenty-first century – with Saucy Jack. Had he been caught, he'd be like so many everyday murderers, all of his nigh-mythical status drained away. Recently, there have been a slew of films based on the subject and even the crime writer Patricia Cornwell positing the unlikely theory that the painter Walter Sickert led a secret life as London's most famous Victorian murderer.

The fascination with the Ripper continues unabated to this day, with Jack remaining eternally malleable. As the facts of the case were never really known (despite a million conspiracy theories to the contrary) and Britain's best-known historical serial killer was never caught, this makes it possible for filmmakers and writers to simply utilise (and create filigrees upon) the genuinely mythic figure he has become. With their keen eye for exploitable properties, it was hardly surprising that the canny Baker and Berman duo would come up with a version of the story prior to their inspiration, Hammer (although the latter studio was to subsequently produce one of the most interesting Jack the Ripper films, Peter Sasdy's *Hands of the Ripper* (1971)). In fact, in 1959, even the very words 'Jack the Ripper' (as the eponymous film of that year was called) were somewhat contentious, as the mere title alone had lain under a censorship interdiction (although John Trevelyan sanctioned the use of the name). The original script that had been considered was firmly rejected, and Baker and Berman once again employed the reliable Jimmy Sangster, who presented for the duo a story which peripherally touched on historical facts, but wove a new and intriguing scenario around them. This screenplay, when realised by the team, was to prove perfectly serviceable, not least when set against a vividly realised late nineteenth-century London. Moreover, the film was stuffed with reliable character actors, including a particularly dour John Le Mesurier (long before he became known as an effete comedy performer) and, in a particularly appropriate piece of casting, the sombre and imposing actor Ewen Solon, who alert viewers might have recognised even in 1959 as the knife-wielding maniac concealed beneath a veneer of respectability (although Sangster threw in a host of red herrings, including a facially deformed laboratory assistant, audiences were beginning to be aware of the tricks that filmmakers played upon them and had become notably harder to fool). Solon's character, Sir David Rogers, fits in with the most commonly utilised notion of Jack the Ripper's hidden identity in movies: a titled professional man whose brusque manner barely conceals his contempt for those around him (particularly women). The motivation given to his version of the Ripper by Sangster was the customary insane hatred of prostitutes and in particular the woman, Mary Clarke, who he believed had given his son syphilis. The actor is given a splenetic speech justifying his murderous activities, but the uncut print of the film (at one time shown on British television, although only ever shown in cinemas in its truncated form) incorporates a twisted sexual motif into his killings – one lingering sequence of mutilation and murder has clear orgasmic undertones for the character. His death (crushed by a lift) occasions the film's only use of colour as the blood of the Ripper seeps through the floorboards in distinctive red hues.

But while the casting of English character actors is as impeccable as ever (such things were in fact the norm both in the Baker and Berman productions and in other studios), the film labours under one of the traditional bugbears of the day – the perceived necessity to import an incongruous American actor in order to sell a film to the USA. Here, it is the young actor Lee Patterson (later to find fame as a TV detective in a variety of shows), whose performance is serviceable enough, although his impressive pompadour is distinctly anachronistic. Like the Boulting Brothers, Baker and Berman shared a variety of creative duties on the film, although Baker was in fact responsible for most of the direction. It was perhaps inevitable that the script (when submitted to the BBFC) would provoke the customary outraged denunciations, with objections raised not just to the grisly killings but also to some 'lascivious' scenes of can-can dancers, which were considered to be too shocking. On this occasion, despite the duo's sympathetic relationship with John Trevelyan, they made an attempt to defend the integrity of the film and resisted the suggested censorship cuts (which included not just the strangulation of one of Jack's victims but also a scene of champagne being poured over an actress' breasts). Foreign buyers of the film had no such reservations, and *Jack the Ripper* was already potentially profitable even before it had run the gauntlet of the British censors. If the film succeeds on a straightforward Gothic level rather than incorporating any kind of interesting subtexts, it is none the worse for that, and given the slew of truly woeful film incarnations of Jack the Ripper, Baker and

Berman's version was one of the more memorable. The success of the film led to the duo considering another historical monster – two, in fact: the Edinburgh grave-robbers Burke and Hare.

By hiring John Gilling to direct *The Flesh and the Fiends* (1960), Baker and Berman knew they would be assured of a highly professional product (they had a long association with the director), and Gilling offered something more, as the director's career (although sporting its share of uninteresting by-the-numbers assignments) demonstrated that he was a filmmaker of real commitment when he found material (often Gothic) that was to his liking. This appeared to be the case with this version of the brutal resurrectionists Burke and Hare, which the director attacked with his customary determination. Anatomist Dr Knox (played by Peter Cushing with somewhat unnecessary facial scarring to suggest his damaged character) is finding that the supplies of cadavers for his medical students are simply not producing what he needs. With a bitter contempt for the local authorities, Knox avails himself of the services of Edinburgh's unscrupulous suppliers of bodies with no questions asked, the drunken and thuggish Burke and Hare. The latter do not take long to realise that time is saved by providing bodies via violent murder rather than the tedious task of disinterment. But they make a crucial mistake when they kill Mary Paterson, a local prostitute whose body is recognised by one of Knox's students, who is the dead girl's fiancé. Things quickly begin to go bad for everyone concerned and a singularly gruesome fate is in store for the two resurrectionists – not least the graphic blinding by torch of Hare (played with reptilian relish by Donald Pleasence). In fact, the film contains echoes of Gilling's earlier work on a screenplay he wrote for Tod Slaughter, *The Greed of William Hart* (1948), and a certain censorship leeway was permitted (such was the kind of trade-off evident in dealings with the BBFC in these days) if the screenplay on the film remained as faithful as possible to the facts of the original case. This, of course, gave the makers plenty of opportunities for brutal, bloody violence and underclass scenes of sexual abandon (the latter, involving topless prostitutes, was not – as mentioned earlier – considered suitable for British eyes), but the BBFC was not persuaded when it realised how trenchantly Gilling and his associates had delivered the tale, and there were further complications when Dylan Thomas' screenplay for *The Doctor and the Devils* (which was owned by Rank) came into consideration as a possible rival, although in the event the latter was not tackled until it finally found its way to the screen some 20 years later in a version directed by Freddie Francis.

Much of the success of the swiftly moving exercise in twisted psychopathology that is *The Flesh and the Fiends* is down to the casting, not least the always-reliable Peter Cushing as Knox. For this role, Cushing brought the same kind of single-minded, almost obsessive quality that he had lent to Frankenstein (with a similar contempt for the obscurantist viewpoints of backwards-looking authorities); what's more, he is able to find (as so often in his career) levels of nuance in the character which elevates Knox above the symbol of evil that the role might have descended to. As the appalling Burke and Hare, George Rose and Donald Pleasence tackle their parts with far more uncomplicated gusto, almost a pre-requisite for delivering such ruthless creatures, and the casting of the formidable actress Billie Whitelaw (now known for her portrayals in the work of Samuel Beckett on stage) as the luckless prostitute Mary was another coup which Gilling took full advantage of (even though her Scottish accent is somewhat wayward). The film's killings are dispatched with the kind of unashamed energy that Gilling was always able to bring to such material, with the death of an elderly alcoholic woman played by Esma Cannon particularly effective – and affecting. Similarly, the dispatch of the mentally subnormal 'Daft Jamie' (played by Melvyn Hayes), killed in a pigpen full of hideous animal noises that matched and substituted for his own, has far more resonance than the simple murders of most horror films. In the event, the film did less business in the UK than Baker and Berman's previous Gothic efforts, and resulted in the duo moving into new territory (including the aforementioned *The Hellfire Club* and the horror send-up *What a Carve Up!* in 1961), but their future prosperity was assured by the production of such TV series as *The Saint* and *The Persuaders*. Recent reissues of *The Flesh and the Fiends* have restored some of the missing footage and it may now be seen as one of the more distinctive entries in the British Gothic cinema during the middle of the last century.

It is perhaps a matter of debate whether or not certain films are British. Take, for instance, Roger Corman's adaptation of Poe's *The Masque of the Red Death* (1964), which features an American director (Corman), star (Vincent Price) and writers (Charles Beaumont and R. Wright Campbell). But the film was shot in the UK, utilising some impressive British talent (including the actors Hazel Court, Jane Asher, Nigel Green and Patrick Magee), along with a British composer (David Lee) and cinematographer (the now-much-respected Nicolas Roeg – the sumptuous visual style of the film is one of the things that makes it one of the more ambitious entries in Corman's Poe filmography). One might also argue that the director's sensibility is not typically American – *Masque*, in particular, is influenced by the work of Ingmar Bergman, who Corman admired inordinately (and whose films he distributed in the USA via his own company). But whatever the provenances of *The Masque of the Red Death*, it can be regarded as an impressive British-made film. With *The Tomb of Ligeia*, Roger Corman tackled the story that Poe had described as his own favourite among his works, and certainly the narrative (in which the protagonist Verden Fell is placed in a hypnotic trance by his apparently dead wife) touches most of the key Poe themes: the hopeless love for a woman whose life is slipping away, the persistence of life after death and (tied into all this) the acrid whiff of necrophilia that informs so much of the writer's work. Filming once again in England, Corman's sensibility is once more finely attuned to the demands of his narrative (the adaptation is by a pre-*Chinatown* Robert Towne) and encourages a more interior performance than Vincent Price is wont to give in this series, suggesting that the struggle against the occult by the central character is perhaps less crucial for him than the struggle against a strong-willed woman.

Certain films in the British Gothic vein have become almost impossible to see because of continuing censorship problems (as much as rights issues), and in the twenty-first century, more people are familiar (if at all) with Robert Hartford-Davis' *Corruption* (1968) and James Kenelm Clarke's *Exposé* (1976) from fuzzy grey-market video incarnations than cinema showings. Both films are heavily compromised (and not just by the extreme and still-unacceptable levels of violence), but both have distinct points of interest. The presence of the estimable Peter Cushing in *Corruption* is surprising; the film, the umpteenth remake of Franju's *Les Yeux sans Visage* (with a coolly demented doctor attempting to restore the beauty of a mutilated loved one) is sometimes uncomfortable to watch given the amount of unrestrained, bloody flesh-ripping that Cushing is called upon to do. Cushing is engaged in a lengthy struggle with a prostitute, ending in multiple stabbings with, finally, the disturbed doctor rubbing his hands over her blood-covered breasts. This is followed by a graphic, unhurried decapitation. The doctor leaves the room with the dead woman's head in his bag, and the camera finally rests on the headless body of a doll. When watching this scene – shot for the 'continental' version – it's easy to see why the actor was the uncomfortable making the film.

Exposé has remained similarly controversial, also re-using a warmed-over plot (in this case drawn from Sam Peckinpah's *Straw Dogs*), but adding a certain visual energy to the proceedings, while some unorthodox casting (Udo Kier, Linda Hayden and porn star Fiona Richmond) adds curiosity value. Even in the more liberal era of censorship available today, both films remain problematic for censors (the Clarke film fell victim to the 'Video Nasty' hysteria).

The last one-shot for consideration here is something special. Viewers of the work of the iconoclastic director David Lynch were not prepared for the understated, classically elegant film of *The Elephant Man* (1980), exquisitely photographed by Freddie Francis in monochrome and showcasing sensitive performances by John Hurt as the tragic, deformed Merrick and Anthony Hopkins as the sympathetic doctor Treves who befriends him. Despite the measured pace and the avoidance of the conventionally gruesome, the film resonates with a perfectly judged Gothic atmosphere.

10
Fresh Blood or Exhaustion?: The 1970s to the Turn of the Century

What is the political stance of the British horror film? Initially, despite the bourgeois-baiting shock tactics employed by filmmakers, the genre shares with a great deal of British crime fiction an impulse towards the restoration of the status quo – but only after the latter has been sorely (and excitingly) tested by the eruption of some attractively destructive primordial force. But when that primordial force has been something other than a mindlessly homicidal monster, the destruction of social equilibrium can usually be found within an establishment figure, most often a doctor or scientist, or a member of the aristocracy (routinely perceived as decadent and corrupt – this is virtually a shibboleth of the genre). Ironically, the political stance of many British Gothic films which so upset the more conservative-minded over the years might even be described (for all their iconoclastic feel) as conservative (with a capital 'C'); an analogy might be found in the mixed signals issued by such right-wing British newspapers as the *Daily Telegraph* and the *Daily Mail*. There is the divided attitude towards the establishment: a certain historical deference set against a nagging feeling that the establishment – though ineluctably and inarguably the natural leaders of society – are wrong-headed and morally bereft, and certainly in need of continual chiding and correction. There is the horrified but fascinated response to the forces that might destroy society (in the broadsheets it might be unrestrained immigration, while in the Gothic film, it is often the disastrous results of scientific experiments). Similarly, comparisons can be drawn between the relief and applause for whatever restores the status quo, though there is always the fatalistic acceptance that such restoration is usually temporary (the right-wing press knows that the left will always be inculcating some strategy to chip away at the moral values in society, while the monomaniacal doctors of the Gothic horror film will forever be attempting to stitch together some new monster). But perhaps what the right-wing press and the British Gothic cinema share most is the simultaneous horrified/fascinated response to what they identify as destabilising forces. It has to be conjured into existence, again and again, so that it might be satisfyingly extirpated.

In the terms in which authority figures such as Van Helsing (as played by Peter Cushing) are presented in the genre, there is a similar dual reaction: these men instantly command respect by virtue of their single-minded character (they are usually presented as a *force majeure*) and their endless stock of arcane knowledge. But while their job is to protect society (often with the aid of the accoutrements of the established church), they are seen as admirable maverick figures, eternally being obliged to overcome the old guard, who are locked in their fustian ways. And the message these mavericks bring is (counter-intuitively) a return to the now-unfashionable values of the day which have been swept away by current thinking; these men have to assert the existence of the supernatural in the face of implacable nineteenth-century rationalism. Van Helsing has good reason to believe in the existence of vampires, even though the burgomeisters and police chiefs he encounters scoff at such notions as being outmoded and superstitious. Was Margaret Thatcher the Van Helsing of the Conservative Party? Was her mission to violently sweep away the moribund Edwardian *ancien regime* to re-establish the true faith, in which moral imperatives were absolutely straightforward? (The flaw in pushing this analogy too far might be the essential humanity that Cushing always invests in the Van Helsing character, however peremptory his behaviour, and there is always a somewhat melancholy sense that he is aware that the innocent must be destroyed or sacrificed in order to vanquish his enemies.) This element of humanity is often freighted into the authority figures of the genre, regardless of how doctrinaire they might at first appear. Take, for instance, Andrew Keir's brusque priest Father Sandor in *Dracula, Prince of Darkness* (1966) – however unyielding (and even Mullah-like) he might initially appear to be, there is a refreshing and very human sybaritic quality to him (he likes his food and wine and the comforts of the body), but we do not doubt that his tensile steel core will be *de rigueur* when it is time to deal with the eldritch evil he will come up against. Politically (and ecclesiastically), in his heart Sandor is clearly conformist.

But after the first wave of Gothic films of the late 1950s, a variety of different political attitudes simmered beneath the surface of the British Gothic film, ironically at a time when the genre had seriously over-extended itself and was running short of new ideas.

The increasingly desperate response to falling receipts for British Gothic product (notably the inclusion of more sexually explicit and graphically violent material), combined with the invasion of a new wave of contemporary horror films from the USA which made much of the British period-set product seem old-fashioned. There was a failure to reinvigorate motifs which had been utilised once too often. The 1970s wave of British exploitation films took advantage of relaxed censorship (including the iconoclastic Tory director and producer Peter Walker) with intriguing political undertones and commentary.

Peter Walker was something of an exotic plant in the field of British genre cinema. Making his mark in the genre of low-budget sexploitation movies, he grew tired of the limitations of this restricted field and moved into the area that proved to be his true métier: grim and remorseless crime committed behind the blinds of British bourgeois society. His main area of attack was hypocrisy, particularly that practised by the establishment, of which no area is spared, from state to church. Surrounding himself with a reliable group of colleagues, his all-too-brief moment in the sun as a filmmaker produced some eye-opening work, notably that involving the character actress who was to be his muse, the remarkable Sheila Keith. Keith had been a standard performer in British TV comedy, but Walker was the first to realise just how terrifying she could be as one of his establishment figures with dark secrets, or suburban housewives with homicidal tendencies. She was given full rein in Walker's movies, then sank back into far less demanding work when he gave up cinema.

The workaday *Die Screaming Marianne* (1971) is basically Walker finding his feet as a director, but has flashes of the inspiration that was to come later, as does the equally under-realised *The Flesh and Blood Show* a year later. But then came the film that marked Walker out as talent to watch.

There are those who regard the director's *House of Whipcord* (1974) as something of a personal testament, and it is best remembered as a wry critique of the more extreme members of the moral majority in society – a favourite theme in Walker's work. But perhaps what works best in the film is the director's utilisation of Hitchcockian elements (notably impeccable timing and cutting for the management of suspense). The result is the kind of film in which the viewer is almost inclined to shout advice to the hapless characters on-screen and a frustrating near-escape for the imprisoned heroine is almost heartbreaking when it is finally foiled. *House of Whipcord* has the British judiciary handing out grim and summary justice, and remains one of the most subversive movies in popular British cinema (not least for its tongue-in-cheek dedication to the self-styled guardians of morality, a dedication taken seriously both when the film was issued and even recently).

With its drab, quotidian settings and evocation of a bleak 1970s Britain, *Frightmare* (1974), in which Sheila Keith is the murderous and corrupt centre of an outwardly respectable bourgeois family, is unquestionably Walker's most fully realised film, successful on virtually every level: as a grisly shocker (including a lethally wielded Black & Decker drill); as a solidly constructed plot, with all the characters – even minor ones – given fully realised lives; and – a *sine qua non* for Walker – as a generous show-case for Keith, who was so often the sinister centre of the director's films.

Here, Keith ineluctably focuses viewer attention tension as the psy-chotic stepmother of a young woman, released from an institution after committing some ghastly crime (the unpleasant nature of which is key to the narrative) and quickly reverting to her murderous old ways, despatch-ing gullible young girls at tarot card sessions with red-hot pokers. Keith's portrayal of barely controlled madness (combined with whimpering insecurity) cleverly walks a tightrope between over-the-top barnstorming (at which she has few peers) and acting of real authority, while Walker plays out his ingenious plot twists with impeccable timing – while delivering a number of really jolting shocks.

Even for the most undiscriminating aficionado of the British horror film, a certain glazed-eyed stupefaction can set in after the ninetieth iteration of warmed-over elements, and in order for the adrenaline to be activated again, it is sometimes necessary to experience that all-too-rare entity: an original re-invention of Gothic themes. And *Frightmare* represented precisely that, despite some sideways step-ping into the overfamiliar. In fact, the deployment of imagination, particularly in the kinetically involving set pieces, makes one forgive any lapses into cliché (ever the customary flaw of so many horror films). The creative and intelligent script by David McGillivray ensures that everything has an effectively edgy quality. As well as being an exploitation filmmaker who delivered the blood-drenched goods that audiences customarily expected from him, Walker was always a pro-vocateur and built into his films casual critiques of modern British society – sometimes subtly and sometimes in an in-your-face fashion. Because of the disrespectable genres in which he worked (first soft-core sex films, then horror films), he was rarely troubled by any critical recognition – a situation that has changed in recent years. But Walker presented problems for his admirers as much as for his detractors. It's a fair bet that most aficionados of the more gruesome horror films were not likely to be habitués of the rubber chicken circuit of the Tory

Party, but the director would frequently make statements that made him sound as right-wing as a rubicund-faced ex-colonel from the shires. What's more, he made confusing noises to the effect that he was pro-censorship, and criticised such films as Stanley Kubrick's *A Clockwork Orange*; these surprising pronouncements unsettled his admirers, particularly as it was hard to see why he regarded Kubrick's film as corrupting – an act of disingenuousness? Or did he realise that Kubrick's film was a more fully achieved piece than anything he himself had managed? His arguments that he tried to keep the incendiary elements of sex and violence separate in his films seemed morally equivocal, to say the least, but he remained a filmmaker of intelligence, coaxing excellent work out of such writers as McGillivray (see Appendix: Interviews), who was responsible for the screenplay what most people consider to be the director's best film, the aforementioned *Frightmare*. The film's narrative begins in 1957, when a husband and wife are committed to an insane asylum after a series of gruesome killings. Fifteen years pass and the audience is shown the couple's daughter Jackie and her rebellious younger sister Debbie living in an acrimonious ménage. Jackie tells a psychiatrist that she is concerned about the behaviour of her antisocial sister, but withholds a gruesome secret: Debbie is taking mysterious parcels to the secluded farm where her stepmother and the latter's husband are living after their release from the institution. What's more, Dorothy has been masquerading as a fortune-teller with a view to attracting people to the farmhouse – and these credulous individuals will have bloody encounters with a variety of murderously wielded domestic tools.

McGillivray told this writer that he was (to a large extent) left to his own devices following the preliminary script discussion as long as he delivered the various elements that Walker required. The influence of the Hammer psychological cycle (which itself sprung from *Les Diaboliques*, Henri-Georges Clouzot's adaptation of a Boileau and Narcejac novel) was always tacitly acknowledged, and the writer was aware that persuasive, unvarnished details of life in modern Britain could profitably be employed to ground his narratives, along with the use of older characters to set against the less interesting juvenile leads – and in the process creating a more plausible texture for the bloodletting which at some point must take centre stage. But McGillivray was also firmly encouraged to push the envelope in terms of the subject matter, coming up with something which would be less immediately acceptable material for the genre – and when cannibalism was mooted as a theme, the confrontational basis of *Frightmare* was born. (An earlier film by the American director Gary Sherman, the highly effective, London-set

Death Line/Raw Meat (1973), had already dealt with this theme with its London Underground-dwelling depraved meat-eaters, as well as including some strongly drawn middle-aged characters, and this film may have been an influence on both McGillivray and Walker.) Such quotidian details of locale in *Frightmare* as a petrol station, a fortune-teller's shabby caravan and the down-at-heel farm at which the killings take place locate the film in a persuasively realised English landscape, as do the unromantically drawn characters, which adds an edginess and sense of reality not often to be found in the modern British horror film.

The packages carried by (and delivered to) the crazed Mrs Yates in the film are a key element of its iconography and are actually used in the poster, in which a smiling Sheila Keith (photographed in such a fashion as to look not quite human) proffers a bloody, dripping parcel towards the viewer, which, as well as rather giving the game away, suggests that the murderous matriarch has all-too-familiar bourgeois preoccupations – the urge to keep things neat, clean and tidily packaged (albeit that the neatly sorted objects in this film are severed human body parts). Walker is also interested in notions of propriety and the responsibility of children towards their parents, however reprehensible the actions of the latter may be. It is a theme which was also addressed by the crime writer P.D. James in one of her most accomplished novels, *Innocent Blood* (1980), which similarly features a daughter attempting to deal with the criminal past of her dangerous, recently released mother (the Moors murderess Myra Hindley is an avatar in both cases).

If Walker and McGillivray are never quite able to make the cannibalism theme function here on any realistic level, this is perhaps an acceptable ingredient in terms of the disturbed psychopathology which is the film's chosen territory; whatever generous interpretation one might apply to the final film, its most pressing imperatives remain those of the ghastly exploitation effort, which both writer and director would happily acknowledge.

When Walker was lucky enough to cast the most apposite actors for his films, the results could be patently successful. Sheila Keith gives her most mesmerising performance for the director as the deeply disturbing (and disturbed) passive/aggressive murderer, while Rupert Davies, one of the most comfortingly familiar of British character actors (notably on TV in a series based on Georges Simenon's sleuth Maigret) also made a prestigious contribution to British Gothic as the abused priest in Michael Reeves' *Witchfinder General*. The two young women at the centre of the film (played by the pretty but uncharismatic Deborah Fairfax and

Kim Butcher) are no more than efficient, but certainly adequate in terms of what they are called upon to do, while the casting of the slightly effete-seeming Paul Greenwood as a psychiatrist who proves to have no ameliorative skills fits in perfectly with Walker's recurrent picture of flawed or misguided authority figures. In the director's universe, such characters are either inefficacious or malign. Walker's mischievous sense of humour was apparent in the film's strapline, 'An everyday story of country folk', a play on the long-running (and deeply anodyne) radio soap opera *The Archers* – as was his wont, Walker took such cosy figures and put flesh-ripping power tools in their hands.

The violence of the film (as so often with Walker) is, despite his aversion to Stanley Kubrick's similar strategies, brutal, shocking and abrupt, its effect heightened by the dynamic of the family at the centre of the plot (which might be said to echo Philip Larkin's famous line 'They fuck you up, your mum and dad'), and precious little comfort is afforded by the conventional underpinnings of society, from religion to psychiatry (the film experienced several attacks for its perceived 'unenlightened' view of mental illness, echoing a similar furore over the unexceptional Boulting Brothers' 1968 film *Twisted Nerve*; the Boultings were obliged to put an apologetic disclaimer at the beginning of their film suggesting that its treatment of mental illness was to be taken on a dramatic rather than a realistic level). But the negativity of Walker's film is very much a part of the fatalistic 1970s ethos which he embraced (and was almost a spokesman for), and he clearly saw evil as a more powerful and effective force than good (if the latter existed in any notable form) – the downbeat elements of his films are significantly resonant. If his completely dismissive view of psychiatry is too tendentious and more than the weight of the narrative can bear – and if plausibility is frequently strained by the overcooked scenario conjured up by McGillivray and Walker, the exuberance with which this tale of bloody dismemberment and cannibalism is delivered cannot be gainsaid. The director had managed to find here the most persuasive contemporary equivalent for the Gothic horrors of earlier cinematic trends, and his own expressed feeling that this was his finest film is not to be argued with.

Inasmuch as the horror film has long been perceived as part of a gimcrack, squeeze-the-punters medium, it's hardly surprising that a variety of freshly minted titles are sometimes used to conceal the fact that a film is not particularly new, but is simply enjoying a dusting-off. Those who tracked down *The Confessional Murders* on the basis that it was a film they are not heard of were to be in for a shock if they were already familiar with Peter Walker's *House of Mortal Sin* (1975); that is what *The*

Confessional Murders, when re-issued for home cinema, actually was, in a new surplice. But the new garb doesn't disguise the fact that this was sadly one of the inventive Walker's lesser efforts, involving a psychotic man of God who shares Norman Bates' matriarchal problems. *House of Mortal Sin* has a Roman Catholic priest dealing with his repressed sexuality by murdering unbelievers and seems topical today as the Religious Right gains ever more ascendancy in both the UK and the USA.

All the Walker ingredients are here, particularly the recurrent theme of the guardians of moral values being themselves corrupt (as in the sardonic dedication of *House of Whipcord* to self-appointed censors) and, as usual, there is a some skilful drawing of peripheral characters (a young priest chafing against the Roman Catholic Church's insistence on clerical celibacy and the working-class mother of a young girl driven to suicide by religious guilt). But somehow the whole thing comes across as contrived – a feeling that becomes inexorably stronger as the plot revelations come thick and fast in the last reel. And the reasons are fourfold:

1. The actress Sheila Keith, normally a reliable delight in Walker's films with her malignant, severe matrons, here struggles in vain with an underwritten part, and the final revelations concerning her role as housekeeper to the psychotic priest are too bizarre for even the splendid Keith to make convincing on any level.
2. The murders (including violent death by such religious icons as incense burner and communion wafer) do not carry the visceral impact Walker usually freights into such scenes.
3. Anthony Sharp, as the demented clergyman, lacks the conviction that Peter Cushing (originally mooted) would have been brought to the part – the peremptory Sharp, efficient enough in one-dimensional parts, lacks the nuance that Cushing might have found in the role.
4. The plot revelations mentioned above are notably implausible and, worse, rather dull. But aficionados of the director may find that there are a handful of crumbs here which will justify an indulgent viewing.

Schizo (1976) was clearly an attempt by Walker to up the ante in terms of horrific content (without, however, a concomitant extra level of commitment to extending the possibilities of the genre on the part of the director) and it certainly succeeded in bringing down the inevitable censorship snips when subsequently issued on home video (later DVD issues have restored the missing footage). The cutting of the film made for at least one curious moment: after a character has had a knitting needle driven through her skull, she begins to slowly turn towards the camera. Why? So that the viewer can appreciate the macabre special make-up effects, of course – Walker always places these centre stage and provided the requisite moments of intense gruesomeness. But the final result of the turning head was deemed too disturbing and was removed. Ironically, an almost identical swivel of a head in a far better film was considered too shocking some two decades earlier in Alexander Mackendrick's Ealing black comedy *The Ladykillers* – when a suggestion is made that Alec Guinness's murderous professor is actually mad, his slow turn towards the camera (presumably to reveal a basilisk stare that chillingly proved the assertion true) was similarly removed. But even with the unacceptable footage restored, *Schizo* is hardly vintage Walker. Despite the title, the film is none other than a slavish *Psycho* clone, but the plot holds few surprises for those who have seen similar material before. Lynne Frederick gives a performance of quite staggering woodenness in a role that really needs a degree of flexibility, but Stephanie Beacham does well enough in support.

A last hurrah for a talented director should make considerable impact, something like (to a use a grandiose comparison) the final chords of, say, Vaughan Williams' Fourth Symphony. Peter Walker's horror career, however, undoubtedly ended with a whimper rather than a bang, which was doubly disappointing – not least for failing to build on what the director had achieved earlier in his career, but also for the lacklustre use of the copper-bottomed cast of horror film veterans assembled for this last film. The degree of anticipation experienced by those who had faithfully followed Walker's career was to be quickly dampened down by the experience of the film itself. There had been a long gap before *House of the Long Shadows* (1983), some five years since the uninspiring *The Comeback*, starring (in a stillborn acting career) the Sinatra-style singer Jack Jones and a progressively more maggoty corpse, and it might have been felt that the director's decision to mine a new vein, traditional Gothic (as opposed to the edgy contemporary variety he had successfully traded in), possessed a fatal sense of disengagement. Here, Walker utilises the cobwebbed paraphernalia of the *Old Dark House*-style narrative, with results that clearly scuttled his customary vein of grisly inspiration. There is a sobering sense of paralysis-choice about what kind of film this is, straddling (as it does) several options: Vincent Price's entrance line (accompanied by a tongue-in-cheek clap of thunder) suggests a camp send-up, but the screenplay by Michael Armstrong (previously responsible for the livelier *The Haunted House of Horror* and *Mark of the Devil*) does not, however, ultimately move in this direction, attempting a balancing act between parody and gruesome seriousness. And the much-vaunted quartet of ageing horror stars (Price, Christopher Lee, an arthritis-ridden John Carradine and a shamefully wasted Peter Cushing) simply don't strike the expected sparks and are given a paucity of material to work with. Walker's in-house prima donna Sheila Keith (standing in for an unavailable Elsa Lanchester) lends to the body-count narrative her usual threatening presence, but this redeeming feature (and a few effectively directed moments) are simply not enough to salvage the whole lacklustre enterprise.

The Wicker Man (1973) was an early proof of the inestimable value of word-of-mouth. Originally buried with little fanfare as a second feature to the Nicolas Roeg film of the same year, *Don't Look Now* (itself drawn from the Gothic supernaturalism of Daphne du Maurier), Robin Hardy's film began to be praised even above the film it supported – with audiences telling friends that they must on no account miss the second feature, something quite different from the more starry piece it accompanied. With its acute response to locale (a Celtic island) and perfectly chosen use of music (the latter folk-based, as befitted the ancient religion of the narrative), the film has reminiscences of Michael Reeves' *Witchfinder General*, but is a very different kettle of fish. Essentially a steadily unfolding clash between an unbending Christianity and a sensuous but ruthless paganism (as represented by, respectively, Edward Woodward's naïve but resolute Christian copper and Christopher Lee's trendily-coiffed aristocratic cult leader Lord Summerisle), the film is unerring in its steady accretion of telling detail, with the destruction of the ill-prepared policeman in the blazing gigantic figure that gives *The Wicker Man* its name becoming ever more inevitable as the film progresses (Woodward's copper is particularly ill-equipped to deal with the sexuality he encounters as part of the cult which reigns on the island – represented emblematically by the nude figures of Britt Ekland, dancing erotically in an adjoining room (body-doubled for nudity) and beating on the wall with her palms, and Ingrid Pitt, who he comes across bathing in a tin bath – no body-doubling for her). The restoration of cut footage from the early part of the film is particularly instructive, as it demonstrates that the Woodward character is already something of an outsider because of his unbending values even when seen among his police colleagues, who regard him askance. *The Wicker Man* is unorthodox in not presenting Christianity as a positive and effective rejoinder to the forces of paganism (and, indirectly, evil); rather, it offers a more nuanced (though critical) vision of alternative religions (with the carefully observed trappings of music and the embracing of unfettered sex) that had previously been seen in such fare, even though, inevitably, such things are of a part with the darker forces that ultimately destroy the protagonist.

Considerably less accomplished films (to put it mildly) than *The Wicker Man* from this era may still have an interest, even if the caveats are many. If there is any doubt that the same film can balance the imaginative and accomplished with the desperately maladroit, Alan Birkinshaw's unique *Killer's Moon* (1978) might be adduced as an exemplar. The absence of any satisfactory DVD issue for this bizarre and quirky British exploitation movie has been much commented upon (since its disappearance after the British 'Video Nasties' hysteria, it circulated in an extremely substandard unauthorised print). But the film has recently become available again, allowing viewers to sample the rather beautiful cinematography in an exemplary transfer. If the adjective 'beautiful' in the preceding sentence might seem a little inappropriate in a tale of psychopathic madmen picking off various victims, a peek at the film will show just how effective director Alan Birkinshaw's treatment of his Lake District locales is (he's better with that than with his actors, who are largely cast adrift). Of course, the plot, a mélange of elements from *Straw Dogs* and *A Clockwork Orange*, is absurd, but that simply adds to the surrealistic tone of the film – which, of course, we now know was pseudonymously co-written by the director's sister, the highly respected novelist Fay Weldon, no less. Now that the furore about video nasties has died down (until another MP picks up DVDs as a surefire way of getting his or her name in the papers with a moral crusade), it's salutary to examine again material that once got people very hot under the collar.

Another film mendaciously re-released under a second title was 1975's *I Don't Want to Be Born* (dusted-off to waylay new viewers under the unimaginative new moniker *The Monster*), but sporting either title, the film, with its plastic, soulless vision of Britain, is further evidence of the fitful quality of director Peter Sasdy's achievement, being an uninspiring conflation of elements from several films, none notably re-energised by the transposition. Everything suggests that Sasdy, having seen the indifferent sequel to *Rosemary's Baby* (*Look What's Happened to Rosemary's Baby* (1976)) decided to make an indifferent sequel of his own. In Sasdy's film, Joan Collins plays (without much conviction) an ex-stripper giving birth to demonic offspring, with Eileen Atkins (hardly a star of Collin's calibre, but a markedly better actress) rising far above her material as a nun who performs the final protracted and unexciting exorcism. The film, set in a glum travelogue London, is riddled with lacunae (how does the initial curse of a malignant dwarf take effect, for instance?). Unlike Ira Levin's carefully constructed original with Rosemary and her cuckoo-in-the-nest baby, no attempt is made at logical storycraft. The smaller parts (the aforementioned Atkins and Donald Pleasence) are nicely played, and the screenplay is frequently surprisingly witty, but the film is still further proof of Sasdy's unfulfilled promise after *Taste the Blood of Dracula* and *Hands of the Ripper*.

The words 'fresh blood' and 'exhaustion' characterise this chapter – and two of the last Hammer *Dracula* movies, regrettably, qualify for the latter noun. Nether film could be said to be a dramatic conclusion to a cycle that has had more than its share of interesting and intriguing work, even though one of these films actually had intriguingly apocalyptic undertones. A sense of desperation is evident by now, with the studio casting around for something new to do with its over-used but profitable franchise character. The modern-day incarnations of the vampire, *Dracula A.D. 1972* (made in that year and saddled with an ill-advised title which now makes the film seem more of a period piece than most of its predecessors) and *The Satanic Rites of Dracula* (produced a year later) were both produced by the same team: Christopher Lee and Peter Cushing starring, with screenplays by Don Houghton and direction by the usually reliable Alan Gibson. *The Satanic Rites of Dracula* is much more successful at finding a contemporary framework in which to set down Dracula's anachronistic evil. In *Dracula A.D. 1972*, Lee (now visibly tired of the role) is virtually a bit player, confined to a deconsecrated church in modern London, greatly reducing his menace, while some trendy teenagers (who were dated when the film was first issued and look positively hilarious in the twenty-first century) half-heartedly act as his agents. But in *Satanic Rites*, the radical notion of having Dracula pose as a mysterious property speculator (the latter-day equivalent of a vampiric monster perhaps) is more fruitful and is matched by the Count's splendidly apocalyptic mission: nothing less than the end of all life on earth and ultimately (a consummation, for him, devoutly to be wished) his own death.

But inspired work was still being done in the decade of the 1970s. The achievement of Christopher Wicking (see Appendix: Interviews) as a screenwriter was generally (as the writer wryly admitted to me) generally compromised and altered in some way, but almost invariably something of his highly individual and unorthodox skills remain in the finished films, which is the case with *Demons of the Mind* (1972), a later Hammer outing directed by Peter Sykes in which a doctor discovers that two children are being kept held captives in their house by their father; his probing uncovers incest and supernatural possession. The film occasionally has glimmers of some of the visual style of the late Michael Reeves, but the plot (a sort of Gothic reworking of *Forbidden Planet*'s 'Monster from the Id') is sabotaged by acting that is either overblown (Robert Hardy, Patrick Magee) or blank and indifferent (Paul Jones, Gillian Hills). But Wicking's customary interest in investigating the darker recesses of the human psyche still leaves its imprint on this flawed but interesting film. Similar compromises vitiate the effect of Wicking's screenplay for a British-made entry in American International Pictures' Edgar Allan Poe cycle, *The Oblong Box* (1969), slackly directed by Gordon Hessler, but this writer and director produced at least one film where the collaboration coalesced into something rich and stage.

Graham Greene's short story 'A Little Place Off the Edgware Road' is possibly his most flesh-creeping entry in the world of British Gothic, and for dedicated Greenians, the very title (the story is about a trip to a cinema that ends in grotesque bloodshed) suggests a deeply unsettling experience. For this writer, it was in a little place off the Edgware Road – in a long-vanished cinema – that I had such a disquieting experience (but of a more pleasurable kind), seeing, on its first run in 1970, Gordon Hessler's film *Scream and Scream Again*, with a screenplay by Christopher Wicking. Like most viewers of the day, I would have had (on entering the cinema) a variety of expectations: the producer was Milton Subotsky, behind the various Amicus anthology movies (of varying quality but always offering something of interest), while the film appeared under the American International umbrella (of which the same might be said). And then there was the cast: the three most prestigious names in horror films of the day: Vincent Price, Christopher Lee and Peter Cushing. The scenario – so far as one can tell – concerned a vampiric killer wreaking havoc in London. All of this pointed to an intriguing hour and 35 minutes, no doubt along generic lines, but delivered with some panache. But while the second half that sentence is true, the actual experience of the film is quite unlike anything most of the stars had been involved in before.

In Wicking's screenplay for *Scream and Scream Again*, there were certainly the requisite horror elements, but the film is actually science fiction. And in the numerous ways that it subverts both the expectations aroused by the genre and even audaciously frustrates what might appear to be its own narrative trajectory, the film is in many respects a rule-breaker; it's not hard to see why the producer (and original writer) Milton Subotsky was unhappy with the rewriting of his work (as discussed in the Christopher Wicking interview in the Appendix). One of the many pleasures afforded by the film is not just the participation of the three starry principals (who, while all excellent, are essentially cameo players; their presence here is as much for marquee value as anything else). The central character is a tough, no-nonsense cop, Detective Superintendent Bellaver, played by the excellent British character actor Alfred Marks, for whom this is something of a career-best. But having established him as a mesmerisingly brusque protagonist, Wicking proceeds to have him fall victim to one of the film's superhuman killers – a premature demise which leaves the audience gasping (and, what's more, rather cast adrift).

The police are on the trail of a young man (played by the haunted-looking actor Michael Gothard) who is prowling the discotheques of London and is possibly the blood-drinking killer who has already murdered several young girls (the first killing in the film is grimly squalid – nasty, unspecified things happening in a suburban tunnel), and the young killer appears to have some connection with the respected scientist Browning (played by Vincent Price). The loss of a hand does not appear to slow the young man down, but then, rather than be apprehended, he elects to choose a hideous death by being obliterated in a vat of acid. And if this narrative were not compelling enough, Hessler and Wicking take us to an apparently separate secondary narrative strand (something almost unheard-of in the genre): we are in some totalitarian central European country, in which top-ranking party officials are being ruthlessly murdered. What's more, back in England, a young athlete wakes up in a hospital to shockingly discover that there is less of his body than when he went to sleep.

The sheer complexity of the various narratives here perhaps reflects the cinéaste tastes of Christopher Wicking, who, like most of his generation, had (he told me) grown up on the challenging films of Alain Resnais and Michelangelo Antonioni, so was excited by the possibilities of non-linear narrative. But an alertness to developments in European art cinema was not the only characteristic that Wicking shared with director Gordon Hessler; both were well aware of the imperatives that a science-fiction/horror scenario such as this would have to deliver a specific location of the source of evil and mayhem (American International would not have been interested in the unexplained open ending of a film like Antonioni's *L'Avventura*, for instance, however ready Wicking and Hessler might have been to attempt such a thing). But the duo were keen to transplant the central engine of the plot some distance away from the alien invasion theme of the original Peter Saxon novel, hence the grim picture of a totalitarian regime which – by extension – the film represents as corrupt authoritarian figures (and the film has more than its share of those). There is also an element of corrupt science (led by Price) that can physically alter the human body and render it overtly superhuman, but while all this functions on the level of keeping the narrative moving inexorably forward, writer and director find time for discussion of notions of power and responsibility (there is an interesting conversation between Price's character and that played by Christopher Lee on the human inability to resist the blandishments of power).

This is not to say that we're talking about a perfectly realised, organic piece of work here. Like all films that attempt to reflect fashion trends over time, the look of the film (which was made in 1969) is now one of its less-endearing features, with the gaudy velvet jackets of some of the male characters and (in particular) the discotheque scenes looking notably dated. But the jittery combination of an arthouse ethos and almost continuous hyper-violence (not to mention female nudity in the autopsy scenes) makes for a peculiarly unique combination – one that is quite deliberately worrying in some aspects (such as the tricky S&M elements in the various murders; an early victim, played by Julie Huxtable, tells her brutal lover that it is necessary to hurt her, but he is to do much worse than that). Performances throughout are exemplary, but perhaps the real find of the film is Alfred Marks, best-known for lending his extremely deep baritone voice and toupéed presence to a slew of indifferent, comedies, but here taking his leading man role by the throat and holding his own against some formidable competition (and, by all accounts, improvising some of his dialogue – and if that was the case, his work was as good as the customary first-rate writing by Wicking). The film's relentless violence occasioned the expected reactions of the day, but several of the more perceptive critics quickly became aware that something much more ambitious was being attempted here than in the average horror film. It is a political movie, and even a film about an alienated modern Britain, and it is a picture of contemporary paranoia which transcends the film's meaningless title. Needless to say, the innovations and initiatives so provocatively presented here were not to be followed up; American International was uncomfortable with what the writer and the director were trying to do, and did not encourage further such experiments.

But if the 1970s were only fitfully successful in terms of British Gothic cinema, another medium still demonstrated that it was possible to showcase ambition and achievement in the field: the cinema's bitter rival, television.

11
The Legacy: Gothic Influence on Television

The history of the many celebrated British television adaptations of Gothic material, such as Jonathan Miller's *Whistle and I'll Come to You* and the long-running *Ghost Story for Christmas* strand on BBC TV, is a prestigious one. Other fondly remembered dramas include the popular adaptations of Charles Dickens' ghost stories and stand-alone single plays, such as Nigel Kneale's genre-stretching *The Stone Tape*. Kneale's significant influence on many of his successors continues to this day with the revived *Doctor Who,* which routinely rewrites and recycles his Gothic and science-fiction tropes.

Television is, inevitably, a less involving medium than the cinema. There is a quantitative difference between the murders committed in crime fiction and films (and not just the so-called 'cosy' variety) and those in the horror film: in the best of the former, murder is committed 'for a reason' (to quote Raymond Chandler's famous line about Dashiell Hammett) rather than simply to provide a body, and the crime genre rarely addresses notions of unalloyed, uncomplicated evil – evil, that is, as a primordial force. The latter, however, is almost a *sine qua non* in the horror genre, particularly where notions of supernatural evil are concerned. Looked at objectively, this may have a distancing function, given (one might suppose) audience resistance to a belief in the reality of supernatural evil, but the concomitant here is the methods of dispatch customarily utilised by the agents of the malevolent. A simple gunshot to take a life is rarely on the agenda, and if a knife is wielded, it is a sizeable butcher's knife, wielded repeatedly and bloodily. Moreover, such carvings are usually in the context of a kinetically designed set piece rather than simply to remove an inconvenient member of the *dramatis personae.* It might also be said that the Gothic cinema's monsters (both those of the human and non-human variety) have a repulsiveness which is not to be found in other genres, principally because there are absolutely no limits for these killers. And perhaps most frightening of all are the intelligent monsters, terrifying because of their sheer acumen, which demands a kind of grudging respect along with the unease. In addition, feelings of sympathy for other human beings are usually extirpated in the context of the implacable behaviour of these violent individuals.

However, considerations of the disruptive force of evil are frequently set in a narrative context that is not dissimilar to that of crime fiction: psychological pleasure granted to an audience by the restoration of normality and order after (in Yeats' phrase in 'The Second Coming') 'the blood-dimmed tide is loosed, and everywhere the ceremony of innocence is drowned' (though the satisfaction that comes from the banishment of evil began to be withheld from audiences in the 1970s).

Leaving aside such considerations of good and evil, there is also the frisson to be obtained from the juxtaposition and ordering of elements within the Gothic genre – elements which may be familiar, but in fact trade on (and sometimes playfully frustrate) the very expectations their familiarity provokes. What's more, even films which can boast only a sprinkling of genuine inspiration amidst a pervasive sense of mediocrity can still provide these pleasures; audiences for such movies are notoriously indulgent and will accept illogicalities and maladroit storytelling, provided that there are other suitable compensations in terms of, for instance, striking visual imagination and pulse-raising dramatic staging. The neglected recesses of horror cinema undoubtedly repay attempts to winkle out and illuminate the imaginative refashionings of Gothic motifs, and aficionados display a welcome lack of snobbery when attempting such acts of excavation.

There is, however, a medium in which the limits of acceptability of the horror film is tested to its limits, and that is the treatment of Gothic motifs on television. Until recently, the Draconian censorship (mostly, that is, pre-censorship) applied to the medium ensured that material which utilised excessive and graphic effects was actively discouraged (the success of Gothic material on TV based on writers such as M.R. James could be more successfully achieved, relying on atmosphere and suggestion more than explicit sanguinary effects).

Certain experiences are ineluctably burned into childhood consciousnesses, and these generational scars are remembered for the rest of the lives of those undergoing such an experience. Some time after the television terrors of the original British *Quatermass* series had made its mark on many a viewer, another truly terrifying television experience was talked about for decades after by those who had seen it and found it a cauterising experience. This was, of course, one of the famous series of BBC films *Ghost Story for Christmas,* of which there were 12 – along with Jonathan Miller's 1968 *Whistle and I'll Come to You,* which is undoubtedly one of the most famous ventures into the macabre ever shown on British television. With Michael Hordern as a fussy academic who unleashes something supernatural and unspeakable, it raised the hairs on many a neck in its original showing – and on the various occasions it has been repeated since. It is undoubtedly the centrepiece of a BFI DVD collection of all 12 ghost stories. Interestingly, a comparison may now be made with the 2010 adaptation of the same story, this time starring John Hurt and directed by Andy de Emmony. Inevitably, highly professional though the latter is, it offers no real challenge to the celebrated original, which still works remarkably well in the twenty-first century, although Michael Hordern's excessively mannered performance has perhaps worn less well.

To impressive viewing figures in the 1970s, the BBC showed this succession of adaptations of the immortal ghost stories of M.R. James, the Cambridge academic responsible for the definitive eldritch stories written in English. The default director for many of these tales was Lawrence Gordon Clark, who supplies insightful interviews for the new introductions in this remastered series. A handful of these classic tales have appeared before, but it is particularly welcome to see them collected together, and it is easy to see why the series was so influential and continues to be; the writer and actor Mark Gatiss (responsible for the new Holmes series *Sherlock*) is an avowed fan. In such adaptations as 'Lost Hearts', 'The Treasure of Abbott Thomas' and 'The Ash Tree', the understated, allusive approach of the personnel involved here pays dividends, with a concentration on the slow accretion of atmosphere rather than any indulgence in more overt horror tropes. M.R. James is not the only author represented here: long before his fame for his work on such writers as Jane Austen and George Eliot, Andrew Davies supplies an impressive version of Dickens' 'The Signal-Man', perhaps being more faithful to the material than he was subsequently to be in the adaptations which upped the sexual content – something which would hardly be appropriate here.

In *Whistle and I'll Come to You,* a sceptical academic (Hordern) discovers an ancient whistle on a beach in Norfolk and ill-advisedly plays it, releasing a terrifying apparition. What is particularly intriguing about Jonathan Miller's adaptation is the suggestion that the monstrous thing (which appears chillingly – and simply – as an ambulatory bedsheet) is a product of the professor's repressed psyche, representing an overlay of then-modern readings of psychosis (sexually related or otherwise) on the chaste original material. However, of course, while James and the other great ghost story writers who followed him could hardly explore such regions, this is not to say that they were not reaching into these dark channels, whether consciously or not. The savvy Miller never twists the material to make any particular points in this area.

'The Stalls of Barchester', directed by Lawrence Gordon Clark in 1971, has Clive Swift coming across a box of papers which were the property of the former Archdeacon Haynes (played by Robert Hardy), locked away since the nineteenth century. Inevitably, of course, they are released. All of the stories are about the unleashing of something unspeakable which wreaks chaos when it is brought into the light – in this case, a clandestine history of bloody malfeasance and supernatural revenge. Once again, a carefully maintained atmosphere is crucial in setting up the eruption into the present.

If the following year's story, M.R. James' 'A Warning to the Curious' (also directed by Lawrence Gordon Clark) is a tad less effective (and hardly as creative in its use of unsettling *mise-en-scène*), that is as much a comment on the sheer adroitness of the earlier teleplays than on any shortcomings to be found in this adaptation.

The reputation of Nigel Kneale's legendary TV sequence of six spine-chilling plays, *Beasts*, has grown immeasurably over the years, fuelled by the fact that (since their initial showings in the 1970s) they were virtually unseeable. Leaving aside the limitations of TV production of the day which have undoubtedly taken their toll (and some infelicitous acting here and there), this series – as with most things that the prodigally talented Kneale attempted – represented the very best that the television medium could achieve, a world away from the idiocies of today's lowbrow programming (Kneale, incidentally, predicted the horrors of *Big Brother* – the Channel 4 show, that is, as opposed to George Orwell's concept). And not only that – such episodes as the remarkable 'Baby' are among the most genuinely disturbing dramas ever made for television.

When the Hammer studios, virtually moribund in terms of film production, inaugurated a new series of television dramas with the *Hammer House of Horror* series in 1980, expectations were not high. The last gasp of the company (before contemporary horror items filling the cinemas drove a stake into its exhausted heart) was this largely underwhelming Carlton TV series, featuring many of the same personnel and actors (Peter Cushing makes a memorable appearance, rising above the by-rote material); if the horror is (inevitably) more underplayed than in the cinema outings, such reliable character actors as Diana Dors and Denholm Elliott more than enliven proceedings over a series of patchy but occasionally accomplished episodes.

The films in the series (there were 13 50-minute episodes broadcast on ITV) that managed to rise above the restrictions of the genre were generally applauded. Created by latter-day Hammer executive Roy Skeggs, the man who kept the brand alive, they were produced in association with Cinema Arts International and ITC Entertainment, and were discrete stories revisiting the themes which the studio had explored so profitably in the cinema: werewolves, Satanists, voodoo curses and witches, along with an acknowledgement of current trends in the cinema such as implacable serial killers (Hannibal Lecter *avant la lettre*) and cannibalism, difficult topics for television which had already caused censorship worries in such cinema films as Gary Sherman's graphic *Death Line/Raw Meat* (1973) and Peter Walker's *Frightmare* (1974). Needless to say, the actual moments of violence in the television series were severely circumscribed, and although there were the customary dissenting voices objecting that such material was never suitable for home viewing, admirers of the horror genre almost invariably felt short-changed by the low-key approach to the horror elements. Nevertheless, certain moments in the series acquired a reputation for genuinely unsettling television audiences, such as a children's party in the episode 'The House that Bled to Death'. The latter episode (directed by Tom Clegg and written by David Lloyd) featured a young family moving into a new house, but finding a terrifying residue from the previous owner, who had murdered his wife. The scene mentioned above showed blood streaming from pipes in the ceiling, an effect which perhaps owed something to similar sequences in the (by then) banned EC horror comics of the 1950s such as *Tales from the Crypt* (for example, a well-remembered story drawn by George Evans and written by Al Feldstein and Bill Gaines, 'Indisposed', which similarly had domestic pipes gushing forth with shredded human remains and blood).

Much attention has been paid to the *Hammer House of Horror* episode 'The Silent Scream', not least because of the presence of Hammer alumnus Peter Cushing as an amiable owner of a pet shop toying with the notion of open prisons but concealing a sinister past (the episode also featured actor Brian Cox, who undergoes a terrifying ordeal). It was directed by the talented Alan Gibson, who was perhaps more successful in television than his attempts to reinvigorate the Hammer style in the cinema had been. Other episodes remembered by those viewing them on their first showings included another sequence directed by Gibson (and written by Ranald Graham), 'The Two Faces of Evil', which was a treatment of the doppelgänger theme after an encounter with a hitch-hiker by a family on holiday. But despite sterling performances by Gary Raymond and Anna Calder-Marshall, the episode (like so many in the series) came across as slightly anodyne, lacking in the visceral charge that the screenplays involved would undoubtedly have received had they been made for the cinema. Nevertheless, a certain interest has been evinced for the series by Hammer aficionados over the years, not least for the contributions of regular Hammer directors such as those mentioned above, as well as the talented Don Sharp (though the latter's 'Guardian of the Abyss', involving ancient rituals and human sacrifice, remains more of a sketch than a finished piece, with the notion of a sinister mirror explored far more effectively in the similar episode of Ealing's *Dead of Night*).

When the follow-up series, with the more pussy-footing (if more honest) title *Hammer House of Mystery and Suspense* first appeared, one of the taglines used in the advertising was 'Hammer lives!'. But if the truth be told, this particular incarnation represented only a kind of half-life – and the company's largely moribund status was only altered to the effect that this series of one-off dramas being commissioned proved, if nothing else, that the Hammer brand still carried connotations. And the relative success of the series demonstrated that the name still worked for audiences wistfully hungry for the macabre outings that used to be the company's stock-in-trade. By 1984, when the *Hammer House of Mystery and Suspense* series appeared on television, the company no longer made full-length feature films, and viewers had good cause to miss those small miracles of atmosphere and imagination produced on often painfully strained budgets.

The first two episodes were handled capably enough by reliable Hammer director John Hough, and as the title of the series suggested, the emphasis was now less on horror than in the preceding series. Of the two episodes directed by Hough, the second, 'A Distant Scream', was by far the best, an imaginative and well-acted ghost story which skilfully sidesteps cliché. Performances were generally well judged, including that of David Carradine (each episode had a statutory imported American star – shades of the tactics employed in Hammer's very first feature films) and the British actress Stephanie Beacham, the latter once again demonstrating the subtle off-kilter approach to her characterisations which suggested there was more to her than her looks. This efficient piece was not matched in terms of quality by the episode 'Black Carrion', which begins promisingly enough with an attempt to track down two Everly Brothers-like pop stars of the 1960s who have mysteriously vanished, but quickly founders on a preposterous resolution (the preposterous can be made viable when presented with conviction, but the actions of a group of villagers in this episode simply has insufficient motivation). Other episodes included the workaday 'Paint Me a Murder', directed by Alan Cooke (and starring Michelle Phillips), and 'The Late Nancy Irving', directed by another Hammer regular, Peter Sasdy. Neither episode shored up the increasingly shaky foundations of the series.

Classic Gothic literature remains grist to the television mill. There are two 'high concepts' in play in *Jekyll* (directed by Matt Lipsey and Douglas Mackinnon in 2007): the extrapolation of Robert Louis Stevenson's split-personality novella into the modern era and the casting of Irish heartthrob James Nesbitt as the eponymous victim of a vicious doppelgänger – one, moreover, who looks not too physically different in his 'Hyde' persona (beyond black contact lenses). In fact, the notion of Jekyll and Hyde in the present day is treated with every possible variation here, given the surprising length of the piece (broadcast on TV in multiple episodes), with much interpolation of ideas that are not to be found in Stevenson, such as sinister organisations manipulating lives and Nesbitt leaving messages for his alter ego (whatever persona he is inhabiting) by tape recorder. The casting of Nesbitt is the selling point here: while his Jackman/Jekyll is dour and low-key, his Hyde is more akin to Jack Nicholson's Joker in *Batman* than anything else, with the verbally playful black humour and psychosis (Barrault's capering, twitching comic monster in Renoir's *Le Testament du Docteur Cordelier* also lurks here). Some may find the horror underplayed (scenes of potential violence are usually cut away from, then subsequently found not to have happened at all), but Nesbitt is value for money, and the audio-visual elements are impeccable (including a rich surround mix).

The use of Gothic tropes in contemporary television drama is endemic – so often, in fact, are the defining elements of the genre utilised that they are in serious danger of over-use and depletion. Certainly, there can be few modern television viewers who have not encountered one or more of the classic Gothic motifs in such shows as the revitalised *Doctor Who* in 2005; after coasting by in a moribund heavily tongue-in-cheek state for several years, the show was granted new life by the writing of Russell T. Davies, who was succeeded by Steven Moffatt and Mark Gatiss, who trod a canny line between the humour which has always been an integral part of the show (while avoiding toe-curling tweeness, the show's besetting sin over the years) and a new level of intelligence and ambition. Although the basic premise of the series is science fiction, the omnivorous appetite for new material has meant that Gothic horror themes have been plundered again and again – and in this regard, the show is a worthy successor to the influential dramas of Nigel Kneale, whose science-fiction character Quatermass frequently encountered menaces that appeared to have a supernatural agency behind them but customarily turned out to be alien in origin. Kneale's television plays such as *The Stone Tape* (1972), mentioned earlier, similarly brought about the forced marriage between science and the uncanny (in the latter, occult happenings are investigated by a scientific team with all the apparatus of modern technology – a notion much imitated since). And speaking of imitation (or, more kindly, inspiration), the indebtedness of the *Doctor Who* series (both before and after its revivification) to the concepts originally created by Kneale is profound, but while older viewers may recognise familiar elements, they will of course be fresh to the large new generation of admirers, and such is the skill with which these notions are generally treated in the new writing for the Doctor that allowances can be very easily made.

The team of Steven Moffatt and Mark Gatiss have also performed radical surgery on Conan Doyle's Great Detective, and *Sherlock* ((2010–), like the duo's other endeavours) frequently dipped its toe into the Gothic, even though the concept of the new show – Sherlock Holmes alive and well in the present century – makes it harder to integrate such elements into a plausible modern setting. However, the series frequently infuses its contemporary scenarios with a genuinely Gothic sensibility, winning over nearly all the dissenting voices bridling – sight unseen – at the concept.

In addition, outside the remit of this book, there are also a slew of American programmes which attempted similar strategies in re-working gothic themes – and in the early twenty-first century, their popularity shows no signs of abating.

12
The Modern Age: Horror Redux

.

The iconoclastic films which rejuvenated the horror genre both in this country and abroad often achieved this task by taking radical new approaches to the genre; millennial horror had a pervasive influence, with an end-of-the-century (and end of time) mindset creating and feeding a fatalistic (often apocalyptic) strain. Visions of apocalypse tied into the revival of the zombie movie, while the massive new success of the vampire genre, both in the cinema and on television, aimed at (and captivated) a younger demographic. Along with these various phenomena, there was a marked growth of knowing parodies of the genre in such films as *Shaun of the Dead*. And the modern horror film enjoys some perceptive and informed attention. The days when a serious critical response to work within the cinema horror genre was considered *infra dig* seem very distant now, and a great deal of intelligent and perceptive analysis is now being applied to the field. But it should be noted that when the direction of so many films in the Gothic genre is dispiritingly pedestrian, aficionados are wont to leap upon the most evanescent fragment of inspiration and inventiveness, possibly praising these felicities more than they merit (perhaps a characteristic of this study?). But such generosity regarding the green shoots of inspiration is unsurprising, given the workaday nature of what we Gothic aficionados are – and have been – presented with so often.

Part of the pleasure for the audience of the Gothic film throughout its history has been the satisfaction of noting standard formulae being utilised (or embroidered upon) in novel ways; comforting acquaintance previously resulting in a certain calcification. By the early twenty-first century, the genre was ripe for change. Utilisation of familiar elements inevitably had resulted in many films falling into certain predictable patterns: most obviously, perhaps, the following scenario: the victim being presented for the sacrificial slaughter and the subsequent dispatching of the malign figure by another interested party (relative, lover, authority figure, etc.), which, in fact, had been the modus operandi of other Gothic-influenced works. It survived into the new century, but was matched by some intriguing new concepts.

There are also the Grand Guignol elements that remain such a crucial part of the mix, notably the demise of the victims in some spectacularly unpleasant fashions. Of course, this reliance on the familiar can have a deadening effect on the viewer's responses, producing a pleasant narcoleptic sensation rather than the sense of unease which (one assumes) might be the filmmakers' intention. And without wishing to sound like the self-appointed moral guardians who talk about audiences' increased desensitisation towards violence, there is the fact that when the macabre elements become the be-all and end-all of the piece (as in, for instance, the *Final Destination* film franchise, which exists for the sole purpose of providing novel and ingenious ways of slaughtering a variety of victims), any sense that what is being presented is anything more than a simple fairground ride is unavoidable. And certainly, as the sheer number of films produced grows ever larger, it seems ever more likely that in the desperate search for novelty, other crucial elements are disregarded.

When the Detroit filmmaker George Romero made the massively influential *Night of the Living Dead* in 1968 (itself influenced by Hitchcock's *The Birds*), he was not just (inadvertently) placing one more nail in the coffin of the increasingly marginalised Hammer-style period film, but inaugurating a new era. The better horror films were not only permitted but *expected* to make a variety of cogent points about modern society (in the case of *Night of the Living Dead* and other works by the director, everything from media exploitation to race and consumerism were grist to the mill). In this respect, British Gothic cinema was perhaps a little slower to realise that not only was work with such (sometimes hidden) levels of seriousness now a possibility when it came to making more ambitious films, but that such 'added value' was to some degree useful in finessing the commercial possibilities of the film (and however serious the filmmaker, filmmakers were always obliged to be concerned with the bottom line – without state subsidies, films simply have to make money). Furthermore, as serious critical attention began to be given to genre product, there was no reason why more intelligent directors and writers should not freight in this extra structure of ambition (i.e. ensuring a film was about something more than simply frightening the audience, as long as they were able to observe that imperative).

In the early twenty-first century, the genre in the UK began to incorporate these newer, more motivated strains addressing, for instance, business ethics, recession-hit Britain and the impact of a bleaker future on the underclass. But perhaps more significantly was the field's greater readiness to grapple with the notion of – and the existence of – evil as something more than a peg on which to hang the narrative.

At a book event with the criminologist and social reformer Ludovic Kennedy (a very civilised affair with wine and canapés), I was talking to the late writer and his wife, the actress Moira Shearer, who appeared in one of the great British Gothic films, Michael Powell's *Peeping Tom*; the latter surprised me when she asked her husband: 'What was that horror film I did with Micky Powell that sabotaged his career?' I reminded her and pointed out its subsequent cult status, of which she seemed unaware.

Shortly after, Kennedy was approached by a friendly-looking middle-class lady who, to our surprise, launched into a passionate diatribe about the ethos of the way he made his living. Her eyes burning, she claimed that his books, examining a variety of murderers and killers, exploited the very worst aspects of human behaviour. His work, she continued, appealed to the crassest and most debased elements of the human condition (grasping her wine glass ever tighter as she railed at him). He listened politely, then gave a carefully considered rejoinder. He suggested that it was essential that we all examine why the monsters and serial killers in society behave as they do, and that an examination of their motives and (crucially) their backgrounds might lead to a more intelligent assessment of how to deal with such people and, in fact, protect society in a way that would not be possible if a discreet veil were drawn over the actions and motivations of such disturbed individuals. 'But you're writing about *evil*', the woman continued, 'And by writing about it you give it what Margaret Thatcher called "the oxygen of publicity"!' At this point, Kennedy realised that he was being forced into a discussion of the nature of evil, and later said to me: 'I wasn't happy talking to her about the subject when it became almost metaphysical – because I'm not really sure that evil exists. Although everything in my experience persuades me that it does.'

More recently, British horror films and younger directors have touched upon this notion – the existence of evil and what form it takes. It is an index of the low esteem in which both politics and big business are held in the early twenty-first century that there is often a metaphorical conjoining of evil with the great and good of society. This is a recurrent theme, particularly in the hybrid horror/crime films of such modern British directors as Ben Wheatley and Sean Hogan. The protagonists in these films are essentially workers, paid to do a job. Professional hitman seems to be a favoured profession in the modern horror film, but they invariably come to as messy an end as any of their victims and sometimes undergo a *crise de conscience* concerning their ruthless world view – the character played by Billy Clarke in *The Devil's Business* (2011), directed by Sean Hogan (see Appendix: Interviews), is an example of this. But these blue-collar professionals are almost invariably employed by wealthy businessman or political types, and their targets are sometimes other privileged figures, even men of the church, somehow implicated in malign behaviour and awaiting their grim fate with a certain resignation (as in Ben Wheatley's *Kill List* (also 2011)). Evil in the modern age is no longer located in foreign aristocracy or supernatural creatures, but in the pillars of the establishment.

By the time of his third film, *Sightseers* (2012), Ben Wheatley's work had started to generate considerable interest, not least because the eccentric Englishness of his films was set against their extreme violence (such as the unrelenting beating out of the brains of a victim in his second feature, *Kill List* (2011), a scene as difficult to watch with its gruelling-to-watch presentation of hammer blows, exposed brain tissue and bloody scalp as a similar bludgeoning in the Gaspar Noë film *Irréversible*). *Sightseers*, however, dispensed of the hitmen of *Kill List* and Wheatley's debut *Down Terrace* (2009), retaining the quirky, Anglocentric approach to language and performance in which the names of fellow British directors Mike Leigh and Ken Loach (particularly the former) were routinely invoked. The demented, 'ordinary' couple in *Sightseers*, played by Alice Lowe and Steve Oram (who also co-wrote the screenplay), may take part in copious bloodletting and violent murder on their eventful caravan trip, but on their initial appearance in the film, critics were quick to point out how much they resembled the desperately unromantic, desperately banal British couple played by Alison Steadman and Roger Sloman in Mike Leigh's *Nuts in May* (1976). And while the psychopathic nature of Wheatley's couple is something new, the other elements that we are shown, an English couple glumly determined to have a good time on their ill-fated holiday even as all occasions inform against them, is a common theme – and in fact the film is more about a certain (sometimes bovine) English *sangfroid* in the face of petty disaster as much as it is about the latent capacities for monstrous behaviour in even the most ordinary of English people.

The beating in of brains with walking sticks and rocks (or even by the use of moving vehicles) in the film is given a blackly comic treatment, some considerable distance from the comedy of embarrassment of the early scenes. And the surrealism of the writing echoes Wheatley's earlier work with such British television comedians as Vic Reeves and Bob Mortimer, who similarly take a wildly off-kilter (though not gruesome) approach to their material. Wheatley is also interested in the contrast of the grotesque happenings of the film with the beauty of the Lake District settings in which it takes place, as stimulating for him as the Englishness of another project, the Civil War drama *A Field in England* (2013). Certainly, after watching *Sightseers*, such comforting British institutions as tram museums and rickety caravans will never seem the same again.

The continuing appeal of the horror genre may perhaps be due to more than a simple sideshow ethic, although it's possible to be too precious about the appeal of the genre on the simple visceral level, as true in 2013 as it was century earlier. But given the under-regarded reputation of British cinema for so long – presenting a slightly restrained, repressed picture of the British psyche – it is hardly surprising that ambitious filmmakers embraced the genre for the leeway it gave them in exploring hitherto inaccessible territory (these explorations are not the exclusive preserve of the horror filmmakers, however; the films of Michael Powell and Emeric Pressburger, with their rather un-English brand of unrestrained romanticism, similarly demonstrated that popular genres might have a resonance beyond the simple narrative level). A more liberal approach in film criticism since the 1980s has allowed a consideration of the genre in a way that simply was not encouraged before (the BFI house magazine *Sight & Sound* rarely covered such genre material, and then often only in portmanteau reviews, e.g. reviewing en masse several films produced by Hammer and its rivals), but the new criticism has consigned such snobbery to the dustbin of history. It might be argued, however, that the establishment view expressed in response to the first 1950s wave of British horror – along the lines 'suitable for sadists only' – is still around, perhaps lurking beneath the surface. Indeed, in some circles it is still considered *infra dig* to express an admiration for this lurid material.

The revival of Hammer Films (after many false dawns) finally took hold with successful product (including the new appreciation of the studio's output via DVD and Blu-ray issues, now seen in a historical context), as well as new films made under the Hammer imprimatur. But have the traditional forms been customised for the new millennium? And is a new level of cliché becoming enshrined in the modern field?

Defences are made of the genre, even by those who are committed admirers, with a variety of caveats built in, almost a preliminary, proactive response to the kind of scorn that such a defence will usually prompt. And anyone who has tried to defend horror films will be well aware of the sanctioned approach: a readiness to enjoy these films, but only on a simple visceral level, with any intelligent reading of the material being firmly sidelined. The pleasures afforded by repeated motifs and the ingenious use of cyclical materials is often dismissed as mere repetition, with little attempt to examine on its own terms how creatively film-makers have re-invented familiar themes. But twenty-first-century fare is beginning to take on new tropes, though its outward accoutrements remain (superficially) the same. It should not be forgotten, however, that the imperative of Gothic horror material is still to disturb – not in the way, for instance, that Ibsen's drama *Ghosts* does, although horror films often similarly deal with the painful unearthing of dark secrets. But perhaps the impetus in the horror genre is simply the extirpation of evil rather than an attempt to recreate an organic, whole human personality. The latter is the function of much great art (although the results are not always successful, the striving must be maintained). Context too is important. In 2012, in a prestigious Nick Dear stage adaptation of *Frankenstein* directed by Danny Boyle, the actors Benedict Cumberbatch and Jonny Lee Miller alternated in the roles of the creator and creature, and the reviews were almost overwhelmingly positive, but this endeavour was in the remit of the National Theatre, with the literary antecedents of Mary Shelley prominently featured, so that none of the dismissive attitudes routinely trotted out for similar adaptions were aired.

Hammer is back (see the interview with the new Hammer CEO Simon Oakes in the Appendix), and one key film, a massive hit, is proof positive of that assertion. James Watkins' *The Woman in Black* (2012) is a significant film for a variety of reasons. First and foremost, it is a demonstration that the elements of the Gothic mythos can still be invested with chilling *force majeure*, even after a million increasingly desperate plunderings have left the genre looking shopworn. The film also demonstrates that a modern sensibility (here on the part of the director, the writer and the star, the winsome Daniel Radcliffe) can be profitably applied to a period genre, although it might be argued that the makers' clearly avowed attempt to play down certain elements (such as period speech) does not work to its advantage, and the film also shows that the accoutrements of the classic Hammer film (notably the sumptuous, evocative period design – here a deliciously cluttered haunted house) are still reliably effective if utilised with intelligence and an appropriate sense of atmosphere. Lastly, of course, it is proof that the imprimatur 'Hammer Films' is still capable of posthumous life, even though one might legitimately argue that the film is only peripherally connected with the golden age of that studio (the new logo, for instance, with a series of comic strip-style images, is more redolent of the pre-credits design of the superhero movies drawn from Marvel and DC Comics, a congruence further brought to mind by the presence of Jane Goldman as the adapter of the novel; Goldman is best known as the writer of the successful film adaptation of the graphic novel *Kick-Ass*). But above all, perhaps, the success of the film (and it *is* a success, both commercially and, largely speaking, critically, though many critics have registered caveats) owes a great deal to the original source novel by the writer Susan Hill.

Who, though, is the real Susan Hill? Is she Britain's best exponent of the classic ghost story? (After a celebrated television adaptation by Nigel Kneale, the stage version of her unsettling novel *The Woman in Black* has been playing on the West End stage since 1989.) Or is she the heir apparent of Anthony Trollope? (Her novel *The Shadows in the Street* is crammed as full of wonderful ecclesiastical squabbles as Barchester Towers, with High and Low Church at each other's throats.) Or is she a practitioner of the police procedural novel, with a doughty copper struggling to keep difficult murder investigations on course? Actually, she is all three – and she is adroit at whatever genre she turns her hand to. But for many, her ghost story credentials are paramount, and there is no denying the protean nature of her material, as the above list of adaptations of *The Woman in Black* comprehensively proves.

James Watkins, director of *The Woman in Black*, was also responsible for the powerful *Eden Lake*, and his film of Hill's novel, despite its highly impressive cinematography (by Tim Maurice-Jones), which perfectly captures its nineteenth-century feel, and Kave Quinn's exquisite production design, has a notably contemporary sensibility, and it is this which is perhaps one of the film's demerits. Daniel Radcliffe, now a post-Harry Potter young adult, adroitly conveys the alienated, vulnerable qualities of the young widower who takes on the job of sorting out the papers of a dead woman in a remote village and finds himself mired (sometimes literally) in supernatural terror. Radcliffe took the decision, along with his director (as James Watkins told me) and writer, to avoid period trappings in his performance, and his dialogue maintains an anachronistic feel, delivered with vaguely estuary English undertones (though never quite undercutting the reality of the situation). But it's hard not to feel that the younger actors who played such juvenile lead parts in Hammer films (from Edward de Souza to Simon Ward), in adopting a clipped, more authentic form of speech, maintained a more plausible period ethos. And while the older actors here (such as Ciaran Hinds as the Radcliffe character's only ally in an increasingly hostile village) has the requisite level of authenticity, the film struggles to accommodate its rather modern-seeming hero. But it is a tribute to James Watkins that all the tried-and-trusted apparatus of the Gothic horror story does not seem like a tired rehash of previous entries in the genre, even when the director borrows some effects from maestros of the past (the eponymous spectral woman's terrifying traversal of a room in a gliding motion without the use of her legs owes something to a similar unnerving floating corpse in Mario Bava's *I Tre Volti Della Paura/ Black Sabbath* (1963), while Jack Clayton's adaptation of Henry James' *The Innocents* perhaps provided the sudden jolting appearance of a dead face at a window).

The Gothic strain used here is one that is perhaps carefully de-eroticised, with the loss of love (in a variety of forms) more significant than any suppressed carnal impulse. Arthur Kipps (the Wellsian name may conjure up images of unhappy shop clerks rather than solicitors, but that is a choice of Susan Hill's) is, to some degree, fertile material for haunting by the woman in black, avenging herself on the village for the loss of her child in her own campaign of child murder. Arthur's own loss of his young wife in childbirth has left him a spectral, almost dead figure even in the land of the living – and James Watkins makes the most of his actor's desolate, haunted blue eyes to suggest his protagonist's disenfranchisement from the real world. And of course, crucially, Arthur has his own beloved son who may become a victim of the vengeful ghost. If the more subtle psychological elements explored in other British Gothic adaptations (such as the repressed sexual hysteria of the governess in Jack Clayton's aforementioned adaptation of Henry James' 'The Turn of the Screw') are not really explored, there is some élan brought to bear in the mechanics of destabilising the audience (in the cinema, the film certainly provides several visceral shocks while avoiding any graphic bloodletting). Most of all, unlike previous attempts at reviving the Hammer moniker, the film makes pleasing connections with the earlier achievements of the studio (Kave Quinn's highly creative production design is something one feels that Hammer's much-loved exponent of that craft, Bernard Robinson, would have relished). But above all else, *The Woman in Black*, for all its infelicities, is proof of the indestructibility of the Gothic genre.

The Hammer brand is appearing – almost virally – in many branches of the arts, including the theatre. At London's celebrated Almeida

Theatre in Islington, an adaptation has appeared under the imprimatur 'Hammer Theatre of Horror' – a version of James' 'The Turn of the Screw' by Rebecca Lenkiewicz (the James story, of course, having been previously – and memorably – adapted for the operatic stage by Benjamin Britten and as the previously mentioned film by Jack Clayton).

Horror from other studios than a revitalised Hammer has found a ready market in the new millennium. It is significant that among modern British films, it is a genre film – one within the Gothic tradition – which depends very much on the specificity of its location (London under siege) to make its points. Danny Boyle's *28 Days Later* (2002) is both a film about London and a film about Britain, and the director's eye for felicities of detail is at all times acute. It is also retrospectively interesting that the director was chosen to put together the celebration of Britishness which inaugurated the London Olympic Games of 2012. The latter exercise was a spectacular exercise in kitsch indulgence, with a great variety of highly disparate elements of Britishness (from Shakespeare to the rap doggerel of Dizzee Rascal) thrown together in a dizzying conglomeration that won almost universal praise from all but the more extreme fringes of the right-wing press (who uneasily sensed a left-wing bias in this celebration of Britishness; more liberal papers were exercised by the fact that Caliban's 'The isle is full of noises' speech from *The Tempest* was bizarrely given to Isambard Kingdom Brunel, played in end-of-the-pier fashion by a top-hatted Kenneth Branagh – thereby presumably touching all possible bases). As a picture of modern Britain, however, *28 Days Later* is hardly more illuminating, but it's possibly more honest and certainly more rigorous than the officially sanctioned orgy of Britishness with which it was felt necessary to open the Olympics ceremony.

The film was written by Alex Garland and (as with most zombie films since Romero's *Night of the Living Dead*) finds a science-fiction rationale for its army of the living dead – although the setting is firmly present day rather than near future, and there are no outward accoutrements of the genre. The film is definitely a Gothic exercise (within realistic parameters) and it is a measure of Boyle's skill that the familiar device of the revivified dead is able to function – and can function highly effectively – in a carefully observed modern Britain, even managing to make some salient points about the latter. The virus which sets the destruction of society in motion is drawn from the same literary tradition as the 'cosy catastrophes' of such British science-fiction writers as John Wyndham and John Christopher, who repeatedly brought about the end of the world while making provocative points about totalitarianism and survivalism (both of the latter shown as ready to fill the void left by the collapse of such institutions as the police and the army). Inevitably, the trajectory of such films (and books) is as follows:

1. Initial catastrophe that lays waste to society.
2. Survival of a durable group of protagonists, always at the mercy of looters or self-styled dictators.
3. Tentative suggestion of some kind of restoration of order from the chaos.

The 'rage' virus that sets disaster loose in *28 Days Later* has been released accidentally and the protagonists Jim (Cillian Murphy), Selena (Naomie Harris) and Hannah (Megan Burns) are obliged to form a new kind of nuclear family, escaping from the chaos of London to eke out an agrarian existence even as planes from abroad attempt to contain the disaster on these shores. A variety of progenitors of the disaster are suggested at intervals (including the attentions of terrorists anxious to bring down the 'decadent West') and Boyle allows the various possible causes to remain in the background. He is particularly interested in a kind of visual surrealism that long attracted surrealist painters to the Gothic genre: an eerily deserted London with evidence of the death and destruction that has swept people from streets is frequently invoked to great effect. Earlier filmmakers had ploughed such furrows before, notably Wolf Rilla in another doomsday movie, albeit on a smaller scale, in his adaptation of Wyndham's *The Midwich Cuckoos* (as *Village of the Damned*), which similarly showed streets bereft of human beings. In fact, a mention of John Wyndham is apropos, as the survival of the character of Jim in *28 Days Later* echoes that of the hero of Wyndham's *The Day of the Triffids*, where the trajectory is similarly from a room in London to the countryside (Terry Nation's impressive television serial *Survivors* (1975) similarly mined his territory with its genetically modified virus).

Boyle's film retains its plausibility over other entries in the genre by making its marauders less like stereotypical zombies (i.e. living dead supernatural creatures) and noting that they are victims of a virus which nevertheless allows scenes of violence and terror to take place against such familiar landmarks as Trafalgar Square (and such scenes are dispatched with real élan, ratcheting up the suspense). But as well as making points about the fragility of the social order, Doyle and Garland are interested in the limits of the family unit. The film features Jim discovering his dead parents who have committed suicide at the beginning of the film, but the movement of *28 Days Later* is towards the eventual restoration of the family unit – and in order to survive, Jim is obliged to strip away all the conventional pieties and received wisdom of 'the family', establishing something new and organic which has the capacity to survive in a rejuvenated form.

As with Terry Nation's *Survivors*, the virus which strips away the fabric of society here ties into other durable fears of the horror film, notably the 'body horror' theme that is seen as the prerogative of the Canadian director David Cronenberg. And, as so often with that filmmaker, the infection here might be seen as a metaphor for the removal of individual autonomy – an all-too-real threat in both the West (under the demands of consumerism) and in Middle Eastern theocratic countries (where any kind of dissent from a religious orthodoxy is punishable by death). If Boyle and Garland are not able to keep cliché completely at bay (and even less so in the disappointing sequel, *28 Weeks Later* (2007)), there is enough thought and intelligence here to ensure that the film functions on a variety of levels – not a prerequisite of the Gothic genre, but always welcome when such an enriching of texture occurs.

Different approaches to the zombie film in the modern age proved feasible. While British-made horror films of the 1950s felt obliged to incorporate an imported American leading man (often past their sell-by date) in order to sell the films in the USA, it quickly became apparent that this supposedly uncivilised audience was not quite as resistant to certain things from the Old Country as had been believed. The producers of the James Bond films had been told by American distributors that the idea of a womanising, sexually voracious Englishman as the hero of a series of spy films would simply not be accepted by US audiences (in fact, in the very first Fleming adaptation, a TV version of *Casino Royale*, 007 had been forced to become the bland yank 'Jimmy' Bond). But while the received wisdom was that a carnally active Englishman was still a hard sell for Americans (at least a heterosexually active Englishman), it was clear that a certain kind of practical, forceful eccentricity was acceptable in English actors (the first breakthrough performers in this movement were Peter Cushing and Christopher Lee, rarely playing Englishmen, but always adopting a precise received pronunciation that made it perfectly clear what country they came from). By the time of the late twentieth and early twenty-first centuries, the eccentric Englishman had become popular on the opposite side of the Atlantic via the charm of such actors as Hugh Grant – and another, less physically prepossessing actor specialising in comic roles (although customarily played straight, the humour coming from his blank, bemused reactions to the situations around him) was proving to be something of an phenomenon: the Gloucester-born Simon Pegg. His alter ego was the director (and co-writer) Edgar Wright, and the duo were to find a particularly fresh approach to British Gothic cinema with *Shaun of the Dead* in 2004. The film played on the same kind of relationship-based comedy that such writers as Richard Curtis had enjoyed such success with in the States.

The eponymous Shaun (played by Pegg) is losing the affection of his girlfriend Liz (Kate Ashfield), as she is exasperated with his torpid attitude to life and their relationship. But the first thing that strikes audiences is the picture of Britain presented here. In fact, although played for comic purposes, the opening scenes of the film showing a dull quotidian modern London (all unreconditioned pubs and identical Asian corner shops) actually presents a vision of Albion unlike that being shown in most other British films of the day (notably those of the aforementioned Richard Curtis, who presented a romanticised, prettified version of the country in which glamorous American leading ladies could sweep stultified Englishman out of their unexciting bookshop existences – as long as they looked like Hugh Grant). But what struck British audiences about *Shaun of the Dead*, even before the bloody mayhem promised by the title was delivered, was that this was recognisably the England in which most of us lived, and the carefully neutered reactions of the characters to most aspects of life have a plausibility and keenness of observation that was not to be discerned in most drama, let alone a comedy such as this. In the film, a night at the local pub ends with the relationship between Shaun and Liz reaching a dead end, despite Shaun's attempts to disprove her (clearly accurate) view of his unchanging, moribund life. But when, the next morning, Shaun and his friend Ed (played by the heavy-set Nick Frost, who has become the slobbish foil to Pegg's only slightly more acceptable slacker) wake up, they discover that Britain is in the grip of a zombie invasion and begin a fraught rescue operation, attempting to save the lives of Liz and her friends David and Dianne from the marauding undead. Also coming under Shaun's now-energised protection (it has taken an assault by the living dead to shake him out of his torpor) are his mother Barbara and unsympathetic stepfather Philip. The latter are played by much-loved British character actors Penelope Wilton and Bill Nighy, the latter in particular now familiar to American audiences no longer resistant to British players. The more middle-class ambience added by these performers (who instantly realise precisely what level to pitch their performances at) helps present a rounded picture of British society, under threat from a flesh-ripping horror – or is it in fact from its own deathwatch beetle, gnawing within?

The malaise that Liz has (correctly) identified in Shaun, as evinced in his inept response to his own life and their relationship, might be read as a more endemic way of thinking, one carried over from the successful TV series which preceded the film, *Spaced*, which ran from 1999 to 2001 and which similarly set a barely sentient slacker ethos (in which the characters make inconsequential attempts to quantify their meaningless lives) against a parody and celebration of the techniques of modern American cinema – which is very much the approach taken with *Shaun of the Dead*. The bloody and graphic dispatch of the zombies in the film (often accompanied by a sardonic comment that undermines the gut-spilling grotesquerie of the images) was actually not a considerable distance from the attitude expressed in the film of which the very title here was a parody: George Romero's *Dawn of the Dead* (1978). And while the mayhem is always funny, death is on the cards for several of the principal human characters, and a pervasive sense of melancholy is never far away. Also built into the film is the knowledge that audiences will be familiar with the wide range of cinematic techniques on offer, serving the function of building tension (bloody siege situations straight out of Romero, who had in turn borrowed such things from Hitchcock's *The Birds*), while every aspect of British society is turned on its head (a running joke is the surprising sight of characters we have seen in normal situations turning up as homicidal zombies, including a checkout girl seen early in the film; this might also be seen as a nod to Romero, who made sure that the zombies did not simply include generically sinister creatures, but individuals transformed from their earlier dull lives and still bearing the trappings of the latter, such as some in blue-collar uniform).

Perhaps one of the reasons for the film's success is its quintessential Britishness, with Shaun's hopeless character in line of descent from such earlier British losers as the comic actor Tony Hancock, presented as articulate and striving, but full of self-deception about their own possibilities to change. Unlike his predecessors, however, Shaun demonstrates the capacity to re-jig his life, and becomes proactive and competent – unlike his earlier self.

Shaun of the Dead also manages to have its cake and eat it, sending up the excitement of zombie destruction (the latter likened to the static time-wasting qualities of computer console games, but also delivering a degree of pulse-raising excitement). The final scene, in which Shaun finds himself playing a PlayStation game with his now-zombified friend Ed, nicely undercuts the progression shown earlier in the film; Ed, now one of the undead, is incapable of change – Shaun has shown that he is, but he clearly has a capacity to slip back into his old ways. Britain may be a backwater, Pegg and Wright may be saying, but that water can either be stagnant or freely flowing – whichever it is to be depends on the kind of Britain we choose.

But not everything that Simon Pegg was associated with turned to gold. The story of Burke and Hare had been the subject of several films (notably John Gilling's *The Flesh and the Fiends*, discussed in Chapter 9), but its use as the basis of a horror comedy in 2010 seemed something of a retrograde step. Pegg played Burke and the physically flexible actor Andy Serkis (who had made a career of creating such motion-capture creatures as Gollum in the Peter Jackson *Lord of the Rings* trilogy) was William Hare. The presence in the cast of such reliable actors as Tom Wilkinson further burnished (one might have thought) the film's possibilities. But was the fact that the director was John Landis a particular asset? The American director had made what is quite possibly the best British horror comedy with the immensely enjoyable *An American Werewolf in London* in 1981, but the particular combination of elements that made the earlier film work had consistently eluded the director in subsequent years – as indeed they were to do (once again) with *Burke and Hare*. In keeping with the utterly unfazeable nature of modern audiences, the new version sets out its stall quickly with a variety of amputations (*sans* anaesthetics), rotting corpses and executions, but it quickly becomes apparent that Landis' once-impeccable grasp of tone has deserted him, particularly as we are invited to dredge up some sympathy for the murderous title duo. Burke and Hare are presented as not-unlikeable, incompetent confidence tricksters as much as drunken body-snatchers. There is an ill-advised love interest added for Simon Pegg's Burke (as opposed to the unpleasant co-dependency of earlier films), and in keeping with contemporary orthodoxy, the really culpable individuals are those (far worse because of their added gravitas and power) located in the establishment, as represented by Dr Knox, the man who pays the duo for their supply of bodies. Tom Wilkinson seems curiously subdued in the role (and certainly offers no challenge to earlier players such as Peter Cushing) and audiences, whether familiar or not with earlier versions, may not find themselves persuaded to be placed on the side of the duo of killers. Having said all this, Landis is still able to pull a variety of irons out of the fire and keeps things moving in a lively end-of-the-pier-style horror show, with a variety of starry cameos which make up for the tiresome anachronisms repeatedly used for comic effect (Landis also appears to have lost the scalpel-like touch of his earlier work, with gags milked to the nth degree). The mixed response of audiences of the film, however, did not tarnish Simon Pegg's lustre at all.

The title of Arjun Rose's *Demons Never Die* (2011) might have suggested a straightforward horror outing, but in fact the film is another in the burgeoning sub-genre of urban youth crime/horror film hybrids which has a sharp and unsentimental eye for its unlovely council house settings and self-destructive teenage protagonists. The young Londoners we see here appear to be less interested in surviving in their drug-ridden backyards than in actually ending their short and brutal lives. But a certain camaraderie grows up between the group, with the aspirant killer Kenny (played by Jason Maza) suggesting that a deal with the devil is one to take seriously, however unspeakable the consequences for the young criminals and those unlucky enough to cross their paths. After a while, the film seems to settle into a standard bodycount movie, with violent death on the agenda for its characters, dispensed by a masked killer (the latter more than a little reminiscent of such figures in the films of Dario Argento and Mario Bava – the film is nothing if not polyglot in its influences), but Rose's film (from his own screenplay) is intelligent enough to suggest that the bloody mayhem on view may be an exteriorisation of the suicidal impulses of the Thanatos-worshipping youngsters. Is the Satanic force of evil here some clever metaphor for the uncaring society which is perfectly happy to see these teenage drains on the social system dispensed of with the least possible fuss for the middle classes? Certainly, Rose details a considerable tally of the social ills blighting the lives of his characters (from family break-up to uncertainties about sexuality). In fact, so detailed is this list of possible pitfalls for the characters that the demonic murderer (or murderers) seems at times to be the least of their troubles. Nevertheless, Rose's ambition – as well as, frequently, his achievement – is to be applauded.

The director Neil Marshall had enjoyed some acclaim for the gritty werewolf film *Dog Soldiers* in 2002, and expectations were riding high for his next film. In the event, *The Descent* (2005) more than matched the achievement of the earlier film and marked Marshall out as a name to watch as one of the key talents of the new British Gothic. As with most of the best films in such genres, Marshall was able to combine the visceral excitement in which the genre traded with a certain level of intriguing subtext. To some degree, the concerns of the film are in line with those first utilised by another British director, John Boorman, in his American-made *Deliverance* (1972), in which sophisticated city-bred types come into violent conflict with rural dwellers – the latter often characterised as being degraded (or in some fashion animalistic) and full of homicidal loathing for their better-dressed enemies. The trajectory of such narratives is usually as follows: edgy encounter between two groups; bloody winnowing out of vulnerable city types; then messy, ineffectual (but finally successful) taking of the initiative by the city characters and surviving the lethal attacks. A given of the genre is the sybaritic, initially carefree attitude of the city-dwellers (invariably entering the wild as part of a holiday), and a certain casual disregard for the way of life of those obliged to live here (usually in squalor), while the city-dwelling individual initially presented as least equipped to survive (cf. the sensitive Jon Voight character in *Deliverance*) somehow struggles through, bloody but alive. Since its first rigorous treatment in the Boorman film, this template has done service numerous times, and audience pleasure comes from the fashion in which variations are wrought on the theme.

To his credit, Neil Marshall has several aces up his sleeve when it comes to reinvigorating this familiar material. While the water rafting at the beginning of this film is clearly a self-conscious reference to Boorman's original, his characters, Sarah, Beth and Juno, are very different, not least because of the different gender chosen by Marshall for his endangered protagonists. This switch in the sexuality of the characters is exacerbated by the fact that their tormentors are specifically male (although one of the 'crawlers' is female, her longevity is brief). The Jon Voight character here, Sarah (played by Shauna McDonald), will be obliged to confront her own innate insecurity and weakness in order to survive. But where Boorman in the original film rarely suggested a commonality between the two opposing groups, Marshall is at some pains to do the reverse here, although the traumatic consequences of survival here are (it is suggested) more likely to alter forever those from the ostensibly 'civilised' background.

The one element not mentioned in the template above concerning the *Deliverance*-type narrative is an acute sense of place, with striking natural locales becoming a setting for terror and dismay; by the end of the film, everything we see has become minatory and unsettling. And inevitably, with the female emphasis of the narrative here, the 'weekend warriors' of *The Descent* cannot escape the Freudian implications of a descent into the Boreham Caverns. A feminist reading of the film might run along the lines of the investigation of the vagina that is necessary for the characters to know themselves thoroughly – in Eliot's words in 'Four Quartets':

> Descend lower, descend only
> Into the world of perpetual solitude,

World not world, but that which is not world,
Internal darkness, deprivation...

And:

... the end of all our exploring will be to arrive where we started and know the place for the first time.

In fact, though, such metaphors are not treated in any tendentious fashion. The Caverns themselves are no less intimidating than the original landscape through which the protagonists travel to reach them, where there is some attempt by Marshall to make the characters seem isolated and tiny within the context of an uncongenial locale.

The women here seem initially equipped to survive even before the appearance of their savage nemeses – they are fit, capable, muscular – although the mislaying of a crucial map suggests an inherent weakness, particularly in the light of the metaphor of the journey (both physical and otherwise).

The source of death and horror in the film are the crawlers, who possess a synergy with their threatening surroundings which make them an implacable enemy. Their barely human attributes place them at one with the notion of a threatening, untamed nature. There is perhaps a suggestion that the inability of the women to deal with this physical threat is due to their being out of sync with nature; despite their apparent fitness for survival, they have lost the crucial abilities to survive, which renders them as cannon fodder for the murderous subterraneans.

It is no accident that the film's central character, Sarah, is a mother, although two of the elements that create that status (her husband and daughter) are both lost to her, and when she is obliged to end the life of her friend (as well as combat her barely human enemies), the thin veneer of civilisation is ruthlessly stripped away, a process echoed in her increasing resemblance to the crawlers. When she is obliged to ruthlessly break the neck of one of the youthful crawlers, her movement towards a synchronicity with the creatures who want to kill her is now complete, and the cesspit of bloody, shredded ragged flesh into which she falls is both a symbol of her final immersion in primitiveness and the sense that she has finally lost all the outward signifiers which mark her out as human. When Sarah finally sees the truth about herself, she is able to blind (with the horn of a deer) one of her antagonists; she now is the one who can see, as opposed to her opponents who have previously possessed a bat-like ability to function in the dark. The self-creation involved in the woman that Sarah becomes is as traumatic as can be imagined, but the immersion in a 'vaginal channel' is significant here, as are the birth metaphors that end the film.

The resuscitation of the Hammer brand also has a literary arm, represented in the new publishing imprint which in 2012 bore the name of the company. And while several books in the new series cheerfully channelled the gruesome goings-on of the Hammer Films in its heyday (such as free adaptations of various films), an index of the great critical respectability given to the field was perhaps the commissioning of such literary writers as Jeanette Winterson to contribute to the series. The latter's *The Daylight Gate* took as its subject the Lancashire witchcraft trials of 400 years ago. Real-life witchcraft hysteria (such as that of an incident in the Pendle district of 1612, in which a woman was obliged to confess her witchcraft and ask for forgiveness) demonstrated that such films as Michael Reeves' *Witchfinder General* (not to mention Arthur Miller's play *The Crucible* with its American setting) had all-too-real antecedents. Witchcraft accusations flew thick and fast, with grim consequences for the accused, as Winterson details in her novel. The writer may be better known for her more respectable literary fare, but (thankfully) does not shy away from the gruesome implications of the narrative in *The Daylight Gate*, even including such insalubrious details as the gang rape of a girl suspected of witchcraft and witch hangings. What's more, Winterson's catalogue of horrors includes male rape and an uncompromising scene involving castration. Inevitably, of course, the writer is keen to infuse her own preoccupations (such as the dangerous implications of faith) into the narrative, and there is no question that Matthew Hopkins (so memorably played by Vincent Price in the Michael Reeves film) is an influence here, as the torturers of the witchcraft suspects take a distinctly non-religious pleasure in their grim work. Perhaps more than her Hammer precedents, the writer's customary concerns are aired – such as a polymorphous sexuality which takes centre stage (notably that of the sexually omnivorous Alice). What makes the book an odd fit for the Hammer imprint is that, despite its catalogue of horrors, the writing in the final analysis is poetic and finely judged rather than an operatic celebration of the horrors on view.

Other contributors to the Hammer Horror novellas series include the controversial children's writer Melvin Burgess (controversial, that is, to some adults who have objected to his frank and unblushing treatment of mature themes in young adult novels – his concomitant standing among his teenage readers could not be higher). *Hunger* features a young woman waking up one morning covered in dirt and attributing her condition to a case of extreme sleepwalking, until reports of a desecrated grave grant her nocturnal perambulations a more frightening aspect. While the novel is suggestive of Hammer only in the broadest sense, its treatment of the awakening of ancient evil is something that might have warmed the cockles of such Hammer alumni as Michael Carreras and Terence Fisher. But Burgess has always been a writer who has a pronounced skill for destabilising the reader, and that particular ability is well to the fore in one of the more impressive entries in this revived Hammer franchise.

The Hammer novella imprint has shown a commendable readiness to embrace non-genre authors alongside specialist practitioners, and a prestigious addition to the list has been Julie Myerson's *The Quickening*, an edgy and unsettling piece (whose protagonists are a honeymoon couple) sporting a gruesome catalogue of murders in an Antigua holiday resort. As with other writers who have contributed to the imprint (including Helen Dunmore and Jeanette Winterson), Myerson has forged something provocative and unusual – a novel, moreover, which demonstrates an unerring grasp of narrative, something that would have received a welcome imprimatur from the company's creative personnel in its glory days. In fact, a book in the genre of the macabre is not such a great stretch for Myerson, whose previous eight novels have shown a taste for the disturbing (it's clear that the writer – who makes no secret of her love of Hammer – is drawn to the supernatural), and *The Quickening* marries a grasp of the exigencies of the genre with the author's own gift for carefully nurtured atmosphere. Martyn Waites has contributed to the list a sequel to Susan Hill's *The Woman in Black*.

So, is British Gothic cinema in rude health at the start of the twenty-first century or subsisting in a half-life like one of the zombies in the current crop of films that refuse to lie down? Certainly, enthusiastic filmmakers are ensuring a steady flow of new titles: *Wishbaby*, *The Zombie Diaries*, *The Living and the Dead*, *The Seasoning House*, *Straightheads*, *Doghouse*, *Tower Block*, *Community*, *Comedown*, *Cherry Tree Lane*, *The Cottage*, *Inbred*, *Wilderness*, *The Bunker*, *Deathwatch*, *Cockneys vs. Zombies*, *Lesbian Vampire Killers*, *The Dead Outside*, *Harold's Going Stiff*, *Wild Country*, *Black Death*, *Beyond the Rave*, *Temptation*, *Chatroom* and *The League of Gentlemen's Apocalypse*.

The critic Kim Newman remarked to me that this list includes a whole slew of tower block/council estate social miserabilism horrors, which perhaps contrast with the very middle-class tone of classical British horror cinema or suggest an industry desperately trying to connect with 'da kidz' – a perhaps doomed enterprise. Has much changed in the last three decades? Does, say, *Long Time Dead* represent contemporary youth as poorly as *Dracula A.D. 1972* did in its era?

In terms of the continuing influence, horror films are currently among the most surefire of genres – although such popularity is inevitably cyclical. In terms of box office (and critical) success, the UK continues to punch above its weight and the revival of interest sparked by *28 Days Later* carries on apace, with several directors proving conclusively that they are no one-hit wonders (Michael J. Bassett, for instance, has directed the memorable First World War trenches-set *Deathwatch* (2002) and the survivalist epic *Wilderness* (2006), while Johnny Kevorkian used a council estate setting for *The Disappeared* (2008)). Other directors have found unusual elements to explore in such areas as business training courses, such as Christopher Smith's *Severance* (2006), and even the urban transport system (the same director's *Creep* (2004) – although the London Underground has already provided fertile territory for the macabre in Gary Sherman's *Death Line* some three decades earlier, both films play on our atavistic subterranean fears, even in as familiar a place as the Underground station).

In such films as *Sightseers* (as discussed above), there is a provocative new mix of gruesome mayhem with the banality of modern-day English life. The characters are not savants or authority figures, but people drawn from the target demographics of such intelligence-insulting reality TV shows as *Come Dine with Me* and *Big Brother*, but who are nevertheless shown as capable of the most appalling violence (a particular exemplar here is Steven Sheil's *Mum & Dad* (2008), which gleefully explored the psychopathic heart of a boring family living in a faceless airport hub, suggesting that dark madness need not be located in baroque settings).

Bucolic rural settings in British horror have been shown to be just as fraught and dangerous as a Liverpool cul-de-sac (in Paul Andrew Williams' *The Cottage* (2008) and Lawrence Gough's *Salvage* (2009), respectively), and while the back-from-the-dead entity of Hammer Films has re-tooled the much-acclaimed Swedish film *Let the Right One In* (as *Let Me In* (2010), although the latter, directed by Matt Reeves, is an American co-production), the director Nick Cohen found a considerable degree of minatory atmosphere in the Norfolk Broads for *The Reeds* (2010). And the benighted past, once such fertile territory for directors like Michael Reeves, is still inspiring filmmakers such as Christopher Smith, whose *Black Death* (2010) presents a distinctly unromantic view of a bloody period in England's past, as bubonic plague lays waste to the population.

What is particularly intriguing about the new wave of British horror is its readiness to investigate *every* quirky aspect of these isles, proving again and again that despite the geographical restrictions of this sceptred isle (compared, say, to the sprawling vastness of the USA), there is still an immense variety of attitude and accent to be mined from John O'Groats to Land's End. The long-cherished fear that British films are often too parochial to be exported is being disproved by the success of several of the newer films in America, although US-friendly elements are often incorporated – a tradition, in fact, which stretches back to the earliest periods of British film horror. And star names help, as Nicole Kidman's lustrous presence in Alejandro Amenábar's multinational *The Others* (2001) demonstrates. But whether or not newer filmmakers re-invent the gruesome tropes of the past or stride into previously unexplored territory, there is no denying that blood is currently flowing healthily through the veins of British Gothic cinema.

Appendix: Interviews

Ingrid Pitt (actress, *The Vampire Lovers*, etc., writer)

A relatively recent phenomenon is the actor who has a successful second career as a writer. If performers have the gift, they can relish this new life as a writer after the glory days of their primary profession are over. Dirk Bogarde accomplished this, and so, in her own way, did the late, charmingly eccentric Ingrid Pitt. Pitt is unquestionably the Queen of British Gothic cinema, even though her actual body of work is small. But such was her huge impact in a few short years that she became a much-loved feature of the film festival circuit and, with an entertaining – if relatively superficial – series of books, a writer who was never to be reviewed in the serious press, but was assured of a healthy readership. Pitt (her real name was Ingoushka Petrov) was born in Poland and is certainly best remembered in the blood-boltered Hammer epic *Countess Dracula* (1971). Her actual genre debut was in the indifferent Spanish *Sound of Horror* (1964), but the real attention came with her performance as the highly sensuous lesbian vampire in *The Vampire Lovers* (1970). It's difficult after so many years to remember the amazing impact this movie had in its day. The film upset the more fastidious critics as well as the moral guardians of the day, and Hammer films (which now look models of restraint, bursting with the cream of the cream of the British acting profession) had many critics reaching for their most vituperative adjectives. However, by the 1970s, the Hammer studio realised that it was losing its capacity to shock – and that was bad news, given that it was ever-conscious of the marquee value of a touch of outrage. With *The Vampire Lovers*, the company upped the ante in terms of sex and violence, with the bloody mayhem of the movie matched by the statuesque, sultry Pitt providing a sensuousness which had previously been relegated to the bosom-heaving victims of Christopher Lee's Dracula. Pitt's now-famous nude scenes inaugurated a new frankness in the genre and transformed the British horror film until William Friedkin's shocking *The Exorcist* (1973) to all intents and purposes drove a stake into the heart of the more sedate British industry. With the misfiring *Countess Dracula*, Pitt took on the role of Countess Elizabeth Bathory, a real-life female monster who, according to some (disputed) accounts, believed that bathing in the blood of virgins would keep her young. After the up-front horrors of *The Vampire Lovers*, *Countess Dracula* (while stylish enough) seemed restrained (a subject which Pitt feels strongly about) and notably underpowered by Hammer standards; indeed, despite her blood-drenched nude scenes, the film did not make the expected impact (even with the sterling support of such excellent actors as Nigel Green and Sandor Elès – see below). Nevertheless, her career continued with appearances in Robin Hardy and Anthony Shaffer's British cult classic *The Wicker Man* (1973) and a notable turn as a ruthless terrorist in the otherwise negligible *Who Dares Wins* (1982).

After those heady days, Pitt became a familiar figure at film festivals celebrating horror and the macabre, with her vampire associations much to the fore.

Her name was added to a book with the unsubtle title of *The Ingrid Pitt Book of Murder, Torture and Depravity* (2003), a lively history of such monsters as the demented Roman Emperor Caligula, the ruthless Torquemada and the murderer of 10 Rillington Place, John Reginald Christie. The grisly cover was an apropos piece of high-culture gore: Caravaggio's study of Judith and Holofernes, with a close-up of a detail showing Holofernes having his head hacked off by Judith's sword as blood spouts onto the pillow. This classical reference is gorily echoed inside by illustrations that are redolent of the most unbuttoned excesses of mid-1950s horror comics. Countess Dracula herself, Elizabeth Bathory, is the subject of the first chapter, accompanied by a picture of the naked Countess ecstatically rubbing over herself the blood dripping from the screaming young woman (also naked) in the spiked cage directly above. While these images may have helped to sell the book, it is a useful and concise history of some of the most memorable monsters of the past, which justified shelf space. But when I interviewed her, getting the ebullient Pitt to discuss her career was initially a little difficult: she talked at length about Christopher Lee, whom she held in high esteem, and was fascinated by the fact that he mentioned that he was related to both Rasputin and Ian Fleming (admittedly, an intriguing interesting genealogy).

Q: Why do you consider that in the field of British Gothic film there are relatively few female monsters?

A: Well, there is the lady with whom I have a certain association having played her in the Hammer movie, Elizabeth Bathory. But a woman who kills on this scale is unusual. After all, the epic killers are usually men – because they have the power which makes it possible to commit mayhem on a massive scale. Caligula, for instance. And in any case, don't you think that men have pretty well cornered the market in monsters? Nevertheless, Bathory was a serial killer on an epic scale, and she really did bathe in the blood of young girls, which she believed would restore her youth. In a remake of the film, I could play her again – but this time as the older Countess. I wouldn't need the latex anymore!

Q: It's a well-known fact that the crime and horror genres have a very large female following. Why do you think that is?

A: Actually, I think it's fear. We are, unless trained in martial arts, less equipped to deal with the threat of violence, and women can certainly relate to that. But as for enjoying that frisson of fear – well in books and films, it's safe. The reader or viewer is never in any real danger. Ironically, when I lived in Hollywood, I spent a lot of time living in fear of being mugged. In fact, I actually learnt karate! But fear is an interesting thing. After my success in the vampire movies, I used to be asked at children's parties to play a vampire and pretend to frighten the kids. While a lot of the children had great fun with this, I quickly realised that some of them were not able to perceive that this was play-acting and were genuinely scared, so I quickly started refusing to do it.

I was the first female predator. It's interesting that now most of those films are regarded affectionately, but they were criticised as beyond the pale in their day. Even the beheading in *The Vampire Lovers* was cut, and most TV prints don't have it. Look at all the beheadings in Tim Burton's *Sleepy Hollow* today! I'm glad to say that the DVD issue has restored the cuts.

Q: Have you ever seen the quote about your own career in Kim Newman's *BFI Companion to Horror*: 'the British cinema was no longer able to accommodate her predatory beauty'?

A: No, I hadn't seen that ... that's really interesting! But it wasn't just me the British cinema couldn't accommodate anymore. When American movies like *The Exorcist* and *A Nightmare on Elm Street* came along, the writing was on the wall for the British period horror film. Now horror had to be very much set in the present day, and those Hammer trappings began to seem old-fashioned. Ironically, that's the very thing that has made the films more and more fondly remembered as the years passed by. But those movies were considered very strong stuff in their day. Except that I always felt that *Countess Dracula*, for censorship and other reasons, pulled its punches somewhat. On the set, I tried to insist they made more of her bathing in blood, but the director Peter Sasdy mentioned censorship, and I think it would have been a far more powerful film if we'd been able to show just how depraved Bathory was. That's actually the case with most real-life monsters and their equivalents in film. Ed Gein, who I've written about, inspired both *Psycho* and *The Texas Chain Saw Massacre*, and did far more horrible things than either of those films showed, but I suppose that it's inevitable such changes will occur.

Q: In *Countess Dracula*, you were supported by one of the very finest British character actors, the late Nigel Green. What are your memories of him?

A: Nigel was wonderful, but he wouldn't take my advice. At the time they were making the film of *Nicholas and Alexandra*, and I suggested that he would be perfect for the part of Rasputin. I told him he should speak to Sam Spiegel, but he said, 'If he wants me, he can come to me'. And he never really got the parts he deserved, although he's wonderful in *The Ipcress File* and *Zulu*. As well as in *Countess Dracula*, of course.

Q: Have you ever suffered from the obsessed, stalker type of fan, as Janet Leigh did after *Psycho*?

A: No, I've been very lucky – that's never happened to me. Thank God! Look at what happened to Jodie Foster ... it's really worrying that people like her stalker are out there.

Q: So what led you to undertake the literary career you've carved out for yourself?

A: Desperation! The parts weren't there anymore, and I was a survivor.

Q: But although the Gothic film (and vampire) industry may have been what made you successful, hasn't it been something of an albatross?

A: No – I don't think so. After all, I find vampires great fun, and the genre has been kind to me.

Q: **Before you began to make your films for Hammer, vampirism had always been something that happened instead of sex. But you ushered in an era in which both could take place. How did you feel about being in the vanguard of this innovation?**

A: Well, when Jimmy Carreras offered me the part in *The Vampire Lovers*, I really did my homework about the phenomenon. And in Le Fanu's story 'Carmilla', there is this strong sexual element. I think the director, Roy Ward Baker, really made it work – although the producers were two lascivious little chaps. On the way to do my nude scene with Madeline Smith, I came out of the trailer with my dressing gown on and nothing underneath, and I saw these guys walking towards me with their heads down. I thought, what the hell, I'll make their day and just flung open the dressing gown. Their reaction was priceless!

Q: **If there is a connection between the sexual and bloodthirsty aspects of those films, is that healthy?**

A: Why not? Sexuality is a complicated thing, and films should reflect that.
(Ingrid Pitt, 1937–2010)

Ramsey Campbell (writer, *The Nameless*, etc.)

Q: **Your work is modern, but despite the contemporary trappings, you're still a part of an English Gothic tradition. Is that something which is consciously in your mind when you're writing?**

A: Seldom consciously – I'm concentrating on the material and doing my best to engage imaginatively with it. There are specific exceptions. 'The Guide' was written as both a tribute to M.R. James and an attempt to demonstrate that his methods are still vital, but the seed of the story was a single paragraph that came to me on a woodland walk – the kind of activity that often lets ideas come to the surface of my mind. Equally, 'The Place of Revelation' was a conscious bid to use the naïve voice that Machen wonderfully employs in 'The White People' to evoke a little of the sense of disquiet and awe he achieved (while my recent novel *The Kind Folk* kept Machen at the back of my mind too). Other echoes are less conscious. The dreadful apparition of an ape in 'The Trick' didn't strike me as related to 'Green Tea' until Jack Sullivan pointed out the similarity, for instance. And would we call Thomas Hinde a Gothic writer – *The Day the Call Came*, for example? That novel certainly influenced some of my tales from paranoid viewpoints.

Q: **Are you more influenced by literary Gothic or film adaptations of the great writers? Or both? Or something else?**

A: Literary, pretty well every time. While I'm generally not conscious of it during the process of writing, I certainly think I'm part (a small one, I should say) of the literary tradition that – in Britain – extends from Radcliffe through Le Fanu to M.R. James, and the parallel one that would include (in my view) Machen, Blackwood, de la Mare and Aickman. I must also acknowledge American influences, including Lovecraft's sense of structure and Leiber's particular kind of urban supernatural tale, where the familiar settings are no longer invaded by the uncanny but produce it of themselves. Films didn't play a great part in my progress as a writer, but I saw two in my mid-teens that did – *Last Year at Marienbad* (which I found hugely disturbing, and wanted to do something similar in prose) and *Los Olvidados*, where it seemed to me that the surreal moments intensified and shed extra light on the realism.

Q: Are the classic Gothic concepts looking a little exhausted from over-use in the cinema?

A: I'd say they rather are, but all it takes is imagination to re-invent them. I'm sure they will survive the trivialising tendency of post-modernism if that should be brought to bear on them.

Q: Which of your own books would you consider closest to the classic Gothic tradition?

A: Very possibly *The House on Nazareth Hill*, a title shorn of the first three words in America. After all, it isolates the young heroine in a Gothic building and puts her at the mercy of a crazed male villain. On the other hand, he's her father, and she's surrounded by a town and by other tenants who don't intervene (my variation on the geographical remoteness of *The Shining* – in my tales the worst often happens in the middle of the everyday). I've never been sure if the book makes its theme of the marginalisation of the female too obvious – it becomes literal in the historical detail, where an inmate of the early asylum the building used to be has to communicate her experience in the margin of her Bible. Anyway, I hope the book does a little in its own way to re-imagine the Gothic.

Q: What would be your choice of the film that means most to you in British Gothic cinema?

A: Jacques Tourneur's *Night of the Demon*. I fell in love with it when I was 14 or barely 15, from the opening – the voiceover, the great Vaughan Williams-influenced score, the wonderfully atmospheric and menacing drive through the night and its outcome. I even like the demon, although its early appearance rather throws off the structure of the film, which is very carefully organised as a process to undermine scepticism. As the film now stands, we have to wait for the protagonist to catch up with what we already know, but that's productive of its own kind of disquiet. I'm fond of *The Haunting* (the Robert Wise version, if I need to say that to anyone), but I think that Tourneur offers more of the lyrical dread both directors learned in their years of working for that champion of understatement, Val Lewton at RKO.

Christopher Fowler (writer, *Hell Train*, etc.)

Another writer who has forged a modern literary version of the Hammer ethos is Christopher Fowler, author of *Hell Train*, a supernatural chiller written in homage to the company. Fowler is eloquent in his autobiographical memoir *Paper Boy* when talking about the appeal of Hammer. 'Horror', he said, 'was, at one time, perceived as an adolescent roadhouse on the way to more sophisticated forms of entertainment, perhaps because the genre appealed at an early age. The young suffer few intimations of mortality, and children are morbidly fascinated by the ideas of death and the supernatural. Each time I read or saw something that I liked, I drove another fence-post into the topography of my imagination, gradually mapping its outlines.

'Horror, however, regained respectability through the sumptuous period pieces that were central to Hammer films. English horror had extended from a civilised background, the world of E.F. Benson, M.R. James and Saki, of ghost stories told over after-dinner port. Ghost and horror stories could be found in household collections all over the country because the literary tradition was respectable. When the first, definitive Hammer *Dracula* appeared on-screen, it had a powerful impact; with no video and no MTV, youthful minds were less saturated with violence – images retained the power to shock. Fast cutting had not been invented. All horror films appeared in double bills (the thinking seemed to be that two horror films equalled one normal film).'

Speaking to Fowler about this own literary revivification of the tradition is instructive. 'Imagine', he said, 'that there was a supernatural chiller that Hammer Films never made. A grand epic produced at the studio's peak, which played like a mash-up of all the best ideas Hammer ever came up with. My notion in writing *Hell Train* was that a young writer goes to Bray Studios and is commissioned to write a Hammer film in a week for Christopher Lee and Peter Cushing. He produces a script about four passengers who meet on a train journey through Eastern Europe during the First World War. As the sinister "Arkangel" races through the war-torn countryside, there is a cocktail of bizarre creatures, satanic rites, terrified passengers and the romance of travelling by train, all in a classically styled supernatural adventure. For me, the Hammer tropes have unexplored possibilities ... but will they be explored in the company's new dispensation?'

Sean Hogan (director, writer, *The Devil's Business*, etc.)

'I tend to be surprised at the influences people sometimes tag me with, as they're often not what was on my mind when I was making a film. It's only when you look back over what you've done – and when interviews like this force you to think about it! – that you start to see some of the truth in what's been said about you. Because I don't deny that the sense of that Gothic tradition is there, it's possibly just that it was so formative for me that I don't even think about it now.

Certainly if you'd have asked me what I wanted to emulate when I was first setting out to make films, I would have said the 1970s new wave of US horror. Those films made a massive impact on me when I was younger, and I imagine that I might have dismissed a lot of the Gothic tradition as old hat at that point. But it's all part of the same road you end up travelling along, and so I can't refute the fact that a lot of that tradition has stayed with me to a certain extent. It then just becomes a question of what else I try to fuse that particular influence with.

I'm probably just a big stew of influences, like most people. I mean, I grew up reading classic Gothic horror – *Dracula, Frankenstein*, a lot of short stories – and then progressed to more contemporary stuff. And I followed a similar path with cinema – I was allowed to sit up and watch the Universal and Hammer movies on TV at a fairly young age, which then served as a gateway to the modern genre era when I was a bit older. So whilst I am more consciously influenced by the contemporary work I saw, I imagine that all that older Gothic stuff is still bubbling under in my head somewhere. Which may be why I'm attracted to trying to reinterpret that sort of material in a modern setting.

I mean, if you look at Cronenberg's genre work, it's obvious that he has absolutely no interest in the Gothic – it's all modern, scientific, clinical. Whereas for me that sort of thing still has juice in it – if you try and drag it into the present day and make it relevant somehow. I think Stephen King talked about a similar thing early in his career – he wanted to emulate what Richard Matheson did by bringing classic horror into the everyday, and by doing so he suddenly made the genre speak to a wider audience – it wasn't stuck in a Gothic castle anymore. And I think the same is still true now. Every now and then you have one of these expensively mounted Gothic period pieces that looks very handsome and finds a wide audience, but that's not what keeps the genre vital. They're not looking forward.

My film *The Devil's Business* represents a synthesis of the crime film and the horror film – but is this kind of cross-breeding necessary in the twenty-first century? I'm not sure: look at the recent success of something like *The Woman in Black*. That was pretty classically Gothic and clearly appealed to a lot of people. But yes, from a personal perspective, I'm always looking at how I might put a spin on the standard concepts. I'm not necessarily trying to re-invent the wheel – if you look at my stuff, the core supernatural tropes are often fairly traditional (ghosts, vampires, the occult), but what I am at least trying to do is offer a contemporary take on them. My formative years were spent watching the 1970s genre films that used horror iconography as a means of addressing the times they were made in, and so I've always been interested in attempting something similar. Not always in the larger political sense, but hopefully the subtexts of the various films I've made – alienation, poverty, class, authority/control – do speak to something in the here and now.

So I suppose the kind of cross-breeding mentioned above is a function of that – an attempt to try and keep the genre fresh and somewhat relevant. And it's also just a byproduct of being influenced by work outside the genre – as many people pointed out, the primary influence for *The Devil's Business* was Pinter's *The Dumb Waiter*. What made that exciting for me was the idea of trying to fuse this kind of existential hitman story with occult horror, with the result hopefully being that you get something you haven't often seen in the genre before. Beyond that, I'm just a big fan of film noir, and it always seemed to me that the kind of existential fatalism you get in those films would also fit pretty snugly within a horror framework. So by pulling in these outside influences, you try and create something new. I mean, that's the way the larger culture works, so I don't see why the horror genre should be any different.

I recently directed a series of short plays, *The Hallowe'en Sessions*, written by such novelists as Kim Newman. The format was the classic portmanteau anthology concept from Ealing's *Dead of Night* to the Amicus films. I am a big fan of the format, and the initial idea of mounting a multi-author theatrical production started with me, so it certainly wasn't just an assignment. I grew up watching and loving those classic portmanteau films, and so the notion of doing that has always appealed. I have also co-directed an anthology film – *Little Deaths* – and that came from a very similar place. Only there we ultimately decided to stay away from the classic portmanteau structure (the stories were simply linked thematically), and so avoided having a framing story or anything similar. Which was probably the right thing to do for that film, but it still left me with the unscratched itch of not having done my Amicus project! So when *The Hallowe'en Sessions* happened, I was very keen to embrace that particular form. In that sense it's probably the most purely nostalgic thing I've done, but it was still a real challenge to pull off, and certainly I enjoyed working with other writers such as Kim. In fact, we're both working on another multi-author project which has kind of sprung out of the ashes of the play.

It's still fairly difficult these days for an independent filmmaker to get the funding necessary to make the films one wants to make. My films have usually done OK – certainly they've had a lot of festival play, been internationally distributed and generally well reviewed – and I'm supposedly at a point now where certain people want to work with me, but then what you find is that they invariably want you to do what they want to do, not what you want to do. You always find yourself butting up against what distributors think is commercial, which of course is what was successful this year. But that isn't necessarily what will be successful next year. And if you make the sort of dark, character-driven stuff that I like to do, then it's always going to be fairly tough regardless – no one's going to give me two million quid to make *The Devil's Business*, but they will happily spend that on a dumb monster movie, just because it seems more commercial to them. Not that the monster movie necessarily makes that money back either, of course.

But the flipside of it is that I've always done what I've wanted to do, which is the freedom that working on lower budgets gives you. I've got a few scripts I'd like to shoot, and none of them need be that expensive. Frankly I'd rather spend the next two years making two or three films I want to do on smaller budgets than making one bigger film that was purely an assignment and that you end up losing control of anyway, which seems to happen quite a lot.

Writing for me is a key element – the influence of such writers as Harold Pinter is something I acknowledge. But the visual is equally important. I always enjoyed writing, but for me it's all part of the same process – it's just about getting the story down on the page first, then figuring out how best to shoot it. I'd like to think that I pay equal attention to both the writing and the visuals, but because so many lousy genre scripts get made, anyone who can string an actable line of dialogue together suddenly gets labelled as being of a more literary bent. *The Devil's Business* was a special case because of how and why it was made – we shot it in nine days with very little money, so obviously the visual design was going to have to be relatively simple. But even then we took a lot of care with the lighting, etc. And if you look at the films I've done with slightly more resources, I think the visuals are there. Certainly it's an area in which I want to push things further, but that comes with having more time and money.

But writers like Pinter and Mamet were certainly a big influence. I just never understood why a genre script couldn't be well written – it's the only part of the process that doesn't cost anything to get right! So in theory what I always wanted to do was to take that and combine it with the sort of visual acuity you get in Hitchcock or Polanski or whoever. Not that you'll ever get to that level perhaps, but that's what you try and strive for. Equally though, I'm not afraid of dialogue scenes. If the actors are good and the scripts are well written, that to me is as enjoyable as anything – some of the greatest scenes in film history are just actors and dialogue. I remember David Cronenberg once said that for him the greatest visual was the human face, and he had a point.'

Sandor Elès (actor, *Countess Dracula*, etc.)

Q: You've done some interesting work as an actor in the field of British Gothic cinema – and being born in Hungary, you did not have to masquerade as a Hungarian in your film work in the same way British actors often do.

A: It's kind of you to say so, but I'm not sure that my work in British Gothic cinema was particularly interesting, or at least as good as it could have been – I tried to do my best, but the two principal films I made in the genre, *The Evil of Frankenstein* in 1964 and *Countess Dracula* in 1971, were hardly the Hammer studio's finest hour, were they?

Q: But you nevertheless saw the working of the Hammer studio apparatus, and worked with some talented people such as your countryman, the director Peter Sasdy, and one of the studio's two most important actors, Peter Cushing. You also acted in the syndicated *Hammer House of Mystery and Suspense*, as well as the 1977 TV series *Supernatural*. And there's Robert Fuest's *And Soon the Darkness* in 1970.

A: Ah yes, for *Supernatural*, I did an episode called 'The Werewolf Reunion' and another by the title of 'Countess Ilona'. And I suppose my other principal connection with Gothic/horror subjects – at least of the psychological variety – was, as you say, *And Soon the Darkness* in 1970. But as to having an awareness of Gothic traditions and such things, I can't really (in all honesty) lay any claim to that. I'm a jobbing actor, and I took what jobs came my way, trying to be professional at all times and give my directors what they wanted. Thankfully, most filmmakers I worked with seemed happy with my work, such as Peter Sasdy, who, as you say, was a fellow Hungarian and with whom I made *Countess Dracula*. Though I wasn't in what I think was his best film for Hammer, *Taste the Blood of Dracula*.

Q: What was the experience of making *Countess Dracula*? Did you consider that you were making a film in the Hammer tradition or bear in mind that it was a vaguely historical subject – something based on the real-life supposed atrocities of Elizabeth Bathory?

A: Well the answer to that is: both. I suspected while making it that the film didn't have a great deal to do with the real-life Elizabeth Bathory, but I think back then we all realised that even if she had not bathed naked in the blood of virgins to preserve her youth (as Ingrid Pitt does in the film), that colourful legend was the most interesting thing about her. Sex and horror – a surefire combination, right? I think it's only recently, though I could be wrong, that the historical facts have been challenged. But then Ingrid and I, in scenes we had together, were hardly thinking of serious historical antecedents – we knew we were making a piece of popular entertainment, and we had fun. She told me, though, that she wasn't particularly happy during the making of the film as she felt that the material should have been tackled with more abandon. And looking at *Countess Dracula* today, she was clearly right – what could have been one of the most outrageous Hammer films, played with real gusto, actually comes across as rather restrained. And who needs restraint in a subject like that?

Q: Did you also feel while making the film that certain elements were being underplayed?

A: Frankly, no, but in all the films I've made, I've never really paid much attention to a vision of the final product – so you're usually surprised that something did not turn out as well as you expected it to. Keeping a vision of the film in mind is the director's job, and I'm happy to leave it to the people who know what they're doing. I know that Michael Caine has said that he never set out to make a bad film (and he admits to having made more than a few) – you're always trying to do your best work, whatever the material, and that's certainly true in my case. As for working in the Gothic genre, I've always had a taste for that – I am Hungarian, after all, and I particularly enjoyed pitching my performances at a certain level. In Gothic horror material, delicate, understated playing is just not appropriate; everything has to be – well, I won't say, larger-than-life, but slightly stylised and certainly not realistic.

Q: Your playing in *The Evil of Frankenstein* seems naturalistic.

A: Yes, I suppose you're right. But to some degree in that film, there was a different dynamic when working with Peter Cushing. Ingrid and I would just spend a lot of our time joking on the set of our film and we were very much contemporaries – I had fun fishing for fangs down her cleavage, for instance. But with Peter, I was very conscious of working with a senior actor of tremendous authority, and I'd already been warned that whenever I was on the screen with him, audiences would only be looking at him. Although, to be truthful, this wasn't just due to his complete command as an actor, I realised. People would tell me he'd do something to draw attention to himself (for instance, he always had some piece of business that would grab an audience's attention and have them looking at him – just the authoritative way he'd handle a surgical instrument, for instance). But that doesn't mean that he wasn't an immensely generous actor, and you knew that in any scene with him, he would do his best in a subtle fashion to make sure that you, too, would look good – although you never forgot who was most important person the scene. And I was most happy with that. I knew I would have been on the losing wicket if I tried to do anything that made me as interesting as Peter.

Q: Did you feel that either of the directors you worked with at Hammer, Peter Sasdy and Freddie Francis, considered themselves part of a Gothic tradition?

A: No, not really. Peter Sasdy was an immensely talented man, but would talk about projects that he desperately wanted to do but could not get the funds for. But whatever he turned his hand to, he did his best with – although it's obvious that he failed to make the film he wanted to make with *Countess Dracula*. Freddie

Francis on *The Evil of Frankenstein* was always competent and professional, and worked very quickly – I think he was very conscious of the studio ethos that you are expected to be good, but you were expected to be economical – time was money. As for being part of a Gothic tradition, I don't think Freddie would have been particularly interested in that. He wasn't an intellectual with any abstract appreciation of such things – just a highly professional filmmaker, and, of course, one of the British cinema's great cinematographers. However, he didn't do his best work in this film and I remember thinking at one time it would be nice to have worked with Terence Fisher in his heyday. It would have been possible, but I would have been a very young actor.
Sandor Elès (1936–2002)

Tim Lucas (writer, *Mario Bava: All the Colours of the Dark*, etc.)

Q: From an American perspective, which film has the most resonance for you in British Gothic cinema?

A: It may seem an odd or even inappropriate choice, but the first title that flashes to mind is Powell and Pressburger's *Black Narcissus* – it has the classic Gothic element of the provincial young woman who goes to an exotic place to serve a purpose, to lend meaning and structure to her life, and finds herself becoming as susceptible to its mystery as to its history. Isn't all Gothic fiction, to some degree, about the power of places and people to change us? *Black Narcissus* also has a parallel to the traditional Gothic totem of 'the tower' and the madness that must be purged from it. Powell and Pressburger's *I Know Where I'm Going!* shares some of the same traits, albeit in a more wholesome way. The stronger counterpart is actually Jack Clayton's *The Innocents*, also with Deborah Kerr. I watched it again recently, after reading Henry James' 'The Turn of the Screw' for the first time, and I found it both faithful, and yet superior, to the novella because it had genuine ambiguity, whereas the achievement of the novella resides more in the artful complexity of the oblique angles it takes to observing the heroine, her psychology and her motivations. The film, I think, is an absolute masterpiece. The only other British Gothic that begins to approach it, I suppose, is Roger Corman's *The Tomb of Ligeia*, which has genuinely classical dialogue by Robert Towne, still one of his finest achievements. Elizabeth Shepherd could not be more wonderful in the film, but would I love to see an alternative universe edition with Deborah Kerr as Ligeia/Rowena, David Farrar as Verden Fell, and Powell and Pressburger at the helm? Yes, I'd have some of that, thank you very much.

Q: Do such films have purchase in the USA today?

A: People seemed to turn out for *The Woman in Black* and they did want to love *Dark Shadows*, whose opening few minutes at least are a marvellous epic in miniature – a compressed trailer for the film the TV series' fans most wanted to see. Most of the films we see in the USA these days are about watching things explode, explosions that make you feel bad, followed by explosions that make you feel good. They cultivate appetites for revenge and [are] not much more advanced than that. I do think American audiences at least subconsciously miss stories that leave them with something to think about and to apply to their own lives. We're told that young people don't seem to have any interest in the past, but I think this is because no filmmaker has come along to make the past seem compelling or relevant to their experience. The classic Gothic stories usually have a strong erotic metaphor for an undercurrent. The protagonist, whether female or male, is usually virginal and formless; they find their identity in a dreamlike surrounding that is commanded by a powerful male or female presence, in an adventure that builds to some kind of climax that leaves them more experienced but haunted and alone. They're like love affairs, in that they sweep up the reader, or the viewer, give them a great transcendent experience, and then take them right back where they were picked up.

Q: Is the Gothic redundant in today's cinema?

A: Redundancy is the great characteristic of today's cinema, and it's at least partly because too many of the cinema's storytellers see movies rather than read stories. George Lucas did a lot of damage when he championed Joseph Campbell and convinced people that all stories followed the same eight or 12 templates. It was a tremendous discouragement to reading, and this from a man whose *Star Wars* is like a junkheap of ideas raided from filmed but also literary science fiction. I found Hammer's *The Woman in Black* competently done but rather tepid, because the earlier British television adaptation had done the job so well, and not so very long ago; a younger or less informed viewer would likely find it more original and less exhausted. I maintain that audiences may be, or may like to think they are, more 'sophisticated' than the old Gothic story templates, because no one can be sheltered or inexperienced in the way of most Gothic heroines in a world where the most untravelled teenagers can show up for their first day of middle school secure in the knowledge that they have so-many-hundred Facebook friends, but basic human needs remain basic. There are still things about human experience that are best absorbed through literary metaphor. Our need for genuinely romantic entertainment is eternal and anything that's well done will find an audience, either immediately or over time.

David McGillivray (screenwriter, *Frightmare*, etc., producer)

Q: You might be said to be part of a 'holy trinity' of 1970s British horror cinema with the directors Peter Walker and Norman J. Warren. Did you see yourselves as exploitation filmmakers or as something more ambitious?

A: I can't speak for the others. But I'd be surprised if they didn't have some ambitions beyond exploitation. Personally I never saw myself as anything other than a hack or a journeyman. It's only now, late in life, that I regret writing nothing of significance.

Q: Who were your own literary inspirations?

A: The writers who scared me as a child were Poe and Lovecraft. But I didn't want to write stories like theirs. I wanted to write like Nigel Kneale about horror affecting the lives of people like you and me.

Q: Did *House of Whipcord's* dedication to the moral majority (who would presumably have loathed the film) come from you or Peter Walker?

A: Walker. That dedication wasn't on the print that was shown at the cast and crew screening. Walker added it after the film had been to the BBFC and the censor Stephen Murphy told him that he believed *House of Whipcord* was an attack on the likes of Mary Whitehouse, Lord Longford and the censorship group the Festival of Light.

Q: *Frightmare* is now regarded as one of the most accomplished horror films made in this country – did it feel like something special when you were working on it?

A: No. We hoped it would shock people. We were very disappointed when it got such terrible reviews and such a short West End run.

Q: Similarly, did you realise quite how iconic an actress Sheila Keith would become because of your films?

A: Walker got on with her very well on *Whipcord* and subsequently she was written into his films. By the time of *House of the Long Shadows* he was well aware of her iconic status. When Elsa Lanchester turned down her role, it went straight to Keith.

Q: Did you feel the loss of Peter Cushing from *House of Mortal Sin* compromised the film?

A: I was thrilled by the prospect of working with Cushing. (In the end I never did.) I felt Anthony Sharp was a poor substitute. His name wasn't going to bring anyone in. But of course he did a fine job.

Q: Who did you find most satisfying working with: Peter Walker or Norman Warren?

A: To begin with I loved working with Walker. He never altered a comma of my scripts. *House of Whipcord* is the only one of my films I can bear to watch and indeed I introduced it at a festival in Edinburgh not so long ago. Later Walker and I began having rows and we parted acrimoniously. I believe my best work wasn't done with Warren. But we never argued. We've remained friends. We still see each other. I went for an Indian with him just recently.

Q: Are you bemused by the far greater regard these films are now held in since their initial reception?

A: I was working at a time when exploitation films had no life after their initial cinema release. Not only was there no video, but there was no possibility of TV sales. I never expected any of these films to be seen again. When they returned on video and later on DVD I thought they would be dismissed as dated rubbish. Of course I'm pleased that some people like them. But I'm always incredulous when they become the subjects of academic theses. Believe me, if I'd been aware of what some academics think I was really writing about, I'd have made more of it.

Kim Newman (writer, *Anno Dracula*, etc.)

Q: Do you feel the shadow of the great literary Gothic tradition when writing your own novels?

A: Yes, of course. Though I think the touchstones of my work tend to be late Victorian/Edwardian horror/fantasy/scientific romance (Wells, Doyle, Stoker, Stevenson) rather than gothic (Radcliffe, Lewis, Maturin, Walpole). Though there's now an air of nostalgia about the turn-of-the-century writers, they were more concerned with being contemporary than with evoking a romanticised past – that's why there's all the stuff about train timetables and Dictaphones. Much of what interests me about that busy period – when so many of our lasting pop culture icons were created in a very few years – is that it was the beginning of so many things we live with now.

Q: How do you distinguish between the canon of Gothic novels as opposed to the film adaptations?

A: I tend to see the great stories/characters of the field as conglomerations – certainly, with Dracula, there's a sense that the idea has outgrown the source novel and is manifested in all manner of interesting, extreme variations that are worth considering. Even Holmes or Jekyll and Hyde have been done over so many times that it's hard not to think of them as genres in themselves.

Q: Should the cinema instigate a moratorium on Gothic subjects?

A: Some approaches to the subjects get tired, but they're now basic essentials – just as every generation has its Hamlet (or Hamlets), there must now be competing, successive Draculas, Holmeses, Dorian Grays, ghost governesses, Frankenstein Monsters, Martians, etc.

Q: Which of your own books would you consider closest to the classic Gothic tradition?

A: If you mean the original flowering of the gothic novel, probably *Drachenfels* (which I wrote as Jack Yeovil; the Yeovil novella 'The Cold Stark House', which explicitly deploys gothic tropes). If you extend it to what we might think of as 'Hammer Films Gothic', then obviously *Anno Dracula* – which has gaslight, vampires and Jack the Ripper – and is an attempt to evoke the genre as if it were a world unto itself. My attempt at playing with classical gothic is the skit 'Mildew Manor, or: The Italian Smile'.

Q: What would be your choice of the film that means most to you in British Gothic cinema?

A: *Taste the Blood of Dracula* . . . maybe not the best film of the category, but it uses the material in an interesting way and does tick almost all the boxes.

Christopher Wicking (screenwriter, *Scream and Scream Again*, etc.)

'There is a part of me that is uncomfortable talking about my work', the screen-writer Christopher Wicking said to me, 'principally because I feel I have to qualify virtually everything I say with a remark: this wasn't my original screenplay. So often, the interesting things I did ended up being changed or compromised, that sometimes I almost felt that anything worthwhile of mine that made it into the final product was almost by accident. But I consoled myself by thinking that far better writers than me – from Scott Fitzgerald onwards – had their work tampered with on its way to the screen.'

Wicking was one of the most innovative and distinctive writers of a particu-larly interesting era in the British Gothic cinema (from the late 1960s onwards), and for nearly a decade he was involved with a variety of unusual films for the British arm of American International Pictures and the home-grown Hammer studios. While delivering the nuts-and-bolts scenarios that his paymasters insisted upon, Wicking was always interested in pushing the envelope and attempting to do something more ambitious and challenging than was generally welcomed in an often hidebound genre.

'It's true to say that I was almost always trying to change the boundaries of the genre with my work, but this wasn't simply because I felt that cliché reigned (although, inevitably, it did most of the time); my reasons were twofold: I love the horror/fantasy/science-fiction genre and wanted to replicate the success of those films which, for me, had achieved something new. Also, it was a way of personally keeping fresh in a creative sense – I was always attempting to think of unorthodox approaches, new angles and new ways of telling stories. And I like to think that I never forgot the key role for a dramatist: keep your characters real, however unlikely the situation.'

As a pupil of London's St Martin's School of Art, Wicking encountered a variety of filmmakers at the college's film society, including the French director Bertrand Tavernier, which led to him writing for a variety of French film maga-zines (including the legendary *Cahiers du Cinéma*). He also began to work for the BBC and was involved with Orson Welles' Falstaff film *Chimes at Midnight* (1966). 'I always wanted to direct', he said to me, 'and it was that impetus that drove me – although in the event, it was writing that earned me my crust.'

An involvement with the late director Michael Reeves in 1968 led to Wicking working for American International on the ill-fated *The Oblong Box*: 'It was to be Mike's follow-up to *Witchfinder General*, and I suspect he was slightly daunted by the idea of topping a film which had had such an impact. He asked if I would work on the new script, but in the event he was never involved, and I ended up working with the producer of the film (who finally directed it), Gordon Hessler. Mike Reeves never had much confidence in *The Oblong Box*, and in the event, Gordon Hessler and myself were able to do only so much with the material. It has its virtues, but it's one of those films which frustrates the audi-ence – for instance, in the massive build-up to the appearance of Vincent Price's facially mutilated brother. The innocuous make-up that was finally used was so inadequate that I remember feeling (on seeing the film) that not since Terence Fisher's devil dog in *The Hound of the Baskervilles* had there been such a disap-pointing revelation – it just looked like a few boils. For me, the best thing about working on the film was the beginning of my association with Gordon Hessler – and both of us really wanted to reinvigorate the horror film. We may not have achieved our aims, but nobody can say that we didn't try. And we had great fun while doing it – although battling with the studio suits was not exactly the most pleasant of experiences.'

Far more successful was the second film that Hessler and Wicking worked on, *Scream and Scream Again* (1970), which – in its radical approach to a variety of genres (the film is a fusion of science-fiction and horror elements) – remains one of the more extraordinary films produced in this country.

'We were handed Milton Subotsky's original script, which, frankly, was not up to much (it was based on a book called *The Disorientated Man* by the pseudonymous Peter Saxon). Writing, frankly, was not really Milton's métier. We began to change things (for instance, converting the alien invasion theme to a totalitarian regime) and did our best to create a really challenging multi-levelled film with a variety of almost discrete narratives. Our efforts were not received well by our bosses (Milton simply didn't get it), but I'm pleased to see that the reputation of the film continues to grow with the years. We subsequently worked on *Cry of the Banshee* (1970), but the final results were deeply compromised – and by this time, the high esteem in which we were held by AIP has become something different, and Gordon and I had to learn to guard our tongues. We had a notion of drawing modern political parallels with the *Banshee* script, but we realised we would have to keep that quiet. About that time, I worked on a screenplay based on Poe's 'The Gold Bug' and it was frustrating when that was not made. My last screenplay for AIP, also based on Poe, was *Murders in the Rue Morgue* (1971) with Gordon, which was also subjected to radical alteration – although, despite that, it's pleasing to see the film still enjoys something of a reputation; writers were able to see what we are attempting to do despite the fact that the final shape of the film did not adhere to our original intention.

A director I greatly admired, Seth Holt, worked on *Blood from the Mummy's Tomb* (1971); he was hired, in fact, at my suggestion – although his personal problems, notably his alcoholism, meant that the film was already in trouble, even before Holt's death during the making – the producer Michael Carreras finished it.'

Demons of the Mind (1972) was another film on which the writer's ambitious attempt at providing texture bore some fruit. 'Yes', he told me, 'I'm fairly happy with that – at least as happy as I am with any of the films I worked on. Certainly more so than the work I did on the adaptation of Dennis Wheatley's *To the Devil a Daughter* (1976), which was a financial failure. Other projects of mine did not get off the ground, but I never lost my enthusiasm for the genre – and perhaps something I write will one day be filmed as I intended it to be.'

Christopher Wicking (1943–2008)

Peter James (producer, *Dead of Night*, etc., writer)

Q: Your horror/supernatural work (which preceded your crime novels) was very modern, but despite the contemporary trappings, you were still a part of an English Gothic tradition. Was that something which was consciously in your mind?

A: Being modern was something I tried very consciously to do. When I wrote *Possession* in 1987, among my biggest influences were the novels *The Exorcist* and *Rosemary's Baby*, and the Polanski film *Repulsion*, all of which had taken Gothic horror themes into modern, elegant, urban settings. To be honest, it was not so much being part of an English Gothic tradition that was consciously in my mind, but being part of the tradition of the ghost story, which far precedes English Gothic. Although I have always loved classic English Gothic.

Q: So literary Gothic was a key influence?

A: Literary Gothic, without question, was more important to me than the movie adaptations. I remember once reading Dennis Wheatley's *The Devil Rides Out* and being so scared by the scene in which the central character puts himself inside a pentagram for protection that I could not sleep all night – I was convinced something malign had entered my bedroom. I think there is something about the way fiction fires your imagination and puts things into your mind that movies can do only rarely. I think the only movie that truly scared me was *Jaws* – I would not swim in the sea for years after seeing it! Undoubtedly the single biggest influence of all for me was Poe's 'The Premature Burial'. That truly terrified me, and I've used the theme of premature burial in two novels, *Twilight* and *Dead Simple*. The really terrible thing is that this used to happen frequently and still does happen occasionally. Did you know that in Victorian times you could pay a fee and have a rope attached to a bell in your coffin for two weeks after you were buried? It is where the expression 'dead ringer' comes from.

Q: Do you tire of the classic Gothic tropes?

A: Inevitably. We go back to the old, but true, maxim about there being only seven plots in the whole of literature. I do have to admit that I am getting very 'vampired out' at the moment. But horror and the supernatural have perennial appeal, and it interesting to see the revival in popularity of the ghost story as we become more secular as a society. But it is incumbent on all of us who write stories or make movies in this genre to be original.

Q: You produced the late Bob Clark's excellent *Dead of Night*, which shared a title with one of the great British horror films...

A: Bob Clark was wonderful to work with and I was very sorry he died, so prematurely, in a car smash some years ago. In truth, it is always hard to raise film production finance. Movies are big, expensive beasts, and the movie distribution world is culturally dishonest. Investors have been ripped off for decades, but having said that, they are still around. There is a superfluity of 'soft' money, i.e. grant money, that can give you up to 40–50 per cent of your budget. There are pre-sales from sales agents. And there are people who want to be in the business sometimes just for the glamour. I remember at the Royal Premiere we had on my last film *The Merchant of Venice* with Al Pacino and Jeremy Irons (before I focused full time on writing), one investor, a rich man who had put in £400,000, said to me afterwards, almost dancing for joy: 'Just to be here tonight, that is worth every penny of my investment!' But the biggest factor for investors is the huge potential returns from horror films. There have been some great low-budget successes – *Paranormal Activity* being a recent example. And my first foray into film finance, also with Bob Clark, was his film *Children Shouldn't Play With Dead Things*, which we made for $50k. Admittedly, that was back in 1971, but it was still peanuts in terms of movie budgets then, and it made very handsome returns. There is another crucial factor today: with the incredible rise in quality of digital recording, films can be made much, much, much more cheaply than ever. Decades on from *Children*, it is still possible to bring in a movie for $50,000. Make a quality horror film at that money and you are very likely to make a profit.

Stephen Volk (screenwriter, *Gothic*, etc.)

'My own work is not exclusively contemporary or period. I've done several scripts set in the nineteenth century, such as the movie *Gothic*, directed by Ken Russell. Personally, I don't think the terms "modern" or "period" are relevant – Poe and M.R. James, after all, didn't write "period"; their stories were mostly set in their own contemporary worlds.

But to think of one's self as part of a Gothic tradition would be a massive burden of responsibility. When I'm writing I don't really say to myself "What will make this more Gothic?" (Unless it is obvious pastiche, such as a faux-Holmes or Poe story.) But to be honest, the way I think – my approach – makes it more or less Gothic anyway. You may as well take it as given. I said to my wife once, if somebody asked me to write a story about a refrigerator, it would be about a refrigerator on a refuse dump and a little boy crawls into it and gets trapped. That's how my mind works, I'm not going to write a romantic comedy – and I've learnt not to be apologetic about it. Not succumb to the snobbery against the Gothic and horror, but just try to get better at it. In one respect I might be conscious of it, in trying to avoid the absolute cliché such as a thunderstorm or looming shadows or creaking stairs. But on the other hand, these are things you have in your toolbox and you take them and use them – or subvert them if you choose.

The fun for me is the element of the expected, and giving this new twists or putting them in a new context – or at the service of an unusual theme, say, the media – which was *Ghostwatch*, which I wrote for television in 1992. Albeit modern and surrounded by television technology, and also partly a satire about television, *Ghostwatch* was basically a haunted house story. It was also about family secrets, and about the past revisiting the present, about a kind of curse – all sorts of things which you could say are Gothic tropes. It is even "epistolary" in nature, in that it uses the exposition of a back story by various televisual devices. Most Gothic tropes are now indistinguishable from horror cinema now – in the public mind, anyway. For me, the challenge of *Ghostwatch* was a good old-fashioned ghost story told in a contemporary way: but there are plenty of indications it is Gothic through and through. It has an eviscerated dog and a cross-dressing paedophile, for God's sake!

Again, when I was writing the paranormal ITV series *Afterlife*, I couldn't help but be aware of certain Gothic elements. Alison Mundy, the troubled medium drawn towards death, is a textbook "spectral woman" straight out of Mario Praz's *The Romantic Agony*. There's the threat of madness, the death of children, the curse, supernatural powers, crime, mystery, the emphasis on certain locations as harbouring evil . . . The interesting thing, in a way, is to just write and discover afterwards how the Gothic ideas – both literary and cinematic – are there.

It's funny. The other day I was at the Royal West of England Academy exhibition in Bristol and there were literally hundreds of paintings on the walls, and the only picture I had the slightest inclination to buy, or even like, was a small oil painting of a house at night with a massive brooding grey cloud over it. It was tiny and insignificant, but something about the mystery of that house spoke to me and the dark power of the sky hanging over it and I thought to myself "That is essentially Gothic" – and I was curious, because even when I'm not working, these are the things that attract me, that mean something to me, because they feel "real". More emotionally real and true than more sentimental images.

I think the "2 Gothic" is a sensibility that you gravitate towards if you are of a certain frame of mind or personality type, probably at a quite young age. My first memory was an illustrated book of the Pied Piper of Hamelin, which terrified me. Followed, of course, by various horrors of childhood fiction, then the Pan horror stories, then Hammer and that Manichaean world of good and evil that it created so magnificently with denizens such as Cushing and Lee. The Gothic lures me in because it chimes with something inside. In fact, deep down, I think the Gothic might be a short-hand for basically describing the external symbolism of an internal state of anxiety – the sort of anxiety where we depressives and neurotics know a storm is coming; we know fear is coming, we know darkness is coming to get us – and as long as we bear that in mind, when it comes, our innate feeling that fear abides will be fulfilled and we will at least be prepared because we have considered the worst that can happen. I think this idea of imminent trauma is captured beautifully in the film *Melancholia* – where the depressive had her dark view of the world confirmed and, paradoxically, found a kind of peace when the world did end. I could relate to that.

My first produced screenplay was *Gothic*, which was made by Ken Russell for Virgin Films in 1986. You could say that script came from a literary source. It was about the famous "dark and stormy night" at Villa Diodati, when Lord Byron and his house guests Dr John Polidori, Percy Shelley and Mary Godwin created the two seminal figures of Gothic literature to come: in other words, the Vampire and Frankenstein. But the thing is, it wasn't ever meant to be a literary approach or a worthy biopic, which is what the critics expected and derided it for not being. The clue is in the title! It was all about Gothic cinema! I remember Timothy Spall trying to get a handle on his character and the style of the film, and I said to him to think of it as a Hammer film. He immediately "got" it. That was my sole intention, really – a Hammer film about the real people who created modern Gothic horror. Not Byron as the multi-faceted character he was in life, but purely as the Dark Nobleman of Gothic fiction. Mary as the winsome virgin. Shelley as the mad scientist. Polidori as the corrupt monk. Claire Claremont as the fatal woman. And it descended, as all Gothic does, to the primal, to the basement of our emotions, to the dirt and the cave and the rats.

As for influences, I love *Frankenstein*. I have no time for anybody who finds it hard to read. It's bliss. Same with Poe. Poe is "our" Shakespeare; he took the Gothic and gave it added depth and psychology. He gave it an element of the real rather than the distancing exotic of, say, *The Monk* or *Vathek* or *Otranto*. "The Tell-Tale Heart" is about people like us, which makes it all the more gripping, even today. I've written fiction about Poe, including my second novella about him. He is simply too good a character not to write dialogue for. I think of him as a cross between Stephen Fry, Robert Downey Jr. and Will Self. I just wish he'd had his own chat show!

To be honest, I didn't read the true Gothic classics (*Vathek, Otranto, Melmoth*) until I was researching *Gothic* and I didn't find them a very exciting read, but I always loved the inherent ideas. The Gothic I grew up enjoying consisted more of the later writers such as Conan Doyle, Machen, the Jameses (M.R. and Henry). But for me the memory of reading the literature is inseparable from their representation on TV and (later) on film. I was spellbound by *Late Night Horror* (BBC2), *Mystery and Imagination* (ITV) and the BBC *Ghost Story for Christmas* series. Then it was the late 1960s Hammers from *The Devil Rides Out* through *The Vampire Lovers* and so on. I was voracious for all kinds of cinema in those days (and still am!) but that era of movie making wove a special spell. In my teens I wanted to write those kinds of films and those kinds of TV series. Amazingly, I am kind of doing so.

There is a point at which the things that were once scary become banal or even comfy by repetition. Kim Newman is great on this. ("If I see another person opening a mirrored bathroom cabinet and when they close it, someone is standing there...") I personally have a crusade against ubiquitous "scare moments" and have had producers literally tell me to put "ten scare moments" in a script, it doesn't matter where and it doesn't matter how. Entirely insensitive to the creation of something that wants to get under the skin and stay there, or be memorable in any conceivable way. But then most producers don't understand horror in the slightest.

Also, the old material becomes worn and rather blunted. M.R. James stories still work when they are told orally, but the whole concoction, by virtue of the passing of time, has a fusty "Werther's Original" feel – more the warmth of an uncle or grandfather than the cold grip of the grave. This just happens through passage of time, and familiarity does breed a certain amount of indifference – although what is remarkable is that such a lot of the effectiveness of the cinematic Gothic remains unaltered. Take half-a-dozen big scary movies in 2012 (*Absentia, Silent House, Sinister*) and a lot of others used the same techniques that were used ten or 20 or even 50 years ago.

But that's all they are – techniques. I think Gothic is more than just a series of techniques and effects. I think the true Gothic technician (by which I mean, of course, the writer) doesn't repeat, but tries to push the envelope. Instead of *The Premature Burial*, what about *Buried*? Instead of *The Pit and the Pendulum* – *Martyrs*? If you work in the Gothic, especially since Poe, your job is to dig deeper, and the Gothic is at the service of the character's interior life. Perhaps it always was. The "pathetic fallacy" is not so far from John Carpenter's contention that "horror cinema is about internal states made external".

I have written a book called *Whitstable*. It features Peter Cushing as a character, and while it's not a Gothic story as such, it is inevitably about Gothic horror cinema to a certain extent. Increasingly, I've found I can't resist going back to examine what it is that's so endearing and compelling to me about the genre I love.

My most Gothic film is, inevitably, *Gothic*. It's a shame the film didn't get the audience it was meant for: not the lit flick crowd but the horror crowd. I think it fell between two stools, but maybe that's inevitable when you try to do Gothic horror and add something a bit different. It also became hard to market *The Awakening* (which I co-wrote) because it wasn't horrid enough for the horror crowd and it was too scary for the art-house crowd (or so it was thought). That one is closer to the Henry James style of psychological ghost story, admittedly, but of course there are Gothic trappings there too. You can hardly have a ghost hunter in a haunted stately home without them!

The film that means the most to me is probably *The Devil Rides Out*, for a number of reasons. Firstly, probably the impressionable age that I saw it. Secondly, right from the opening bars of James Bernard's music, it is absolutely gripping, and you are straight into the story, with no build-up, no faffing around. The tight screenplay by Richard Matheson is an exemplary adaptation, and I loved the fact that the forces of good and evil are aligned against each other in a wonderfully new but essentially Hammer universe. Integral to the success of the movie is precisely what made the best Hammers work – the sincerity of the playing. Christopher Lee is magnificent, and the world of black magic exceptionally well rendered. I would still rather watch it than re-watch *The Exorcist* any day.

If you are asking me for the moment that means most to me, it would have to be the old "Douglas Fairbanks" moment (as Peter Cushing describes it) from *Dracula*. The physicality of it is just superb. The run down the table. The tearing down of the curtains. (Producer's note: why didn't Dracula nail the curtains in place? He doesn't need to open them.) The candlesticks held by Van Helsing in the shape of the cross. Again, Peter Cushing inhabiting that absolutely vital gravitas that made even the most outlandish of his films absolutely convincing. To me, the image is the epitome of someone saving us from evil – supernatural or otherwise – and maybe, in the end, that's all we ever want or hope for.'

Simon Oakes (President and CEO, Hammer, *The Woman in Black*, etc.)

'It's over four years since I (and my colleagues) took the initiative of bringing Hammer Films back from the dead. It was undoubtedly a labour of love – the films have long been part of my consciousness, and I grew up watching them – but it was also a business decision channelling what I felt were sound commercial instincts. There is absolutely no denying the fact that the Hammer brand is still indelibly printed on the British consciousness, long after the company stopped making films. It struck me that over and over again, I had been aware of the way the very name was short-hand for a particular kind of British Gothic – and even defined the very medium of horror itself. I felt that (with the right handling) there was a way to revivify the brand.

We made a variety of films which we are shot through with the Hammer ethos – or a modern version of it – and it was, of course, the fourth film we made, *The Woman in Black*, that proved so immensely popular. Of course, Susan Hill's book has been an extremely durable hit on the West End stage, and we did have an ace in the hole with Daniel Radcliffe – coming on board with an audience keen to see what he would do post-Harry Potter (backed up by such heavyweight older British actors as Ciaran Hinds) – but, frankly, we were not expecting such an amazing opening for the film, though we were (it goes without saying) pleased when it became such a phenomenon.

We have, however, now made a rod for our own backs. Having brought back Hammer with the kind of success that would undoubtedly have made Anthony Hinds, Michael Carreras and co. proud, we are inevitably obliged to follow it up and prove we can do it again. And that's precisely what we're planning to do now; we have some very interesting projects in preparation.

The concept of Hammer horror is, of course, very different from what it was in the company's heyday – and horror films don't (generally speaking) seem to provoke the furore of moral outrage they once did. There is a reaction to what people now describe as "torture porn" movies such as the *Saw* and *Hostel* franchises, but I never wanted to go down that particular route in any case. I said to myself: if Hammer were still making movies in the twenty-first century, what would they be doing now? How would they have adapted? Adapting was something they always did – and prided themselves on doing. And it's clear to me that they would not have taken, say, the *Saw* route. We wanted to keep the essential spirit of the company, avoiding repetitive bodycount movies – so our remake of the Swedish vampire movie *Let the Right One In* (as *Let Me In*) was an attempt to do something different, while retaining the essence of Hammer, as was the Irish set cult thriller *Wake Wood*.

We are inevitably obliged to bear in mind the times we live in – to some degree, Hammer lost its audience when films such as *The Exorcist* and the urban myth movies became the new face of horror, and we are aware that the pressure is on us to always be innovative and inventive. What's more, we can't channel any Hammer personnel from the past – after all, the only Hammer icon who was still making movies in the twenty-first century is, of course, Christopher Lee.

Hammer was not just about Gothic horror; the company made a successful strain of psychological thrillers (such as *Taste of Fear* – which was called *Scream of Fear* in the US). We have many areas to work in. We appreciate that we've given ourselves a very difficult task, but that challenge is very stimulating. And in the end everything we do comes from a position of affection and admiration for the Hammer ethos. We plan to do it justice – and prove that the British Gothic horror film can work on audiences just as powerfully and insidiously in this century as it did in the last.'

Selected Filmography

28 Days Later, 2002, directed by Danny Boyle
28 Weeks Later, 2007, directed by Juan Carlos Fresnadillo
An American Werewolf in London, 1981, directed by John Landis
And Now the Screaming Starts!, 1973, directed by Roy Ward Baker
And Soon the Darkness, 1970, directed by Robert Fuest
Asylum, 1972, directed by Roy Ward Baker
The Awakening, 2011, directed by Nick Murphy
The Beast in the Cellar, 1970, directed by James Kelly
The Beast with Five Fingers, 1946, directed by Robert Florey
Beyond the Rave, 2008, directed by Matthias Hoene
The Birds, 1963, directed by Alfred Hitchcock
Black Death, 2010, directed by Christopher Smith
Blackmail, 1929, directed by Alfred Hitchcock
Blood and Roses (Et Mourir de Plaisir), 1960, directed by Roger Vadim
Blood from the Mummy's Tomb, 1971, directed by Seth Holt and Michael Carreras
Blood of the Vampire, 1958, directed by Henry Cass
Blood on Satan's Claw, 1971, directed by Piers Haggard
The Bride of Frankenstein, 1935, directed by James Whale
The Brides of Dracula, 1960, directed by Terence Fisher
The Bunker, 2001, directed by Rob Green
Burke and Hare, 1972, directed by Vernon Sewell
Burn, Witch, Burn, see *Night of the Eagle*
Captain Kronos: Vampire Hunter, 1974, directed by Brian Clemens
Cat Girl, 1957, directed by Alfred Shaughnessy
Cat People, 1942, directed by Jacques Tourneur
Chamber of Horrors, 1929, directed by Walter Summers
Chatroom, 2010, directed by Hideo Nakata
Cherry Tree Lane, 2010, directed by Paul Andrew Williams
Children Shouldn't Play with Dead Things, 1973, directed by Bob Clark
Circus of Horrors, 1960, directed by Sidney Hayers
The City of the Dead, 1960, directed by John Moxey
A Clockwork Orange, 1971, directed by Stanley Kubrick
The Comeback, 1978, directed by Peter Walker
The Company of Wolves, 1984, directed by Neil Jordan
The Confessional Murders, see *House of Mortal Sin*
Corridors of Blood, 1958, directed by Robert Day
Corruption, 1968, directed by Robert Hartford-Davis
Countess Dracula, 1971, directed by Peter Sasdy
The Crawling Eye, see *The Trollenberg Terror*
Creep, 2004, directed by Christopher Smith
The Creeping Flesh, 1973, directed by Freddie Francis
Crimes at the Dark House, 1940, directed by George King
Cry of the Banshee, 1970, directed by Gordon Hessler

The Curse of Frankenstein, 1957, directed by Terence Fisher
Curse of the Demon, see *Night of the Demon*
The Curse of the Werewolf, 1961, directed by Terence Fisher
The Dark Eyes of London, 1939, directed by Walter Summers
Daughters of Darkness, 1971, directed by Harry Kümel
Dawn of the Dead, 1978, directed by George A. Romero
The Day of the Triffids, 1962, directed by Steve Sekely and Freddie Francis
Dead of Night, 1945, directed by Alberto Cavalcanti, Charles Crichton, Basil Dearden and Robert Hamer
Dead of Night, 1972, directed by Bob Clark
The Deadly Bees, 1967, directed by Freddie Francis
Death Line, 1973, directed by Gary Sherman
Deathwatch, 2002, directed by Michael J. Bassett
Deliverance, 1972, directed by John Boorman
Demons Never Die, 2011, directed by Arjun Rose
Demons of the Mind, 1972, directed by Peter Sykes
The Descent, 2005, directed by Neil Marshall
Devil Doll, 1964, directed by Lindsay Shonteff
The Devil Rides Out, 1968, directed by Terence Fisher
The Devil's Business, 2011, directed by Sean Hogan
Die Screaming Marianne, 1971, directed by Peter Walker
The Disappeared, 2008, directed by Johnny Kevorkian
The Doctor and the Devils, 1985, directed by Freddie Francis
Doctor Blood's Coffin, 1961, directed by Sidney J. Furie
Dog Soldiers, 2002, directed by Neil Marshall
Doghouse, 2009, directed by Jake West
Don't Look Now, 1973, directed by Nicolas Roeg
Down Terrace, 2009, directed by Ben Wheatley
Dr Jekyll and Mr Hyde, 1931, directed by Rouben Mamoulian
Dr Jekyll and Sister Hyde, 1971, directed by Roy Ward Baker
Dr Terror's House of Horrors, 1965, directed by Freddie Francis
Dracula, 1931, directed by Tod Browning
Dracula, 1958, directed by Terence Fisher
Dracula A.D. 1972, 1972, directed by Alan Gibson
Dracula, Prince of Darkness, 1966, directed by Terence Fisher
The Earth Dies Screaming, 1964, directed by Terence Fisher
Eden Lake, 2008, directed by James Watkins
Edgar Allan Poe's The Conqueror Worm, see *Matthew Hopkins: Witchfinder General*
The Elephant Man, 1980, directed by David Lynch
The Evil of Frankenstein, 1964, directed by Freddie Francis
The Exorcist, 1973, directed by William Friedkin
Exposé, 1976, directed by James Kenelm Clarke
The Face at the Window, 1920, directed by Wilfred Noy
The Fall of the House of Usher, 1949, directed by Ivan Barnett
A Field in England, 2013, directed by Ben Wheatley
The Flesh and Blood Show, 1972, directed by Peter Walker
The Flesh and the Fiends, 1960, directed by John Gilling
Frankenstein, 1931, directed by James Whale
Frankenstein and the Monster from Hell, 1973, directed by Terence Fisher

Night of the Eagle, 1962, directed by Sidney Hayers
The Nightcomers, 1971, directed by Michael Winner
Nightmare, 1964, directed by Freddie Francis
The Oblong Box, 1969, directed by Gordon Hessler
The Old Dark House, 1932, directed by James Whale
The Omen, 1976, directed by Richard Donner
The Others, 2001, directed by Alejandro Amenábar
Paranoiac, 1963, directed by Freddie Francis
Peeping Tom, 1960, directed by Michael Powell
The Phantom of the Opera, 1962, directed by Terence Fisher
The Plague of the Zombies, 1966, directed by John Gilling
The Premature Burial, 1962, directed by Roger Corman
The Psychopath, 1966, directed by Freddie Francis
Quatermass and the Pit, 1967, directed by Roy Ward Baker
The Quatermass Xperiment, 1955, directed by Val Guest
The Queen of Spades, 1949, directed by Thorold Dickinson
Rasputin, the Mad Monk, 1966, directed by Don Sharp
Raw Meat, see *Death Line*
Revenge of the Blood Beast, 1966, directed by Michael Reeves
The Revenge of Frankenstein, 1958, directed by Terence Fisher
The Satanic Rites of Dracula, 1973, directed by Alan Gibson
Scars of Dracula, 1970, directed by Roy Ward Baker
Schizo, 1976, directed by Peter Walker
Scream and Scream Again, 1970, directed by Gordon Hessler
Scream of Fear, see *Taste of Fear*
Severance, 2006, directed by Christopher Smith
Shaun of the Dead, 2004, directed by Edgar Wright
Sightseers, 2012, directed by Ben Wheatley
The Skull, 1965, directed by Freddie Francis
The Snake Woman, 1961, directed by Sidney J. Furie
So Long at the Fair, 1950, directed by Antony Darnborough and Terence Fisher
The Stranglers of Bombay, 1959, directed by Terence Fisher
A Study in Terror, 1965, directed by James Hill
Sweeney Todd: The Demon Barber of Fleet Street, 1936, directed by George King
Tales from the Crypt, 1972, directed by Freddie Francis
Taste of Fear, 1961, directed by Seth Holt
Taste the Blood of Dracula, 1970, directed by Peter Sasdy
The Tell-Tale Heart, 1960, directed by Ernest Morris
Theatre of Blood, 1973, directed by Douglas Hickox
To the Devil a Daughter, 1976, directed by Peter Sykes
The Tomb of Ligeia, 1964, directed by Roger Corman
Torture Garden, 1967, directed by Freddie Francis
The Trollenberg Terror, 1958, directed by Quentin Lawrence
Twins of Evil, 1971, directed by John Hough
Twisted Nerve, 1968, directed by Roy Boulting
The Two Faces of Dr Jekyll, 1960, directed by Terence Fisher
Vampire Circus, 1972, directed by Robert Young
The Vampire Lovers, 1970, directed by Roy Ward Baker
The Vault of Horror, 1973, directed by Roy Ward Baker

Virgin Witch, 1972, directed by Ray Austin
Wake Wood, 2011, directed by David Keating
What a Carve Up!, 1961, directed by Pat Jackson
The Wicker Man, 1973, directed by Robin Hardy
Witchcraft, 1964, directed by Don Sharp
Witchfinder General, see *Matthew Hopkins: Witchfinder General*
The Woman in Black, 2012, directed by James Watkins
The Wraith of the Tomb, 1915, directed by Charles Calvert

Index

Films are followed by their year of release in brackets.
The terms 'Hammer' and 'Hammer Films' are not listed in the index. Index entries are included for individual Hammer films, books, etc.

.